LANGUAGE, STATUS, AND POWER IN IRAN

Advances in Semiotics
Thomas A. Sebeok, General Editor

LANGUAGE, STATUS, AND POWER IN IRAN

WILLIAM O. BEEMAN

INDIANA UNIVERSITY PRESS • BLOOMINGTON

Manufactured in the United States of America

Library of Congress Cataloging-in-Publication Data

Beeman, William O.
Language, status, and power in Iran.

(Advances in semiotics)
Bibliography: p.
Includes index.
1. Persian language—Social aspects—Iran.   2. Persian
language—Discourse analysis.   3. Iran—Social life and
customs.   4. Communication—Iran.   I. Title.   II. Series.
PK6224.75.B44   1986   491'.55'019   84-48490
ISBN 0-253-33139-0
1 2 3 4 5   90 89 88 87 86

CONTENTS

v

PREFACE

The present work arises from a series of strong intellectual convictions that I have maintained for several years concerning the nature of expression in language and its relationship to general semantic theory, combined with problems in the ethnography of communication for Iran which have needed attention for some time.

As will be evidenced in the discussion that follows, it is my feeling that the proper focus for linguistic investigation which hopes to uncover significant interesting information about meaning in culture centers on the functioning of creativity and rhetoric in language usage. If there is a central hypothesis that has been generated from this conviction for this study it is that meaning is a creative negotiated social process rather than a property of words, social events, or other organized cultural phenomena. The principal tool used in the rhetoric of meaning-creation is the variability existing within the codes of any communication system. The principal communicative feature that furthers the rhetorical process is the natural ambiguity existing in any interactive situation. Accordingly, it is the social use of stylistic variation to achieve concrete ends in Persian that becomes the focus for the present study.

In pursuing this line of investigation, a rich set of cultural linguistic processes is opened up for study. Among these are humor, courtesy, persuasion, insult, irony, and charlatanism, all of which involve sophisticated semantic manipulations within social interaction situations.

Primary field work for this study was carried out in Gavaki (not the actual name), a large village about thirty kilometers from Shiraz. There I was supplied with quarters in the house of a former resident, a building that had been turned over to the village for use as a center for the village association and as a preschool center during the morning. Other outsiders who occasionally spent the night in the village, such as the health and development corps members, were also quartered there. Teachers in the local school generally commuted daily from Shiraz.

In this study I was interested in working in a rural community where standard Persian was spoken. This proved to be very difficult. Even as close as I was to the city of Shiraz proper, the speech of the villagers differed significantly from that of urban residents. The problem is the same in other regions of Iran. Indeed, in only one area—around the city of Gorgan in the northeastern part of the country—did I find rural residents whose speech approximated standard urban varieties. In one sense this diversity is not surprising. Rural areas in Iran have traditionally been for the most part isolated from urban centers. The semifeudal system in the country before land reform insulated rural agriculturalists to a large degree from urban markets and from extended intercourse with urban residents.

The village is largely an agricultural community with a few secondary crafts practiced by the citizenry. The population of the village has declined steadily in recent years. At present there are 340 households in the community, which had an approximate population of over 3,000 in the Iranian census of 1966. The present population is difficult to assess properly since there are many persons who can be said to be living both in the village and elsewhere, such as Shiraz. Any Friday, when most offices and shops in the city are closed, numerous individuals appear who have houses or property in the village, but who for one reason or another are not resident during the week. These people come to the village for religious holidays, to attend weddings and other rites of passage, and to maintain social ties. Once these individuals have left the village, however, they play only a peripheral role in the day-to-day community affairs.

The persons I was primarily concerned with consisted of resident male agriculturalists, agricultural laborers, merchants, and craftsmen as they carried out their normal, everyday interactions with each other. Women's society was for the most part inaccessible to me, although I was able to collect some information on women's interaction patterns in the village through two excellent female field assistants I had recruited from the student body at Pahlavi University.

In contrast to the village situation, I also maintained an affiliation with Pahlavi University in Shiraz, where I had an office in the Department of National Development. My affiliation with the University provided me with the opportunity to be a participant observer in another setting altogether from that of the village: the interaction situation of the University itself, including interactions among students, among instructors, between students and instructors, and between faculty and students and the servants and other persons providing maintenance for the upkeep of offices and grounds.

The third situation in which I was an active participant observer during my stay in Iran consisted of a large-scale planning project, being carried out in Fars province, in which the University was a participant. The governor of the province, the chancellor of Pahlavi University, various members of the faculty, and various members of the Iranian Plan Organization met at regular intervals in groups of varying sizes to discuss the project.

All of these field situations presented the opportunity to observe semiclosed communication situations of various complexity. This is to say, observable interactions in all cases had historical antecedents that it was possible for me to detail to a fair degree. Further, except in the case of the governor's commission, it was possible for me to observe or obtain an account of virtually *all* of the interactions that certain individuals engaged in for several days on end. In addition, after six or seven months' residence, I had enough background information and acquaintance with the individuals involved to be able to begin to understand the history of an interaction. I was also able to understand to some degree their aspirations, fears, dislikes, annoyances, and predilections within the total framework of their interactions with others.

Thus, the principal emphasis in field work in all three situations was to raise my own participation level in the groups to the point where I would be able to discern as participant the probable antecedents and outcomes of each communication situation of which I was a part. I would then be noting continually, and as carefully as possible, through either tape recording or written record, the linguistic and nonlinguistic elements present in individual communication events. My desk at the University filled with little dated notes about brief interaction encounters. I covered a large amount of the governor's own notepaper with cryptic scribbles, not about the development plan he was trying to implement but rather about who was talking to whom and what speech forms they were using. Finally, I was able to obtain hours of mundane conversation recorded on tape and in my field notebook. From the village where I stayed I obtained greetings; discussions about crops, marriages, and recent village happenings; gossip; inconsequential banter; interactions between people working together; and social talk during weddings, dinners, and religious ceremonies.

Having done all of this, I must declare that the recording of mundane interactions is without a doubt the most tedious and difficult of jobs. Anthropologists are not used to focusing attention on routine everyday interactions. Field notes commonly consist of transcripts or accounts of directed interviews with individuals; observations of various kinds of processes; and accounts of highly marked events such as weddings, religious ceremonies, or public disputes. Some of the rarest anthropological field data is that on persons routinely interacting with each other.[1]

The routine of everyday life, even in a cultural setting that is relatively unfamiliar to the observer, gradually causes the most repeated, and therefore the most significant, phenomenal elements to fade into the background and become dis-attended. One has to strain to attend to pronoun usage, hesitation words, significant pauses, particular word usage, body distancing, gestures, and posture precisely because they are what contribute to making the event normal, comfortable, and routine. However, they are the backdrop against which all significance in a given encounter is measured. There is no doubt that more advanced recording techniques than I was able to use would have provided a much richer body of data from which to work. Because of financial limitations, however, this was simply not possible. There is some question, too, about whether routine interactions could proceed in an Iranian village with a movie camera or videotape camera pointing at individuals. Roberts et al. (1956), in their *Zuni Daily Life*, have demonstrated that material of value can be collected by continual recording of events, but the recent National Educational Television project, "An American Family," demonstrated that persons being filmed were still conscious of the camera even after a long period of familiarity with the filming situation.

From this body of material and from my previous and continued acquaintance with Persian society, I have constructed a set of formulations of general principles of Iranian communication. After defining these, I attempt to demonstrate how these principles are realized in terms of actual stylistic variants in conversation. Some of these stylistic devices vary from group to group; that is, the behavioral realization of one principle may be somewhat different in a university setting from what it is in a village setting. This does not, however, negate the validity of the principle itself, as I have mentioned above in my discussion of macro- and micro-communication communities.

Finally, I explore the ways that language can be used as an active, strategic tool in social interaction. Through this perspective it becomes possible to see how meaning is created in interaction, rather than being simply a reflex of a given situation.

This kind of analysis is difficult and, almost by definition, imprecise. The best we as researchers may be able to do at this point is, in Geertz's sense, to pursue "thick description"—interpretation of what we see using the best, most informed reasoning we are able, by virtue of our acquaintance with the cultures we are attempting to elucidate. The facet of Iranian life I have chosen to try to elucidate is particularly slippery—so much so that there is little in Iranian literature itself, in all of its vastness, that deals with it. Only a foreigner would be so audacious.

ACKNOWLEDGMENTS

This research was supported in part by the Wenner-Gren Foundation for Anthropological Research, whose help is gratefully acknowledged. I was sponsored in Iran by the Ministry of Science and Higher Education, the Institute for Social Studies and Research of the University of Tehran, and the Department of National Development of the University of Shiraz (formerly Pahlavi University), which also provided me with aid in the form of field assistants: Houri Beheshti, Minoo Eghraghi, Ali Mansurian, and Hamid Taleb-Nezhad, all of whom contributed greatly to the present work. Subsequent research on popular theater traditions was supported by a grant from the Iran Bicentennial Committee, and the Iranian Center for Traditional Performing Arts, Festival of Arts Center, National Iranian Radio-Television. Among my many valued colleagues in Iran, the late Nader Afshar-Naderi, Isma'il Ajami, Ali Bolukbashi, Mohammad Bagher Ghaffari, Farokh Ghaffary, Reza Khaki, Mahmud Khaliqi, Hushang Keshavarz, David Marsden, Hosein Meisami, Mohammad Mir-Shokra'i, Assad Nezami, Javad Safi-Nezhad, Khosro Shayesteh, Manuchehr Shiva, Mohammad Tavakoli-Yazdi, and Firuz Tofiq gave me particularly useful support.

I have been encouraged and inspired in this enterprise more than I can acknowledge by my friend and graduate advisor, Paul Friedrich. Friedrich's vital work on fundamental aspects of cultural linguistic processes in Russian, Tarascan, Ancient Greek, and Indo-European, coupled with his keen sense of significant problems in cultural and semantic theory, has continually honed the cutting edge of my own arguments. Careful readers will not fail to note the inspiration that Friedrich's work has provided for this analysis.

I am indebted also to Professor Heshmat Moayyad, who taught me Persian to the level of skill that enabled this study and provided many insightful critical perspectives and much encouragement throughout the work. I am especially indebted to Catherine Bateson, Michael M.J. Fischer, Byron and Mary Jo Good, Frances Harwood, McKim Marriott, John Perry, Brian Spooner, and several anonymous press readers, who all read earlier drafts of this work and improved it greatly through their comments. Thanks also go to Howard Aaronson, the late Lloyd Fallers, Ray Fogelson, Clifford Geertz, Erich

Hamp, James McCawley, Manning Nash, David Schneider, Michael Silverstein, Milton Singer, Terry Turner, and the late Victor Turner for helping me to develop a useful set of conceptual tools. Many thanks to Harriet Mayerson for her painstaking typing (and re-typing) of the manuscript.

My late father, W. O. Beeman, and my mother, Florence O'Kieffe Beeman, have encouraged and supported me continually throughout my career. There is no way for me to adequately express my thanks to them. My brother, Jim, and his family and my sister, Adele Blue, have always seemed to enjoy my adventures more than I have. I'm glad to give them a lot to talk about.

I would like to mark a debt in this book to an intellectual community of great strength. Although my former graduate studies were completed at the University of Chicago, the formal cast for this work was conceived at the University of Pennsylvania, where I was resident in 1970. At that time I was thrown into one of the most vital groups of scholars I have ever encountered, consisting of Ray Birdwhistel, John Fought, Erving Goffman, Dell Hymes, William Labov, David Sapir, Bob Scholte, John Szwed, and the late Sol Worth. These individuals would likely deny that they ever met all together as a group. Nonetheless, the atmosphere at Penn was electric at the time I was there. Communication passed through students these men had in common and through other informal means. The community broke up shortly thereafter through death and a sad set of shortsighted personnel decisions, but even a decade later, I am still sustained by the energy that was generated there at that time. I hope these people will recognize their influence on the pages that follow.

Another debt of thanks goes to my friends at the Institute for the Study of Languages and Cultures of Asia and Africa, Tokyo University of Foreign Studies, Japan. Through the good offices of my friend, the noted anthropologist, Masao Yamaguchi, I was invited to the Institute in 1981–1982 as a Visiting Research Professor. The stimulation and excellent facilities of the Institute would be hard to duplicate anywhere in the world. The Institute provided me with the means for finishing the final draft of this manuscript, as well as many other projects, and the wonderful opportunity to know Japan.

For my fine Iranian friends everywhere, I have not so much a dedication as a wish. At this writing, Iran has passed through an epoch-making revolution and seven years of astounding transformation into an Islamic Republic. The insights gained in the field work done for this study helped me to understand these events in a way that I feel few non-Iranians could.

For this reason, and for many others too numerous to mention, I sincerely hope that all Iranians may attain their grandest aspirations and achieve their fondest dreams, for themselves and their nation— a country that will always own a part of me.

A NOTE ON TRANSLITERATION
AND TRANSCRIPTION

The transliteration of Persian into Latin characters is a continual problem for scholars since no standardized system exists. Arabic transliteration modes, such as utilized by the *International Journal of Middle Eastern Studies* and other specialist journals have the virtue of representing an unambiguous transliteration of Arabic script in Latin letters but provide little in the way of commonsense representation of the sounds of Persian.

The present volume has a particular set of problems because it is a linguistic study, involving *transcription* of spoken Persian as it is pronounced, as well as an anthropological study, dealing with historical and cultural material, where Persian words are *transliterated*. The conventions for transcription and transliteration are different and occasionally inconsistent. Therefore in rendering Persian into Latin text I have chosen a middle way, using a set of conventions tailor-made for the requirements of this book. They are admittedly less than satisfactory. Both Iranologists and linguists will find the system too inexact, and other readers will doubtless find it pedantic.

I have chosen to use a single character *æ* to represent the Persian "short a" and let an unmarked "a" represent the Persian "long a." Other works commonly represent both sounds with the same letter, with no diacritical mark to distinguish them, or represent "long a" as *ā* and leave "short a" unmarked. No distinction is made in the transliteration of Arabic ز , ذ, ض, and ظ . All are transliterated as *z*. Arabic س, ص and ث are transliterated as *s*. Arabic ت and ط are transliterated as *t*. Arabic ه and ح are transliterated as *h*. I have preserved one orthographic distinction throughout the work where text has been transliterated which has no basis in phonological realization. Arabic " 'æyn" (ع) is transliterated as " ' " (e.g., *'ozr*), whereas Arabic "hæmzeh" (hamzah) (ء) is transliterated as " ' " (e.g., *ra'is*) in non-phonological discussions. These two sounds are the same in modern Persian. In Chapter 5, which concerns phonology, only one orthographic symbol is used to represent both in phonemic and phonetic transcription: /'/ or [']. A similar convention is used for Arabic "ghæyn" (غ) and "qaf" (ق). In phonetic transcription in Chapter 5, both are rendered, when appropriate, as [ğ]. "Qaf" has another phonetic transcription in cer-

tain cases, [q]. In other parts of the book, when "ghæyn" is transliterated, *gh* is used. "Qaf" is transliterated as *q*. Initial Arabic "alef"
(١) is indicated only for its vowel quality and not as a hæmzeh (')
(e.g., *ested'a* not *'ested'a*). A fuller discussion of the sound system of
Persian is contained in Chapter 5, especially in Tables 1 and 2.

Many common words not normally rendered with diacritics, such
as common place names, names of well-known historical and literary
figures, and some literary works, are presented as they normally are
in English, with standard English orthography when contained in
discussions of Iranian history and culture (e.g., Pahlavi, not Pæhlævi).
A superscript ˇ is used in transliteration to indicate an unpronounced
orthographic symbol preserved in modern Persian in some words,
such as *xˇastæn*.

LANGUAGE,
STATUS, AND
POWER IN IRAN

I

INTRODUCTION
THE ARCHITECTURE OF IRANIAN
VERBAL INTERACTION

For centuries, Iranian society and civilization have held a fascination for both scholars and laymen, one that shows no signs of abating. It is noteworthy that with all that has been written about the art, architecture, literature, and military and political history of Iran, the field of interpersonal social relations has been one of the prime areas of interest to commentators from outside the country. This is hardly surprising for those who have lived for any time in Iran, for the quality of social life there differs significantly from that of even its closest neighbors.

The advent of the Iranian revolution in 1978 marked a new upsurge of interest in Iranian culture and civilization. The United States was suddenly forced to confront Iranian civilization directly, and Americans found themselves totally unprepared for the task. The cultural logic employed by Iran in its political dealings with the United States was incomprehensible to many Americans in the postrevolutionary period. With the taking and seemingly interminable holding of fifty-three United States diplomatic personnel as hostages in 1979–1981 with no clear structure for negotiating their release, Americans found Iranian behavior even more difficult to understand.

The key to understanding Iranian social and political institutions lies in an understanding of the dynamics of interpersonal behavior. It is through the intricacies of face-to-face interaction that power is negotiated, alliances are made, action is made incumbent on individuals, and choices of strategy are decided.

Iranian interpersonal behavior has an unmistakable aesthetic dimension—skill in interaction is greatly appreciated in assessing an individual's worth in society. The sense of this aesthetic dimension leads inevitably to metaphors. The elaborate weaving and intertwining of designs in the finest Persian carpets; the extraordinary complexity

1

of rhyme, meter, imagery, and word play in classic Persian poetry; and the intricate improvisatory sweet-sadness of melodic line in traditional Persian music all convey some of the feeling and texture of everyday social interaction. It is not unreasonable to compare interpersonal relations in Iran to art, for negotiating the webs of everyday personal relations and interaction situations requires consummate skill for even those born into the system. Consequently, there are rewards for the adept and setbacks for the clumsy.

Because a great deal rides on an individual's adeptness at communication, verbal skills and the use of language take on great importance in every person's life. Not surprisingly, too, words are rarely uttered or received idly. A person's verbal performance becomes pregnant with import as the listener, practicing the skills he or she possesses as a communicator, tries to register every nuance of the verbal performance and interpret it successfully. To do otherwise would be less than prudent.

"Meaning" in Linguistics and Anthropology

As an outsider trying to understand these intricacies of communication, I was brought to grips with some of the most pressing theoretical problems in the study of language today. Analysts of language in the twentieth century have largely maintained a conceptual separation between "language" on the one hand and "social context" on the other. This separation has resulted in a distinction in the study of meaning between "semantics" and "pragmatics"—the former dealing with questions of reference, truth-value, verifiability, ambiguity, and other topics that are dealt with largely within the linguistic system apart from its realization in actual use. "Pragmatics," a rather specifically defined area of semiotic function for Peirce, Dewey, and William James (cf. Bean 1978: 1–3), has now taken on the role of residual category for some linguists—a box for all those messy things that cannot be dealt with using formal structural analytic principles acting on a closed linguistic system. To quote one recent textbook on semantics, "Within the domain of pragmatics . . . fall topics such as metaphor, stylistics, rhetorical devices in general, and all the phenomena relating what we might call thematic structure—the way in which a speaker presents his utterance" (Kempson 1977: 192).

The Iranian linguistic situation presents a genuine challenge to this doctrine of separation. The elements of language and context cannot be assigned fixed relationships to each other, as is so often implied in theoretical writing about language. Neat rules that unambiguously link a nonlinguistic phenomenon with a linguistic form cannot be formulated without destroying the reality of the linguistic situation. On the contrary, both language and context are negotiable, interpenetrating, and fluid. In many ways Iran can be described as a nation of Humpty-Dumpties in Alice's looking-glass world—not only making *words* mean exactly what they want them to mean, no more and no less, but also making *contexts* mean what they want them to mean.

Early in my research I came to the conclusion that in order to understand the nature of language and communication in Iran, I would have to stop addressing myself to problems like, "What is the full range of referents for *x*?" or "What are the selective restrictions on the use of the verb *y*?" in some culturally neutral (hence artificial) analytic framework. Instead, I would have to address myself to a set of far more basic and salient questions, such as, "How are Iranians using their language to make themselves understood? How are Iranians establishing the criteria for interpretation of their language in interaction with others? In short, how are they creating the cognitive framework within which such closed-system functions as 'reference' and 'verification' operate?"

In this regard, I found full support in the line of inquiry opened by "speech act" theorists Austin (1962) and Searle (1969, 1979). Searle in particular reminds us that even functions that linguists consider properties of semantic and syntactic systems, such as reference or predication, are in fact accomplishments of speakers. One must fulfill set conditions in communicating in order to use a lexical item or utterance in such a way that it "refers" to some other item, and these conditions are not logical but behavioral. Halliday (1973, 1978) and Silverstein (1976) take this a step further and argue strongly for giving such speaker accomplishments a central functioning role in grammar.

Thus, the theoretical requirements of the analysis of language in Iranian interaction seemed not to be met through much of traditional linguistic thinking on the subject of meaning, which seemed unnecessarily narrow and fixed. But these requirements were likewise not met by traditional anthropological approaches to the same topic, which seemed unnecessarily broad and equally fixed.

Meaning as a concept in anthropology has had a long and sometimes exclusive association with the concept of the symbol. Indeed, the culture concept itself has been described alternatively as a "system of symbols" and as a "system of meanings" with great frequency in recent years. Schneider covers all bets and identifies it as "a system of symbols and meanings" (Schneider 1976: 198).

Symbols seem to be of two types in anthropological literature. On the one hand, they are concrete presentational phenomena—images, verbal or sound representations, or complex enactments (cf. Turner 1969, 1974; Douglas 1966, 1975). On the other hand, they are sometimes treated as something far more abstract, as in Schneider's use of "coitus" as a symbol in American society (Schneider 1976: 216). Symbols conceived at this level are not themselves concrete, but rather serve as the reference point for innumerable concrete representations. The work of Levi-Strauss (e.g., 1963, 1966) and Dumont (1970) also largely follows this usage.

Whether concrete or abstract, the symbol is thought of in functional terms as the mechanism that links concrete sensory phenomena with "meanings" in the cultural system. Symbols are seen as polysemic in that they represent many meanings. Meanings are in turn multire-presentational: they are reflected in a multitude of concrete and abstract symbols. This looks like a jumble, or perhaps a jungle, considering Turner's *Forest of Symbols* (1967), where this view of symbols is presented in perhaps its most elegant form.

Out of this tangle of polysemy, the task of the anthropologist seems to be one of discovering two structural orders: first, the structures that order the worlds of meaning and representation, and second, the structures that associate the two worlds with each other (cf. Schneider 1968a, 1976; Geertz 1966, 1973).

This anthropological view of meaning suffers from somewhat the same difficulties encountered in the linguistic views cited above, in that it assumes that there are such things as "meanings" which pre-exist the situations in which they are realized in communication. This view ignores the abilities of individuals to exercise control over the interpretation of the symbols they use. It is at least in part due to the fact that symbols are used and presented in a wide variety of different ways by individuals in society that polysemy is seen by analysts as a "property" of symbols.

Deixis and the Interpretation of Meaning

Deixis is a term that has been used in recent years to refer to those elements of language that "express the relationship between the utterances produced and the social, temporal and physical setting of the speech act" (Bean 1978: 8). This includes a wide range of elements whose interpretation depends on the situation of the individual producing a given utterance (cf. Fillimore 1966, 1968, 1971a, 1971b).

Thus, in simple terms, the pronoun "I" can be assigned referential meaning only when one knows who is using it. In other words, the referential meaning of "I" is different for every speaker. Similarly "here," "now," and other such orientational words have different referents every time they are used.

Understanding the fundamental nature of deixis in language establishes an important principle in the understanding of meaning, for it eliminates the rigidity that comes from assuming that words and other cultural symbols have fixed referential associations or fixed usage. Deictic elements are never fixed. For this reason they have been termed "shifters" by Jespersen (1922) and Jakobson (1957).

Jakobson and others who have discussed the role of these "shifters" in speech focus on their *indexical* qualities. However, as Silverstein (1976: 33–34) and Bean (1978: 9–11) point out, shifters have both indexical properties, in that they are existentially connected with the objects they refer to, and symbolic properties, in that the nature of their reference to any object is established by convention.

Beeman (1971, 1976a), Irvine (1974), and Silverstein (1976) have added an additional dimension to this discussion of shifters by pointing out that they may be used in various creative, performative, or strategic ways. One important aspect of this function is to highlight which of the multitude of aspects of the context of interaction, particularly the "cognitive aspects," will be of essential importance in determining the course of a given interaction. Silverstein points out that these creative uses:

> . . . can be said not so much to change the context, as to make explicit and overt the parameters of structure of the ongoing events. By the very use of an indexical token, which derives its indexical value from the rules of use setting up the indexical types, we have brought into sharp cognitive relief part of the context of speech. In some cases, the occurrence of the speech signal is the only overt sign of the contextual parameter, verifiable, perhaps, by other, co-occurring behaviors in other media, but nevertheless, the most salient index of the specific value. . . . Social indexes such as deference vocabularies and constructions, . . . are examples of maximally creative or performative devices, which, by their very use [sic] make the social parameters of speaker and hearer explicit (Silverstein 1976: 34).

These sorts of insights reveal something of the enormous complexity in any interaction, where literally any aspect of the context of
speech may be brought into focus, made a main point of contention
in interaction, or redefined by skillful speakers. Emmanuel Schegloff
points out that even the use of shifters indicating place, such as "here"
and "there," requires careful attention on the part of speakers. Since
many formulations of place, for instance, in answering the question
"Where are you?" would serve as acceptable replies,[1] the speaker must
choose on particular occasions which terms to select and which to
reject. The aim of this is to " . . . direct attention to the *sorts of considerations* that enter into a selection of a particular formulation, considerations which are part of the work a speaker does in using a particular
locational formulation, and the work a hearer does in analyzing its
use" [Schegloff 1972: 81 (emphasis mine)]. Thus Schegloff is stating
in another way the point made above, that selection of alternative
formulations in speech is a method of directing attention to significant
factors in the context of interaction that affect both the production
of messages and their interpretation. I will return to the question of
variability below.

Appropriateness and Effectiveness

Work carried out on creative aspects of speech, as cited above, has
presented an important argument against one longstanding bias in
linguistic literature: the assumption that a speaker's choice of alternative possibilities in speech is somehow an automatic response to his
contextual environment. That is, given that a speaker is placed in a
given environment, his speech will, chameleon-like, adjust perfectly
to the social, historical, and environmental factors that surround him.

There is no denying that speakers do adjust their linguistic production in interaction, but the fit between communicational style and
contextual factors is rarely predictable through a calculus of the environmental factors alone. In the end, the principal controlling factor
is the intent of the speaker himself—that is, the aims that the speaker
wishes to accomplish in the course of interaction, in conjunction with
those contextual factors.

The context provides some of the elements the speaker has to work
with in creating communication. As in Schegloff's formulation above,
speakers select the factors from the context of communication that
they wish to designate as significant in interaction with others. One

may choose to give special emphasis to age difference, or disregard the fact that interaction is taking place in a formal setting. One may ignore the fact that those one is talking to are utter strangers, or one may draw heavily on the fact that one shares a kin tie with them.[2]

When more than one speaker is taken into consideration, it can be seen that a whole matrix of communication strategies is at work, with each individual vying for control of the definition of context. Moreover, the state of affairs during the course of interaction is continually shifting, as each new action or behavioral element generated by speakers becomes part of the context.[3] This makes the task of the ethnographer one not of describing the communication forms that are produced, but of demonstrating how communication forms are used by speakers to solve problems that arise in conveying meaning to one another.[4]

The problems of speakers may be thought of as falling into two broad categories. The first is the problem of *appropriateness*; the second, the problem of *effectiveness*. Speakers ideally aim to make their speech both appropriate and effective. This is the problem I take up below.

The theory of communication that underlies this study posits for members of a society a core of shared interaction conventions that are used by individuals in accounting for themselves in face-to-face encounters. These conventions may be categorized in two ways. *Prescriptive conventions* are operations in communicative behavior that reinforce a state of affairs that will be perceived by individuals in interaction as normal or expected. By conforming to these prescriptive interaction conventions, individuals meet criteria of *appropriateness* in their dealings with others. *Strategic departures* are operations in communicative behavior that violate expectations in systematic, interpretable ways in order to accomplish specialized communicative tasks, such as persuading, expressing emotion, joking, threatening, or insulting.[5] By skillfully adjusting their speech between prescriptive conventions and strategic departures, participants in interaction are able to excel in *effectiveness* in communication.

Criteria of appropriateness are, in this schema, what one might call accounting "standards." They may be thought of as "if-then" propositions. One can often meet criteria of appropriateness by fulfilling the "then" side of the proposition and leaving it to others to assume or deduce the "if" side. For example, if one sees two people kissing in public, it is assumed that (1) they know each other well enough to be kissing and (2) social convention tolerates kissing in places where it is likely to be observed by others. The kissing is the "then" side of the proposition, and the account that they know each other and that kissing is socially tolerated in public is the "if" side. Even if two people kissing in public are questioned, they can usually account for their actions by supplying the proper "if," usually a cultural rule or convention. Such a dialogue might go like this:

A: Hey, you two can't kiss here.
B: But we're married. (*If* you're married, *then* kissing in public is appropriate).
A: Still, you can't do that here.
B: But we're newlyweds. (*If* you're a newlywed, *then* kissing your spouse in public is even more appropriate).
A: But this is Saudi Arabia. (*If* you are in Saudi Arabia, *then* kissing between males and females is inappropriate in public, even if you're married.)
B: You're crazy! This is New York City! Bug off or I'll call the cops! (*If* you're in New York City, *then* saying you're somewhere else is inappropriate).

By reasserting what is normal and expected, appropriateness as an operation reinforces stability, continuity, and predictability of any given interaction context.

By contrast, effectiveness as an operation serves to alter elements in the context and thereby the context of interaction itself.[6] Thus effectiveness in communication offers a way of altering an expected relationship between message *form* and message *interpretation* (cf. Chapter 2) by forcing a change in the parameters that serve as guides for that interpretation.

Skill in effectiveness consists of being able to depart from an expected pattern and thereby make incumbent on communication a new basis for understanding that conforms to the variant pattern being presented. It is a skill of maneuvering, moreover, since departures from expectations are never absolute. The skillful communicator must be able to shift from conformity to expectations, to minor departure, to radical departure, depending on the assessment of all other communication factors. The new basis for understanding is drawn from the possibilities existing within the communication repertoire of individuals engaged in interaction. Thus, effective communication brings about a shift in belief or conviction concerning the identity of established variable factors within the cultural communicative system.

For example, given two possibilities for identifying speakers in communication, one high-status, the other low-status, a skilled communicator might use linguistic variables that are appropriate for use with high-status individuals in order to convince a listener that he or she, the listener, is higher in status than the speaker, even though this may not be true. By so doing, the speaker creates a basis for understanding in the interaction where the listener is established as a high-status person and the speaker as lower in status.

In Iranian interaction, the above operation and many others related to it can be seen to be present. As will be discussed in Chapter 2, the exercise of *zerængi* ("cleverness, wiliness") can be seen as a means of effecting control of message interpretation. Thus a person who is *zeræng* is using operations of effectiveness in his interaction.

Iranian communication stresses the ability to employ skill in both appropriateness and effectiveness. Other societies, that of Japan for example, place great stress on appropriateness, but distrust the operations of effectiveness.[7] Thus it is possible to see how these seemingly universal operations can be realized differently in different cultures.

In contrasting appropriateness and effectiveness, then, the former can be seen as the ability to move toward predictable usage and the latter to vary from predictable usage in order to establish a revised framework for interpreting the elements of interaction. There is a paradox involved here, since effectiveness in communication also involves movement toward predictability—not the predictability of original expectation, but that of revised expectation. By shifting ground, the skillful communicator forces others in the interaction to "make his unpredictable behavior predictable" by supplying the new set of assumptions and identifications that will render his behavior understandable. This is a challenge to the communicative and interpretive skills of all involved and part of the intricacy, artistry, and amusement found in interaction.

Two major works dealing with the dynamics of language in interaction have been completed by John Gumperz since the present study was conceived and written. Gumperz's work (1982; Gumperz, ed., 1982) is of importance for this study because it is the first study to come out of the American sociolinguistic tradition of the 1960s to give a central place to creativity and variation in sociolinguistic routines. As he writes, " . . . we need to begin with an understanding of how linguistic signs interact with social knowledge in discourse" (1982:29). This assumes that speakers have knowledge of their social environment, control of their linguistic repertoire, and some knowledge of the probable effects of their use of one form as opposed to another. This contrasts sharply with "survey sociolinguistics," which is merely descriptive, making no attempt to take speaker control into account.

Gumperz, as I do in this study, gives a central place to speakers' ability to control the variables of their language to achieve goals in interaction "without reference to untestable functionalist assumptions about conformity or nonconformance to closed systems of norms" (ibid.).

Gumperz is primarily concerned in both of his books with the interaction that takes place between linguistic communities; thus much of his work deals with questions of "bi-lingualism" or "variety switching." The present study deals with the control of stylistic variation within a single language.

This study also takes a different tack from Gumperz's work in that it emphasizes symbolic aspects of the variation found in the language of Iranian interaction. Hierarchy and feelings of intimacy or distance in Iranian interaction are treated then not only as sociologically verifiable facts or aspects of social knowledge, but also as cultural leitmotifs, with important symbolic components that are not limited to the realm of social interaction, but that pervade all of Iranian cultural life and provide meaning for a wide variety of "things Iranian," from pronouns to political protest, from religious drama to royal prerogative.

Iranian Basic Schemas

Persian is a language with a very simple grammatical structure and a rich set of stylistic variables that help individuals to convey accounts of their feelings. An individual has many choices in speaking that must be determined on "pragmatic" grounds, as discussed above. It is a function of all parties in interaction to come up with the correct interpretations for what is said.

Iranian society (like all societies everywhere) provides for basic frames that clue individuals to appropriate language behavior for any situation. These frames provide a cognitive map that helps define what is normal and expected.

The basic dimensions of Iranian society are not terribly complex in a structural sense, but they provide for a rich play of linguistic expression. Two broad arenas of symbolic cultural contrast play a major role in Iranian life. The first consists of the opposition between the *internal* and the *external*, and the second consists of contrast between *hierarchy* and *equality*. The *internal* vs. *external* contrast will be treated at length in Chapter 4 and the *hierarchy* vs. *equality* contrast in Chapter 3. Nevertheless, a brief preliminary discussion of these two symbolic structures may be useful at this point.

The basic orientation of interaction frames consists of a continuum, with situations that are considered more *internal* at one pole and situations considered more *external* at the other.[8] The contrast between *internal* and *external* is pervasive in Iranian thinking and governs many other aspects of national life.

In philosophical terms, the *internal* is often referred to as the *baten* and is revealed as the seat of man's strongest personal feelings. Though it is the seat of passion, the emotions and feelings contained there are generally positively valued, and their expression on appropriate occasions is not only socially sanctioned, but frequently demanded.

The *baten* is also the center of social peace in its theoretical architectural form, the *ændærun*. This is the space within the household that is the most private, the most secluded. It is the seat of family intimacy and is where the women of the family may find safety from the outside world. It is the place where events are the most predictable; therefore it is the place where one can allow the freest personal expression.

The *external* is by contrast the realm of the relatively unpredictable and likewise the realm of controlled expression. It is the realm of politesse and of proper conversation and behavior, where one's true feelings must be held in check, where a proper public face must be put on one's words.

The philosophical realm of the external is labeled the *zaher*, and it is considered a necessary concomitant of life. Nevertheless, it is not highly valued in moral terms. The *zaher* is the realm of corruption and of worldly influences, but it is also a buffer for the delicate world of the *baten*. Thus one may not value the *zaher*, but one must know how to operate in it. The admonition, *zaher-ra hefz kon!* (protect external appearances!) is widely given and widely heeded, since by maintaining the external aspects of one's behavior, one can remain out of danger and protect and control the *baten*.[9]

The *zaher* has its physical reflex in architecture as well. It is the *birun* or *biruni*, the public reception areas of the household where strangers may be entertained without endangering the private space of the family. The *ændærun* and *birun* of the household are, to a degree, portable. The Tehrani family going on a picnic takes its *ændærun* with it to the outdoors by bringing carpets, cooking utensils, a samovar, and the accouterments of home. A person traveling to another town will have innumerable locations available where he or she can be in an *ændærun*—put on pajamas, nap, and eat around a family dinner cloth (*sofreh*)—usually in the home of relatives or close friends.

The feeling of being in an inside/*ændærun*/*baten* situation vs. an outside/*birun*/*zaher* situation is a matter of subjective judgment, depending on a calculus of factors, much as those identified by Friedrich in his classic studies of Russian pronominal usage (1966, 1972).[10] One judges a particular situation based on location, the company one finds oneself with, the topic of conversation, and so forth, down the list.

As was stated at the beginning of this section, and as will be argued at length in Chapter 4, the two situations represent poles on a continuum. An individual feels situated somewhere between the extremes, neither totally "inside" nor totally "outside" for any given instance of interaction. This basic orientation forms the social canvas against which the interpretation of communication takes place.

Persian contains a number of stylistic devices that automatically help individuals signal each other concerning many aspects of their assessment of their relationship. These stylistic devices principally deal with contrasts between relationships of *hierarchy*, which are *status-differentiated*, and relationships of *equality*, which are *status-undifferentiated*.

Hierarchical differentiation seems to be a nearly universal feature of human life, but in some societies, such as India (Dumont 1970) or Japan (Lebra 1976), hierarchy takes on special symbolic significance. There are few societies that take the obligations of status as seriously as does Iranian society. Persons placed in a position of superiority should ideally rise to that position and retain it by fulfilling obligations toward inferiors that ensure their support and respect. Inferiors in turn retain their ties to specific individuals in superior positions by reciprocal observance of obligations of their own. In contrast to the hierarchical orientation in Iranian society are ties of intimacy and equality between individuals. These ties involve mutual obligations of such a severe and absolute nature that they often prove impossible to fulfill.

Social behavior between superior and inferior tends to revolve around patterns of mutual exchange. The obligations incumbent on a superior in a hierarchical relationship prescribe that although demands may be made of inferiors, rewards and favors must also be granted to them. In general, the superior individual is bound to those in an inferior role by a concern for their general welfare and a desire to provide them with opportunities for advancement, comfort, and benefits. When this concern is genuine, the relationship is stable and indeed may even embody great affection. In such cases, polite language and compliments, glossed in Persian as *tæʿarof* (see Chapter 3), may be entirely genuine and sincere expressions of regard, rather than mere exploitative linguistic strategy (cf. Hillman 1981: 238).

Relationships of equality likewise involve exchange in the same manner; the difference is that in equality relationships the exchange of goods is non-status-marked and absolute. The ideal situation is one where two individuals involved in an intimate relationship anticipate each other's needs and provide all for the other without thought of self.

Relationships of equality and those of inequality can be deeply satisfying in Iranian life. Moreover, obligations in both kinds of relationships are absolute, the ultimate fulfillment coming from a willingness to enter into total self-sacrifice in meeting the needs of the other person. This is true of the superior, who must care for dependents, even if ruination results; the inferior, who follows a leader in all respects, even to death; and the comrade, who gives all for the sake of an intimate companion.

As with internal vs. external orientation in Iranian life, status differentiation in personal relationships tends to lead to organization of experience on a sliding scale, with idealized absolute goals at both poles. Few people can fulfill the obligations of social relationships as described above, but as cultural ideals they inspire and direct positively valued behavior.

Style in Cultural Communication

Both internal vs. external orientation and status differentiation constitute communicative dimensions for Persian speakers as well. They serve to orient the kinds of linguistic signals that participants in interaction must use to inform each other of their assessment of their relationships to each other.

Just as every action is an account of itself, every communication can be seen as imposing a commitment to a state of affairs on the part of participants. Bateson pioneered this approach, in which every communication can be seen as having a "report" and a "command" aspect respectively (cf. Ruesch and Bateson 1951: 179–181). Watzlawick et al. summarize this difference usefully: "The report aspect of a message conveys information and is, therefore, synonymous in human communication with the *content* of the message. It may be about anything that is communicable regardless of whether the particular information is true or false, valid, invalid, or undecidable. The command aspect, on the other hand, refers to what sort of a message it is to be taken as, and, therefore, ultimately to the *relationship* between the communicants" (Watzlawick, Beavin, and Jackson 1967: 51–52). In Persian such signaling is carried out largely through stylistic variation in language. This stylistic variation includes the pronoun alternation analyzed by Friedrich, but much else as well, affecting a whole range of linguistic factors—phonological, morphological, and syntactic.

In Chapter 5 interactional aspects of the sound system in Persian will be examined at length. To cite one example, there exists a definite contrast in the speech of speakers of standard Persian between word final consonant clusters on the one hand and a reduction of those clusters to single word final consonants on the other hand. In comparing the speech of individuals in different contexts it is possible to demonstrate that such an alternation is correlated with different contexts of usage; a speaker's use of one form or another is significant in the interpretation of communication events in which that person participates. In interpreting what the role of such alternation is in the communicative event, however, one must have much more information.

One can identify two ranges of applicability with the presence or absence of reduced final consonant clusters. One range of applicability is associated with speakers' perceptions of significant information about the nature of the totality of the communication event in which they are participating. This is correlated in Iranian cultural contexts with feelings about the relative internal or external nature of the interaction context.

The second range is associated with speakers' perceptions about the similarity and dissimilarity of persons with whom they are engaged in interaction in comparison to themselves. This correlates in Iranian culture with judgments of the relative superiority, inferiority, or equality of those individuals in relation to the speaker.

Sound reduction in speech is a reasonable reflex for judgments about context and relative speaker status, because it reflects clearly the amount of total differentiation in communication that appears necessary for interaction to proceed successfully. Linguistic sound systems may be thought of in terms of their communicative functions. As Ladefoged (1974) has maintained, there are two competing bio-behavioral tendencies operating on the structure of a given sound system: first, the principle of least effort for the speaker, which pushes the sound system toward decreased differentiation; second, the principle of least effort for the listener, which pushes the sound system in the direction of maximum differentiation.

There are some situations where the listener's need for maximum differentiation is increased, particularly those situations whose course and outcome are less predictable, in a pragmatic sense, than others. An interaction between individuals exhibiting a low degree of communality, for example, requires a much higher degree of specification in the code to render a message comprehensible. In such situations, the sound system must be more highly differentiated.

Some social situations involve a great deal of communality or knowledge among speakers about all aspects of the interaction: situation, background and potential actions of other participants, messages likely to be transmitted, and so forth. This "casual situation" needs functionally less formal distinction in the communication code to relay a particular message.[11]

The behavioral factor that allows the transition from greater to less formal specificity within the sound system is redundancy. Redundancy in speech tends to be increased in less predictable situations, where the principle of least effort for the listener takes priority. Redundancy is decreased in more predictable situations, where the principle of least effort for the speaker takes priority.

In Persian one sees consonant cluster reduction as a clear response to these questions of context. In complex, socially differentiated social situations, all possible sound distinctions in the language are used in precise ways. Redundancy increases, thereby reducing the unpredictability of the situation.

In Chapter 5 a general account will be given of the phonemic structure of the language. It will then be argued that there is a tendency toward general reduction of consonants in some styles. When consonant deletion occurs, there is a tendency toward general reduction of vowel length as well. Consonants that are eliminated are those that are the most frequent in combinatory sequences and therefore most redundant in terms of the information they convey and the distinct forms they help to distinguish. Reduction in vowel length is seen also as the elimination of a redundant phonetic feature in Persian. One result of the application of both of these stylistically marked processes is to effect a shift in the pattern of syllable structure in the language from a predominantly Arabic syllable pattern to a pattern more characteristic of words of Persian origin.

The shift from verbal style in which consonant deletion and vowel length reduction are practiced to verbal style where they are not is shown to correspond with contextual shifts outlined in Chapter 3. As contexts shift from externally oriented (termed "Pole A") situations to internally oriented ("Pole B") situations, consonant deletion and vowel length reductions occur more often. Since the contexts are cognitively determined, it is largely a function of individual perception whether a speaker is carrying out interaction which is more oriented toward Pole A or Pole B.

In Chapter 6 of this study I will present some of the basic patterns of morphological stylistic variation in Persian. In general, morphological stylistic differentiation is most apparent in the verbal and pronominal systems. Though verbal/pronominal variation seems to be the predominant indicator of differentiated interpersonal "status" relationships in many languages, Persian exhibits a distinctive pattern for this variation.

In Persian the great bulk of variation falls on the separable nonverbal components (adjectives, nouns, nominalized verbs and adverbs) that combine with verbal auxiliaries to make the large number of compound verb forms found in the language, as well as on the personal endings attached to verbs. In considering the morphological construction of the Persian verb, it is possible to see that these two systems are the only ones available to exhibit stylistic variation, since variation in other components of the verb produces changes in aspectual reference. Pronouns are the other area of morphology that exhibits stylistic variation.

Pronouns and verbs in Persian are oriented in three directions that correspond with basic orientations in social relations. The first orientation reflects relationships of inequality and involves a process of "other-raising" vs. "self-lowering." Basically, one uses terms that serve to place oneself in an inferior status and the other person in a superior one. These consist of a series of substitutions for neutral verbs and pronouns. Thus self-reference may use the expression *bandeh* (slave) in place of the neutral pronoun *man* (I). Reference to the other person in interaction may substitute the verb *færmudæn* (command) for the neutral verb *goftan* (say). Relationships of equality use parallel terms. Both parties will use the same pronouns and verbs, and these tend to be rougher and less refined as intimacy between the parties increases.

The important aspect of these linguistic stylistic materials is that they are used differentially, depending on the context in which interaction takes place. It is thus the interplay of cognitive context, in terms of general orientation to inside vs. outside dimensions, with human orientation toward status and equality that creates the interactional grammar for the expression of emotions in Iranian life.

In Chapter 7, I will attempt to deal to some extent with stylistic variation in the structure of discourse. In Persian there are numerous places where remarks can be prefaced, where speakers can alternate, where hesitations can be made, where interruptions can occur, and so forth. Each of these functions in discourse can be carried out by an array of phrase forms that are stylistically marked. A description of the structure of the flow of discourse constitutes a kind of "syntax" of the interaction process (cf. Schegloff 1968, 1972). However, individual choice in the use of variables available constitutes an important aspect of performance in structuring the parameters of interaction, i.e., in the management of messages, as treated in Chapter 2.

Stylistic variation of this sort consists of phrases operating within discourse as insertions at points that correspond to major breaks within the syntactic structure of sentences (cf. Moyne and Carden 1974). Further, these variants are seen to contribute not to the literal message of the utterance, but to the performative aspect of the utterance. This is to say, they contribute little in determining *what is being said* but quite a bit to *what is being done by what is said.*

The phrases themselves are constructed using as a base those lexical units that vary most often within the morphological system. These phrases are further subject to the variation that exists within the sound system of Persian. In this way, the three principal arenas of stylistic variation can be seen as both separate and interrelated.

Chapter 8 will return once more to the question of aesthetics and shows how language skills are used in popular theater and in revolutionary rhetoric. This final chapter demonstrates how these skills play upon the same broad cultural structures that determine stylistic variation.

Iranian Interaction Semantics

In the chapters that follow, I attempt to go beyond simply reporting regularities of the application of communication principles such as those previewed above in order to explore the specific web of social logic that characterizes particularly Iranian principles of communication. In doing this it is necessary to differentiate that which characterizes human interaction in general from that which constitutes the "stuff" of normalcy in a particularly Iranian context.

I would agree with Sapir that a set of common structured perceptions must underlie the common linguistic habits of any interacting community (Sapir 1949: 15–16). In line with this, I will attempt to show below that the web of social and cultural institutions in extra-linguistic situations in Iranian society corresponds with a set of orientational frames for individuals when they enter into interaction with each other—a set of cultural maps of socially significant phenomenal territory.

These orientational frames serve as sensitizing devices for individuals. It helps them to sort out from the infinitude of phenomena available for attention in any given interaction situation those that are culturally significant—to recognize, in Bateson's terms, "the differences which make a difference" in any situation. It helps them select the significant information from the past that bears on the immediate interaction event. Moreover, it gives them the basis for predicting the probable outcome of the event.

The process is a pragmatic fusion of selected elements from the individuals' preacquaintance, present, and potentiality, resulting in concrete behavior that the individual expects will be interpretable by others—interpretable preferably in some way that corresponds with notions of how one's actions *should* be interpreted to fulfill one's own expectations about the outcome of the interaction.

This formulation fairly well guarantees that individual pieces of behavior, if abstracted from social and cultural context, will be uninterpretable by an analyst. This is, I believe, as it should be. From the point of view presented in this formulation there can be no semantics of language used in interaction that is not in some way interpretive semantics. Further, interpretation must proceed from as full a knowledge of all elements contributing to the contextualization of the presentation of an individual communicative element as possible.

Arguing in favor of an interpretive interaction semantics is fully in line with a great deal of current thinking in linguistic theory. If one is willing to allow that the number of sentences that can be generated by speakers of a given language is infinite and that this infinitude proceeds from a set of specifiable formal elements, it would seem profitable to base the study of semantics on the assumption that an infinitude of meaning may be generated within the parameters of the application of specific principles of social interactional logic in which linguistic units are only members of a single class of contributing elements. The broad Iranian cultural classification of events into internal and external spheres and grouping of interaction partners according to relative status dimensions show how an interactional logic may be constructed, one that is based on pan-human dimensions of classification but retains the unique flavor of an individual culture.

This study centers not so much on principles as it does on speakers, however. Individuals' creative use of their own language is ultimately the mechanism that determines meaning in interaction. In the case of Iran, these creative usages have themselves crystallized into recognizable interaction styles that are often misinterpreted by outside observers.

The interaction styles of Iranians involve the patterned use of stylistic variables available for choice within a given interaction frame. Thus there is a double sense in which we must use the word "style" in speaking about Iranian interaction. On the one hand, Persian presents stylistic alternatives to speakers; on the other hand, speakers' strategies in using those alternatives crystallize into interaction "styles."

Chapter 2 will deal with the broad management of messages in Iranian life that give interaction the particular quality and flavor we can identify as Iranian style. Within the broad patterns of message management, the fine workings of the use of stylistic variables find their place, like jewels in a fine setting.

Language and Magic

As this discussion proceeds, it will occur to most readers that the kinds of processes and patterns I deal with throughout this study are not specific to Persian nor to Iran. The degree to which these communicational phenomena are pan-human will be difficult to ascertain until more complete studies are made of other languages in the same vein.

The field of linguistics in recent years has been emerging from a period of narrow focus on a model of language that has been highly abstracted—denuded of its active component and thus stripped of flesh and blood. The next decade is likely to be a time of reintegration of the many diverse areas of inquiry that focus on the study of language, in order to begin to understand how language works in affecting the course of human events for individuals and larger groupings in human society.

In the discussion that follows I refer often to the need to focus on the ways language affects the conditions for its own interpretation. This has been one of the concerns of the traditional academic discipline of rhetoric. Being an anthropologist, I would like to suggest a more provocative framework: language as magic.

Magicians are able to transform reality. Likewise in the performance of communicative acts, individuals are able to transform time, place, thought, and intention. One moment I am unconvinced, and then, with a few words, I enter a new state of conviction. One moment I am unmarried, and then, with a few words, I am transformed into a married person. One moment I find myself in an uncomfortable, formal social situation, and then, with a few words, everyone laughs, the situation itself changes and becomes more comfortable, looser. One moment I have no pressing needs in the world; the next, after talking to a skilled salesman, I feel I will not be able to live another moment without buying something he is selling. This is truly magic.

Iranians are masters of their own communication magic to a great degree. In knowing how to use the resources of their own language in conjunction with their knowledge of society and its dynamics, they are able to negotiate and even transform an uncertain world with skill and grace. Though all men are able to do the same in their own tongues, it may be a particular Iranian skill to be able to carry out this magic with an elevated sense that raises the enterprise above mere pedestrian communication and into the realm of art.

II

THE MANAGEMENT OF MESSAGES

Components of Speech

Jakobson's highly influential article, "Linguistics and Poetics" (Jakobson 1960), provided a schema for the study of speech that has been more or less assumed and elaborated on in subsequent investigations in the ethnography of communication. Jakobson's discussion need not be repeated here, but his list of "constitutive factors in any speech event"—Addresser, Addressee, Context, Message, Contact, and Code— along with their relative functions—Emotive, Conative, Referential, Poetic, Phatic, and Metalingual—remains more or less central in the investigation of speech in interaction.

Hymes has elaborated on Jakobson's schema to a considerable degree in several publications (Hymes 1964, 1966, 1972, 1974), and a highly detailed expansion of this basic core of factors has been suggested by W. P. Robinson (1974). However many factors are included in an analytic taxonomy of communication events, the basic message form remains at the core of all analysis. As Hymes has, to my thinking, quite correctly maintained, "It is a general principle that all rules (for speech) involve message form, if not by affecting its shape, then by governing its interpretation" (Hymes 1974: 54).

When message form is taken to be the central factor in the specification of communicative events, then the general principles of communication one is led to formulate for a given cultural system will be framed in terms of the interrelationship between a given message form and some other factor or factors. Additionally, as can be inferred from Hymes's statement above, culturally specific principles of communication involve statements about not only the shape of message form but also its interpretation.

Hymes's schema for the study of speech makes a clear distinction between message form and message content (1974: 55). Though they are closely interdependent, they vary with regard to each other in any given system of communication. In this chapter I present that body of general communication principles operative in Iranian interaction that have to do with the interrelationship of message form to message content. Subsequent chapters will present information that deals with the relationship of message form to other communicative dimensions.

Uncertainty and Insecurity in Iranian Life

One theme that continually appears in literature on Iran has to do with the great insecurity or uncertainty of social life. Marvin Zonis's important and highly enlightening study of the Iranian political elite (Zonis 1971) cites numerous Western writers who point up the pervasive, manifest insecurity of the Iranian citizenry. Indeed, Zonis himself declares insecurity and uncertainty a basic orientation of the elites he is studying as demonstrated in correlations from an extensive questionnaire administered to those persons.

If we were to attempt a communicational definition of certainty or to ask Americans to delineate exactly what they mean by certainty in human relations, it is likely that we would get such statements as, "I feel certain when dealing with X; I know that he is honest; he means what he says" and "I am certain in my life situation because I am sure of the rules of the game; I am able to understand what is being communicated to me; I know the score."

Indeed, satisfaction in completing a particular communicative act in the United States often involves all parties involved "knowing the score" when it is completed. If questions remain unresolved, individuals will frequently press for additional information by which they can correctly interpret the message forms they receive from others. In short, one important principle of communication in the United States involves a tendency for individuals to try and arrive at a single set of interpretive criteria for understanding the relationship between message form and message content, and this can be glossed as "certainty."

Nico Kielstra in an unpublished paper (Kielstra n.d.) argues for a dialectic approach to the analysis of social relations in Iran. He implies that Westerners interpret Iranian human relations as characterized by insecurity or uncertainty because they fail to understand that one possible form that a system of social life may assume is one where action is subject to interpretation based on sets of values that may be diametrically opposed. Thus, "to observers directed by their culture and training to think in unambiguous one-dimensional terms, the fluctuation between opposed sets of values and the manifestations of these fluctuations in actual behavior could easily give the impression of uncertainty in human relations, while for a Persian such fluctuations are the predictable result of variable conditions and are therefore not very uncertain or unexpected" (Kielstra n.d.: 6).

In the Iranian village of Gavaki there was continual difficulty in determining who would serve as the *kædkhoda* (official) of the village. Essentially the problem reduced to a conflict in values of the sort Kielstra cites. The difficulty revolved around the fact that the *kædkhoda* would be the one individual who government officials would be in contact with in their dealings with the village.

On the one hand, the majority of the villagers, who were for the most part small landowners and day laborers, wanted a person to represent them in government dealings who would not misrepresent their interests. On the other hand, they were anxious to have an individual serve as *kædkhoda* who was powerful, effective, and able to entertain urban officials on their occasional sojourns to the village. Unfortunately, the few persons who were powerful, wealthy, and effective enough to deal with the government were also large landowners who were likely not to want to operate in the best interests of the small landowners (indeed, large land-owners as a group had already proven to be extraordinarily adept at manipulating village land allocation and other economic affairs to their own advantage and to the detriment of small landowners).

The end result was that two individuals came to be known as *kædkhoda* (but see below). In conversation, depending on the content and nature of the discussion, either one or the other of the men would be referred to as *kædkhoda*.[1] The regional government of Shiraz was not willing to confirm either man, as both were unacceptable as village officials for differing reasons, but the villagers were unwilling to select others in their place. Eventually, however, regional government officials came to deal with both men on an unofficial basis, depending again on the nature of the business to be transacted. The two *kædkhodas* would each have been happy to have had the issue resolved in his favor (because this would represent an increase in status and power), but they were perfectly able to live with their official status "in limbo," each acknowledging tacitly the authority of the other in its proper context.

To further add to the complexity of the situation, the former *kædkhoda*, who had been designated by the former landlord, was still

resident in the village. Whereas he now had none of the influence
that he once had, he lived in the best house and had the greatest
amount of land of anyone currently residing in the village. In the
situation where the regional government had not designated an "official" *kædkhoda*, he too was still identified as *kædkhoda* in particular
contexts, although he himself denied that he had any authority when
questioned by me.

An outside observer would be told on one occasion that one individual was *kædkhoda;* on another occasion that another of the three
was *kædkhoda;* on yet another occasion that two, or all three, held
office; and finally, on some occasions, that the village didn't have a
kædkhoda at all. These multiple versions could be given as an account
of the *kædkhoda* situation by the same individual on different occasions.
Far from reflecting manifest uncertainty, the eventual state of affairs
demonstrated the flexibility with which villagers were able to deal with
the demands of different situations and value systems. Only an outside
observer determined on knowing "the single truth" about the matter
would try to fix on any one statement about the *kædkhoda* as the actual
state of affairs. The villagers knew better.

As stated in the last chapter, however, the impression of uncertainty
in Iranian life is based on observations of a core of regular phenomena
in interaction and can be stated as a *principle of communication:* the
relationship between message form and message content cannot be
interpreted according to any single set of criteria.

The former shah was, as one would expect, a grand master in the
use of this and other communication principles in Iran. As Baldwin
(1967) has written, "Without a doubt, the Shah leads most of his
countrymen in the art of Persian politics . . . refusing to crystallize
issues to the point where definite choices are made, thus disappointing
or offending someone; never allowing any individual to become too
powerful or too popular; never being so publicly identified with events
that it is impossible to shift the blame onto others; and cultivating an
ambiguity in political life that softens critics by pretending to espouse
their hopes while reassuring vested interests by rarely carrying out
promised reforms" (Baldwin 1967: 19).

It is of some interest to note that the same principle is highly operative in the traditional doctrines of the state religion, Shi'ite Islam,
and in the classic poetic tradition that pervades the Iranian "great
tradition" to so tremendous a degree. Speaking of the former, Fazlur
Rahman writes:

The principle of esotericism upholds the idea of a double or even multiple interpretation of the Qur'anic text. Side by side, with the "external" meaning of the Scripture, there are other "hidden" levels of meaning. . . . The principle of esotericism has also affected the Sufi (mystic) interpretations of the Qur'an and sometimes such "inner meanings" are carried to a pure arbitrariness of interpretation. No group of Muslims, however, have committed such unbridled arbitrariness in applying this principle as the Shi'a on the whole. Almost in every word of the Qur'an a reference is seen to the "holy household of Ali" or to later Imams. The idea that there must be some link between the symbol and the symbolized, which must bestow plausibility, or at least intelligibility on the interpretation, is simply not recognized. (Rahman 1968: 211)

Archer and Archer, in discussing the stylistics of classic Persian poetry, note much the same sort of phenomena among the classic writers:

The ambiguity of sex, since there is no gender in Persian, is too much fretted over. . . . The incessant questioning—is a male or a female being referred to?—burkes an important stylistic point, namely that the inspecificity of gender is a deliberate stylistic artifact, evidenced (if evidence is needed) by the fact that poets (and not only the grosser ones) can be quite ambiguous when the need dictates. . . . The uncertainty is the effect; it adds a further level of meaning to the poem. The effect of this accretion of meaning is not easy to gloss; the alternate play of terse many-layered epithet and diffused referents generalized (e.g. love and love-object) without making purely abstract; at a less polite level linguistic resource is employed economically (whatever the length and embranglement of the total work) to tease, distract, mislead, force uncertainty and thereby heighten aesthetic satisfaction. (Archer and Archer 1972: 18)

In dealing with the language of interpersonal interaction, one class of criteria seems to stand out in the interpretation of messages, however. This is that component of communication that Hymes labels *ends*, understood both in terms of goals and in terms of outcome (Hymes 1974: 56–57). This does not negate the general principle, however, that within the general communication system interpretation according to multiple criteria is the rule. Where "ends" are the basis for the interpretation of messages, interpretation is based on cognizance of multiple ends.

To provide an example related to the situation above regarding the *kædkhoda* in the village where I was resident, I was interviewing one man concerning village personalities. His old father was present in the room, as well as several other persons. I came to a question regarding one of the persons who was known as *kædkhoda*. The old father said, "Of course, he is the *kædkhoda*, and so, ..." Before he could finish his statement his son interrupted, saying, "What are you saying? Hajji Sayyid Hussein (the former landlord's representative) is *kædkhoda*." When his father tried to remonstrate, the son shouted him down again.

I had recorded this interchange on tape and later asked several persons (including the others who had been in the room) what they thought had been going on and why this dispute had come up. There was general agreement that the son wanted to demonstrate respect in some sense for Hajji Sayyid Hussein. Agreement about the nature of the message content in relation to the message did not extend beyond this. Two persons felt that the son, my informant, wanted to be identified as a person who was not opposed to Hajji Sayyid Hussein; another felt that my informant associated me with that same person and was trying not to let his old father offend me by according a less important person (one of the other *kædkhodas*) higher regard than this important village resident. Two others in the room felt that my informant was trying to be regarded himself as an important person, but they differed on the reasons. One felt that the informant was generally a person who had aspirations above his true status in the village. The other felt that the informant was being made to feel important by being interviewed by me, and this action—contradicting his father and defending a high-status person—was a reflex of his reception of his elevated status at that moment. The third additional person in the room claimed that the informant probably wanted some favor from Hajji Sayyid Hussein and hoped that I would put in a good word for him if I had the opportunity.

I then confronted two other sets of informants with this set of interpretations of the original event. I expected at that point to get some set of judgments about which persons had the correct interpretation of the original event. Instead, I was treated to a long set of explanations about why my *secondary* commentators had said what they did in response to my request for information about the nature of the original interaction. However, when pressed to give a judgment about the validity of the various explanations, my tertiary commentators were unable to come to a clear decision about the best interpretation. Several of the explanations sounded reasonable to them. One finally said, "I cannot know the inner state (*baten*) of another man. I can only know *my* inner state. He has to protect his own external appearances (*zaher*). The question of what his intent is is useless (*bi-fa'ideh*). I only need to know what affects me. In the end, I would wait and see what he does; then I would understand what he was doing when he said that."[2]

What is striking about all of this is that none of the commentators felt that my original informant was making a simple statement about who was or was not the *kædkhoda*. What he *said* was felt to be quite different from what the statement was *about*. Further, the bases for assessing what the statement was about were highly variant, depending on what the individuals felt the speaker's view of the ends of the conversation were. That their statements were subject to the same sort of interpretation by still a third level of commentators made the situation all the more remarkable.

The Clever Dissimulator

A widely cited "trait" of Iranians that has an enormous support in literature and anecdote is "cleverness" or "wiliness" (*zerængi*).[3] The archetypical example of the clever and successful individual in society has been Morier's *Hajji Baba of Isphahan*. Although Hajji Baba was created by an Englishman, his adventures have been translated into Persian and are well known.[4] A more indigenous figure is Mullah Nasr od-Din, whose many clever dealings have been the subject of countless apocryphal stories. Additionally, popular stories abound with the clever sayings and doings of famous poets, kings, and court figures down through the ages.

Zerængi is indeed an ability that many aspire to, but its practice need not, as many have claimed, indicate that Iranians are sneaky. If we begin with the premise developed in the previous section, that one important principle of communication in Iran is that the relationship between message form (what is said) and message content (what the message is about) cannot be interpreted by a single set of criteria, then an important tension is set up between the person initiating communicative behavior and the person interpreting it. Stated as a rule for communication, one might say that *zerængi* is an operation on the part of an adroit operator that involves thwarting direct interpretation of his own actions or deliberately leading others to erroneous interpretation of those actions while being able to successfully interpret the actions of others. Since cleverness of this sort represents a

skill, it enters into any interpersonal situation as a potential, foreseeable communication element. A person who is *zeræng* may try to create
a disposition on the part of others to interpret the code elements in
communication in a particular way, by influencing their perception
of these situational elements. Thus, he may ingratiate himself to another person in order, for example, to increase the possibility that
certain messages, such as requests or petitions, will be received favorably or to forestall certain other behavioral acts, such as verbal or
physical abuse (cf. Beeman 1976a).

Cleverness of this sort has an institutional reflection in the practice
of *tæqiyeh*[5] (dissimulation), which grows out of long Shi'a Islamic tradition. Shi'ism became dominant as the state religion only during the
Safavid reign of Shah 'Isma'il in the sixteenth century. Before this
time, Shi'ite believers were authorized to practice dissimulation if their
life or property should be in danger when they were under persecution. Fazlur Rahman declares this to be one of two characteristic
Shi'ite doctrines, the second being the esotericism mentioned above:

> . . . the early doctrinal evolution of Shi'ism is still very obscure. In the
> frustration caused by repeated political defeats and successive perse-
> cutions suffered by Shi'ism in its early phase, the movement went
> largely underground and this subterranean activity on the one hand
> rendered it liable to the influence of all kinds of heterodox ideas and,
> on the other, it produced two principles, one practical and one theo-
> retical, but both closely allied, that have become characteristic of Shi'-
> ism. The practical principle is that of dissimulation of belief (taqiyeh).
> This principle, in its mild form, was permitted also by orthodoxy. . . .
> Under the law of "relaxation and firmness" however, orthodoxy insisted
> on high moral integrity and affirmed that "firmness is superior to
> relaxation." With Shi'ism, on the other hand it became a cardinal prin-
> ciple to dissimulate belief not only under direct and express danger to
> life but in a generally hostile environment. Further, such dissimulation
> is not merely allowed, it is an obligatory duty of a fundamental order.
> (Rahman 1968: 210)

Rahman and Haas both maintain further that these two characteristic Shi's doctrines—*tæqiyeh* and esotericism—are directly related to
each other. As Rahman notes, "God in revealing the Qur'an has also
operated on the principle of *taqiya* [*sic*]" (Rahman 1968: 211). Haas
maintains the notion that Shi'ism answers the national aspirations of
a downtrodden Persian people and in its esotericism answers fundamental national needs built up through centuries of historical
tradition:

No doubt in the recesses of their souls the Persians, at least those of the first century after the Islamic conquest, identified themselves with the persecution and martyrdom of Ali and his house. They, too, were a defeated and humiliated people whose rights and deepest convictions had been violated and trodden upon. . . . Dissimulation could [thus] claim another esoteric function—that of hiding the highest spiritual truth from the contaminating contact with a hostile world; only in this way could the secret truth be passed on from generation to generation unspoiled by foreign elements.

It is this idea of the *ketman* [taqieh] which agrees especially with the whole character of the Shia—that of mystic and in essence secret doctrine. In this religious sphere is the most powerful cause of the change which to all appearances occurred in the Persian mind, giving the Persians their distinctive characteristics. In Sufism the Persian spirit maintains its purity. The Shia, on the other hand, is an admirable, but inevitably only partially successful attempt to discard Islam; it is psychologically speaking, more of an escape than a solution. It is understandable that the long period of national decline and dismemberment, with its uncertainties, was also very likely to foster such a mentality. (Haas 1946: 134)

Considering the analogy to Shi'ite religious tradition made above, the exercise of *zerængi* should be clearly understood not to be operative only in situations of self-interest. Whereas it is often seen and exemplified in situations where personal gain results, the employment of *zerængi* may often incorporate aspects of true altruism. One young fellow in the village where I was resident attended high school in Shiraz. He was not very bright but had nonetheless been promised the opportunity to marry his pretty cousin when he graduated from high school. The first thing he did each year was to change high schools, so that no one in the village was ever quite sure which one he was attending. He then would bring his reports home at odd or irregular times, so that his parents had no idea of when to expect his grades. In time he was able to convince his parents that he had actually graduated, when in fact he had failed his final examinations. He eventually was married to his cousin and had enlisted in the army before his parents were finally informed in a totally unexpected manner that he had in fact not graduated and indeed had not even advanced to the final class in high school, having failed his examinations the year before as well. When I had a chance to question him about this, he told me that whereas his parents were enormously irritated initially (to say nothing of his uncle, who expected a high-school graduate for a son-in-law), they were eventually convinced by their neighbors and relatives that his extraordinary *zerængi* in the whole matter more than offset his lack of filial duty, and that now he was married with a good dowry and a reasonable position in the army, they should be quite satisfied. Indeed, they had now become quite confident of his success in life. His own feeling was not that he had "put one over" on his parents, but that he had been sure that he would never be able to finish high school from the beginning and he simply wanted to arrange things so that his parents would never have to find out when he eventually was failed, to spare them pain and embarrassment.

One arena for the exercise of female *zerængi* is the area of marriage brokerage. The village expression for the woman's role in this exercise is "making the way clear." One of the few areas in which I was able to make inroads into the workings of female society in Iran was on the subject of marriage arranging, which women were ready and willing to talk about. Indeed, having brought off a successful matching of two individuals was as important an accomplishment for a woman in Gavaki as making a financial killing for a man in the bazaar or elsewhere. The woman's chief duty was to let the other family (usually the family of the girl) know that her family was interested in marriage, and to get from the other person fair indication that the proposal would not be turned down. Although the men of the family must meet and make a formal declaration of intent, the guarantee of success in the measure must be obtained by the woman beforehand. The woman must never be in a position, however, of actually having made an offer. She is enjoined from doing so, as a woman, by custom. More importantly, however, an offer made and then refused would cause great embarrassment for the family. Thus there must always be the possibility that the woman could deny that a particular message form in her interaction with another woman constitutes the suggestion that marriage be contracted between the two families.

Related to this is the reluctance of some Iranians of my acquaintance to send telegrams to their relatives. As one man told me, "If I telegraph my mother and tell her that I am delayed in getting home, she will immediately assume that I am near death. Therefore it is better to tell her nothing or to cable her that I am well and will arrive as expected." Because of the common practice of breaking the news of a tragedy in stages, my friend wanted to spare his mother the antic-ipation of progressively worse and worse telegrams by not sending what would be interpreted as the first in a series. In both the marriage brokerage and this situation, the clever individual is able to forestall a correct or definitive reading of the relationship between message form and other components of the communication act as a hedge against foreseeable disagreeable outcomes of that act.

Attempts to practice *zerængi* can sometimes backfire (although, to be sure, persons who are not able to manage interactions in a clever way are by definition not very *zeræng*). An extremely common theme in Persian popular films concerns persons who masquerade as someone they are not or fail to reveal the "true" state of affairs in an attempt to effect personal gain, or forestall disaster, and are caught. In one popular film of 1972 called *Bæd Nam* (*Bad Name*), the heroine hides her shameful profession as a nightclub dancer behind the guise of being a nurse. She carries a black bag and goes to the hospital every night in her *čador*,[6] only to proceed from there to her real job in the nightclub. She falls in love with a man from a "respectable family" in the neighborhood but is found out by one of the neighbors. The end result was that she had to break off her marriage and leave the neighborhood in shame.

Another film, the internationally acclaimed *Gav* (*The Cow*), based on a story by the great contemporary Persian writer, Gholam Hossein Sa'edi, centers on a villager who has a great attachment for his cow. While he is away from the village, the cow dies. The villagers, knowing how much the owner loves his animal, determine to conceal from him the fact that the cow has died. Instead, they tell him the cow has strayed. The owner on his return is confronted with a seemingly impossible fact. He knows that the cow wouldn't stray away from the village; still, he can get no one to tell him otherwise. Eventually, he becomes insane and assumes the identity of the dead cow. When the villagers tell him finally that the cow has died the situation has really become dire; he can no longer be brought back to his senses.

One recent popular film in which the exercise of *zerængi* is highly successful is a marvelous farce released in 1974, *Sazeš* (*Accommodation*). The protagonist is a poor fellow trying to scrape up enough money to marry by working as an actor in a lower-class theatre and as a part-time sneak thief. One evening he breaks into the apartment of a woman who is mistress to a local city politician. The thief overhears the woman's lover tell his wife on the phone that he was detained by an old friend, a doctor then resident in Europe but visiting Iran. The next day, the actor-thief shows up at the politician's home, introduces himself to the wife as that doctor, and allows himself to be persuaded to stay in the home as a guest of the family—where he proceeds to attempt to blackmail the politician. However, he eventually attracts so much credence in the neighborhood in his role as doctor that he is elected to the political post of the man he is blackmailing.

Whom Do You Trust?

Another common observation about Iranian society that is closely related to those I have cited above concerns lack of trust in human relationships. As Zonis notes of the Iranian elite, "As a group . . . [they] are beset by mistrust. They mistrust the motives of other Iranians, their families, their children, and most likely, themselves, at least partially because they are unable to control their environment and places within it" (Zonis 1971: 283). He is certainly correct in his further observation, "that mistrust is a characteristic mode of interpersonal relations in Iran about which virtual certainty exists among students of Iranian politics" (Zonis 1971: 272; cf. Ajami 1969a: Ch. 9; Baldwin 1967:16; Binder 1962:258; Westwood 1965; and many others). However, the notion of mistrust can easily be described nonpsychologically as another corollary of the principles of communication we have been discussing thus far.

Mistrust seen as an attitudinal feature implies that other people are so unpredictable that one never knows what malevolence they are going to inflict on one, or how they are going to fail to support one's interests. If we consider mistrust from the standpoint of communication, we see that what we term mistrust is better thought of as an index of relative communicative maladroitness, i.e., the person we read as being mistrustful is in fact unable to interpret the actions of another to his own satisfaction. Taken in this sense, mistrust becomes the reciprocal of *zerængi*. That is, one person is successfully concealing his motives and true actions from another person, who is perhaps able to ascertain that *something* is going on, but he is not sure what. If this is coupled with a communicative habit whereby one comes to expect detrimental actions and bad news to be revealed in stages (as illustrated in the previous section), a clear pattern of expectation of bad news from individuals about whose actions one knows little is set up. In this light, it is interesting to note that the English word "mistrust" is difficult to translate into Persian and is best handled by a paraphrase.[7]

In this respect then, "mistrust" would seem to have much to do with the pragmatics of communication operative in Iranian social life, but little necessary connection with the actual personalities of Iranians.

To illustrate with an example from American life, no one insists that American women one might find in a singles bar are all gullible by nature because they may react to a verbal "line" given out by a male. The line, the possible reactions, and the status and roles of the participants are all part of the pragmatic communication expectations of the interaction participants. Similarly in Iranian communication situations, where obscurity and multiple meaning are highly valued,[8] one does not expect to be able to divine the motives of those more *zerœng* than oneself. But, lacking a complete reading, one follows the expected stages of message presentation to their worst outcome as a matter of course in the normal pragmatics of interpretation.

Understanding that the behavior observers have been labeled so often as "mistrust" is in fact a feature of communication should help considerably in unraveling that seeming anomaly that crops up again and again in the literature on Iran, where individuals seemingly "love" their relatives, yet "mistrust" them at the same time. Indeed, my experience has been that even dislike is not closely tied up with uncertainty about the potential action of others. Individuals in the village where I lived who were indicated to me as "bad" people, or people one did not like, did not attain that status because they were not trusted or were suspect in their actions; they were disliked rather for specific past deeds that had concrete bad effects.

Thus we are faced with the proposition, unsettling to Americans, that one can hold genuine affection for some people on the one hand and yet be convinced that they are practicing *zerœngi* that one cannot detect on the other hand. In the United States, where direct dealing is a sign, if not the proof, of friendship and affection, this situation may seem bizarre. Nevertheless, the following example points up a typical case where the expectation of secret dealings in no way interferes with the mutual feelings between the two parties.

A druggist with whom I was acquainted in the city of *Mœšhœd* had an "apprentice"—a young fellow who kept the shop when the druggist was away and helped out generally. The relationship between the two was really quite amiable. I was curious about the druggist's accounting procedures, since he never seemed to make a record of his receipts, and was surprised to learn that he kept no books at all. I then asked him if he didn't think that his apprentice might be stealing money with so loose a system. He answered that he was certain the fellow was stealing money, although he didn't know how much or when— in fact, he had never seen him steal or even noticed a shortage. I was somewhat surprised and asked him how he knew that the apprentice was stealing. He replied that, after all, all apprentices steal *something*, and this was an unusually excellent apprentice—the best he'd ever had—because not only was he a good worker, but he stole so little, and so cleverly, that he, the owner, was never able to detect it.

The Changing Ethic of Message Management

The discussion that has proceeded thus far in this chapter has centered on an important central communication principle in Iranian interaction involving the relationships between message form, message content, and the abilities and skills participants in interaction use in managing interpersonal communication. In the United States, where one aims for unequivocal, direct communication in so much of everyday dealing, the notion of a communication system that aims in exactly the opposite direction, toward multiple interpretation and indirect communication of both content and intent, may seem strange.

There is no question that this system of communication was at one time a source of great confusion to American government officials and businessmen in their dealings with Iran (see Millspaugh 1925, 1946; Baldwin 1967). When I first began my acquaintance with Iran in 1967 as a normal employee in the business community, there was enormous frustration among American expatriates who had to do work with the Iranian government and commercial community. Businessmen couldn't understand why, when they were told something, something else seemed to happen; why excuses were made when action was wanted; and why business dealings had to be so complicated. On the other side of the coin, Americans became known for both their honesty and their short-term gullibility. I myself was asked to make judgments about matters of importance because, "being an American," I would tell the truth.

Before the overthrow of the shah in 1979, a new breed had developed on the international government and business scene in Iran. Trained in American universities, these new young Iranian executives and managers understood American business practice and were able to deal with international businessmen on a basis that they could understand. The demand for American business school graduates in Iran had increased tremendously in the 1970s. Indeed, a satellite of the Harvard Business School[9] was established in Tehran in 1972 under royal sponsorship, with essentially total autonomy in its administration, admissions, procedures, and training techniques (not the case with other institutions of higher learning). These new young entre-preneurs came into the practice of business with communication skills and ideas that were quite different from those of their fathers and grandfathers in the bazaar.

Postrevolutionary Iran has shown, nevertheless, the extraordinary degree to which the traditional system of communication and inter-personal conduct has remained entrenched. The new principles of communication developed for use with foreigners still remain, adding yet another level to the complex system of communication already existing in the country and demonstrating a growing realization that individuals in Iran must learn to deal with expanding networks of social relational systems as they enter into dealings with the interna-tional community on their home turf.

The ability to manage messages in an adroit manner, to be *zeræng* in communication, requires skill in perceiving and registering those things that are significant, the ones that matter in the course of an interaction, and in using those language skills that exist in the inter-action code to their best advantage. In the chapter that follows, I will examine the principles of communication that govern the relationship between messages and the relative status of participants.

III

THE MANAGEMENT OF
INTERACTIONAL
PARAMETERS
PEOPLE

Perception, Attention, and "Status" in Interpersonal Interaction

The section that follows deals with principles of communication that affect the interrelationship between participants in the communication act and message form (cf. Hymes 1974: 56). Because my approach to the class of human interrelations often characterized as "status relations" is not a standard one, I will take a few paragraphs to deal with some epistemological issues fundamental to the analysis that follows.

I maintain, as a basic tenet underlying this study, that interpersonal status in interaction is directly related to the quality and nature of the selective perceptions that individuals have of each other in communication situations, as well as to the patterns of expectations one builds up predicated on the complexes of individual phenomena one chooses, is led, or simply happens to perceive at any given moment. I suggest that at each point in the discussion, perceptions of status may vary, depending on the set of phenomena being attended to at the moment of interaction. It follows then that if perception within the interactional field is fundamental to the use of varying stylistic elements in interpersonal communication, we must also speak about the nature of attention.

Attention is often thought of as a physiological process. It was Peirce alone who conceived of attention as a link in logical processes, however. He characterized it as follows:

> [A]ttention is the power by which thought at one time is connected with and made to relate to thought at another time; or, to apply the conception of thought as a sign, that it is the pure *demonstrative application* of a thought sign.

> Attention is roused when the same phenomenon presents itself in different subjects. We see that A has a certain character, that B has the same, C has the same; and this excites our attention, so that we say "*These* have this character." Thus attention is an act of induction; but it is an induction which does not increase our knowledge, because our "these" covers nothing but the instances experienced. It is, in short, an argument from enumeration. (Peirce 1955: 179)

Peirce goes on to connect the notion of attention developed above with the notion of habit. By Peirce's account, a habit arises from the generalization of the performance of a particular act via the stimulus arising from the neural associative sensation of having done that particular act on several occasions to a *generalized* occasion of which the *particular* occasions are a subset. Thus, "the formation of a habit is an induction, and is therefore necessarily connected with attention or abstraction. Voluntary actions result from the sensations produced by habits, as instinctive actions result from our original nature (Peirce 1955: 179).

Peirce's notion of attention and habit dovetails nicely with the proposition, developed earlier, that meaning in interaction arises from the conjoining of selective perceptions in the immediate situation with select items of preacquaintance and selected projections of the consequences of the immediate situation. Attention and habit constitute the process whereby such linkages become repeated and generalized over a range of situations.

When considering the nature of social reality for individuals engaged in interaction, the position I have adopted thus far has been closely akin to that of George Herbert Mead, Herbert Blumer, and other "symbolic interactionists." The symbolic interactionist position espouses a view of society based on interactional models as opposed to one based on organizational models. As Blumer maintains:

> [S]ocial organization is a framework inside of which acting units develop their actions. Structural features, such as "culture," "social systems," "social stratification," or "social roles," set conditions for their action but do not determine their action. People—that is, acting units—do not act toward culture, social structure or the like; they act toward situations. Social organization enters into action only to the extent to which it shapes situations in which people act, and to the extent to which it supplies fixed sets of symbols which people use in interpreting their situations. (Blumer 1969: 87–88)

Combining the two perspectives—those of Peirce and the symbolic interactionists—it becomes possible to make a statement such as the following: Selective perception of, or attention to, phenomenal elements in interaction is a habitual inductive process that links, through generalization, particular situations under a single categorical rubric. Although individual interaction situations can be thought of as essentially unique, the processes and organization of social life can generally be thought of as shaping situations to the point that similar phenomena will be present and available for attention over a wide range of separate situations.

The most common form of interpersonal interaction involves exchange between individuals. Thus, situations in which similar kinds of exchange occur may be generalized under a single rubric. Similar phenomena that occur in such exchange situations can also be singled out for attention within those situations. Some of those phenomena may be seen as attributes of the setting itself. However, the relationship between the situation and the phenomena that occur within it is a dynamic one. That is, if a situation is defined as being a particular *kind* of situation, participants will tend to selectively perceive phenomena that will support that definition. This adds another dimension to Peirce's notion of attention: a *deductive* dimension. Put simply, people not only practice induction in the process of generalization through selective perception, but also deduction in the process of selective perception through *accepting* a generalization.

In either case, the reference point—the point of fusion of interpretation for the individual (and thus the locus of meaning)—is not in the individual attributes that one perceives but rather *in the generalization that one induces to, or deduces from.*

With this realization, we are freed in a discussion of general principles of communication in Iran, or in any community, from having to center our discussion on the particular phenomenal attributes that all actors in interaction attend to in their selection of stylistic variants in interpersonal situations. It is for this reason that I have tried throughout this discussion to avoid the formulation of "rules" in dealing with conversational practices in interaction. Rules of usage, as I pointed out in the last chapter, cannot represent what individual speakers actually do in interaction, based as they are on schemes of interrelationships of features or of attributes. For example, formal rules of usage cannot account for the strategic ironic, humorous, or derogatory use of language.

In describing the characteristics of social differentiation in Iran that are relevant in governing behavior in interaction, I have purposely moved away from descriptions in terms of categorical status dimensions, such as high/low status. This avoids the problems of having to specify every component that makes up high status or low status. Such an exercise is probably futile anyway, as Geertz has observed in declining to carry out such an analysis of Javanese culture (Geertz 1960: 258).

Rather, I choose to describe social differentiation in terms of the quality and ease of the flow of exchange that obtains between two or more people and the communication principles that the persons engaged in interaction use as basic orientations in their attempts to harness, divert, and regulate this flow. Selective *attention* to social attributes and characteristics that others possess are the clues that allow people to develop their skills in human relations. However, in any system where there are adroit and maladroit operators, we must assume that some are better at picking up and using this information effectively than others. The principles of communication that orient people to each other in interaction are like highways on a map of the territory of human relationships. Once one has a clear view of the map and its relationship to the territory, one can negotiate those roads with some ease.

Dimensions of Exchange in Iranian Interaction

If we consider the dynamics of exchange in Iranian life from the perspective of an individual actor, we see him performing three basic functions in his dealings with others:

1. providing action for others
2. providing material goods for others
3. stimulating others to provide either goods or action

In Iran, exchange of this sort can be unequivocal and unmediated or qualitatively marked. This is to say, there are ideally, on the one hand, potential relationships that persons can engage in that involve unbounded, unmarked exchange of goods and action—where mutual demands for action can be made in a direct fashion. There are, on the other hand, relationships where transfer of goods or action and stimuli for goods and action are qualitatively marked in exchange.

The first of the two kinds of exchange can be thought of in perceptual terms as interaction where two persons are defined as being, or perceive themselves to be, close, equal, similar, or intimate in terms of some clear common dimensions. This feeling is conveyed by the

Persian term *sæmimiæt* or the adjective *sæmimi*—used primarily between persons who define themselves as friends, *dustan* (singular *dust*). In this kind of exchange, as well as in the other kind, an *ethic* is implied. (I mean to use ethic in the sense of an aesthetic and moral ideal against which all interactions of this sort are measured, both by the parties involved themselves and by outsiders.) The ethic is one of communality, merger on a spiritual and material plane, and absolute reciprocity. This will be discussed more fully below.

The second of the two kinds of exchange can be thought of, again in perceptual terms, as an interaction where two persons perceive themselves to be dissimilar or unequal. In this relationship, one party takes the part in exchange of

1. providing favors,
2. providing rewards, and
3. stimulating others to provide goods or action through issuing orders.

The other party takes the part in the exchange of

1. providing service,
2. providing tribute, and
3. stimulating others to provide goods or action through making petitions.

The two roles in the exchange situation are reciprocal. If one person is thought to take the first role, the other must take the second. Though the relationship here may seem to resemble Brown and Gilman's "power semantic" (Brown and Gilman 1960), Iranians speak of persons in the first role as *bozorgtær* (bigger, greater) or *balatær* (higher). As we will see below, the idiomatic identification of the two roles is significant for behavior both because it is stated comparatively and because it uses images of size and height.

The ethic implied in both the first and second role in this kind of exchange can be thought of as one of *symbiosis*. In the first role it consists of the duty that proceeds from *noblesse oblige;* in the second role it consists of the duty that proceeds from *gratitude, submission, obedience, and respect.*

In both the first and second kinds of exchange, the ethics involve obligations of an absolute sort between the parties involved. In the best of all possible worlds, then, if everyone were established perfectly in one or another of these relationships with all persons within his acquaintance, exchanges and interactions would flow perfectly and smoothly, for everyone would know how and in what way he must fulfill his duty to God, himself, and others.

The ultimate fulfillment of duty in *both* kinds of relationships is total self-sacrifice—the sacrifice of one's life. Therefore it is not surprising that concepts of sacrifice and self-martyrdom play such a central role in Iranian religious and secular literature, common central elements of speech [*gorban-e-šoma* (short for "I would be your sacrifice"), *jan-nesar* (life sacrificer), used in place of the pronoun "I" and many others], and the propensity of many Iranians to attempt suicide in situations where honor or duty to another is at stake.[1]

Unfortunately, the world is not so constituted that everyone knows his exact position vis-à-vis others. Thus, as one would expect, a good deal of energy in interaction over both the short and the long term is spent on trying to establish mutual relationships in interaction. However, the situation is rare indeed where persons are totally unknown to each other and cannot establish some sort of relationship to each other, on the basis of the activity that brings them together, the characteristics they can observe about each other, or the skill that either or both may have in imposing role definitions on the other person. Such situations, when they do occur, are characterized by noninteraction or real jockeying for position.

As a Persian-speaking foreigner in Iran, and occasionally having to deal with people on a business basis, I was often terribly difficult to place within the interactional scheme (this is true with, of course, most foreigners anywhere). In being associated for a short time with a University Institute in Tehran, I was in the peculiar position of wanting to be on friendly terms with people whose work I was directing, to the point where I would visit in their homes and socialize with them informally as well. This caused a great deal of discomfort for some, since in an Iranian office persons are not invited to socialize in the homes of subordinates, or decline if they are invited. One may accept an invitation from a superior, however, and is under pressure to socialize with one's equals on both an invitational and an informal basis. One who traffics with everyone or will accept any kind of accommodations is labeled colloquially *darviš*, likening him to the holy mendicants who traditionally operate outside the confines of the normal system of social relations.

This was no less true in the village, where I deferred to nearly everyone and made overtures by becoming *sæmimi* with a variety of individuals from all ages and income groups. This might have turned out badly, resulting in my being excluded from most interaction situations. In my case it turned out well, in that in the community I ended up having free access to nearly any house for informal socializing and was invited to participate on all formal occasions. My ambiguous status was marked, however, by a decided disinclination to involve me directly in events as they were occurring or in conversational interchange, except at my initiation. For my purposes, this was all to the good; I was welcome but disattended except when I chose not to be. Requests were not made of me, and I was not allowed to make gestures that would include me within the social interchanges of the village.

I wish to emphasize here an important distinction between intimacy between perceptual equals and intimacy between perceptual nonequals. In both cases, spiritual attraction is and can be very great. However, between perceptual nonequals, the ideal of spiritual merger is thought to be attainable only ideally. The tension in the search for such a spiritual merger is embodied in the figure of Jalalu'd-din Muhammad Rumi (b. 604–d. 672/1273), known in Iran by the name Maulavi and generally acknowledged as the greatest Sufi mystic poet. Rumi's attachment for the dervish Shamsu'd-din Muhammad of Tabriz, generally known as Shams-e Tabriz, whom he acknowledged as his master and spiritual guide, formed the creative tension for much of his work. As Ritter states:

> The physical beauty of the dervish and his exorbitant mystical-narcissistic assertions on the more exalted spheres of the Beloved (ma'šuq) captivated Maulavi completely. Because this ecstatic love-relationship aroused the antipathy of the disciples, Shams in his indignation departed for Damascus; but he eventually [returned] . . . only to arouse a fresh storm of protest that resulted in his being compelled to leave the place again (645/1247). No one knew where he had gone and Maulavi searched for him in vain. The latter's longings and anxiety on account of the Beloved made of him a great poet. By identifying himself with the vanished Ma'shuq he finds him again. It is not he himself who sings his songs, but the teacher, personified in him. . . .
>
> The lyrical work Kulliyyat-i Shams-i Tabriz "The Collected (lesser) Poems of the Sun of Tabriz" . . . is one of the most prodigious achievements in poetry. From beginning to end the undercurrent of the songs is formed by the mysticism of the identification of Subject and Object, flowing on the one hand into pantheism and on the other into self-deification, "with strong emphasis on the narcissistic motif of the identification of the Self with the Object of Love and of Mergence with Him (Ritter 1933: 91)." (Rypka 1968:240–41)

Intimacy between perceptual equals is perhaps better likened to the relationship between individual members of a Sufistic order who are engaged together in a common quest. An archetypical example of this is exemplified in Faridu'd-din Attar's (d. ca. 627/1230) extensive allegory, *Mantiqu-t-Tayr* (*Conversation of the Birds*).[2] In this allegory, thirty birds attempt a quest for the fabulous mythical bird-God, Simurgh—an allegory for the search of the Sufi body for Truth. In the end, however, the birds' search for unification with the exalted object of love becomes a discovery of their collective selves. As Attar points out, the Simurgh is in the end just that: thirty (*si*) birds (*murgh*). I repeat some of Browne's paraphrase of the final passages from the work below:

> Through the reflection of the faces of these thirty birds (si murgh) of the world they then beheld the countenance of the Simurgh.
>
> When they looked, that was the Simurgh; without doubt that Simurgh was those thirty birds (si murgh).
>
> When they looked toward the Simurgh, it was indeed the Simurgh which was there.
>
> While, when they looked toward themselves, they were si murgh (thirty birds) and that was the Simurgh.
>
> And if they looked at both together, both were the Simurgh, neither more nor less. . . .
>
> They besought the disclosure of this deep mystery, and demanded the solution of "we-ness" and "thou-ness."
>
> Without speech came the answer from that Presence, saying: "This Sun-like Presence is a Mirror.
>
> "Whosoever enters It sees himself in It; in It he sees body and soul, soul and body.
>
> "Since ye came hither thirty birds (si murgh), ye appeared as thirty in this Mirror."[3]
>
> (Browne 1906: 514)

Sufism in Iran in a very real sense embodies the direct denial of the social as well as cognitive differences existing in the mundane world. Thus it is not surprising that in the Sufistic literature, the highest form of enlightenment is a state in which the individual differences of an equal status collectively (the first exchange relationship treated at the beginning of this section) and the differences between unequal subject and object, superior and inferior, master and student (the second exchange relationship) are obliterated, effecting a total merger of consciousness on all levels: that which is termed Annihilation in God (*Fana fi'llah*).

Relations of Equality: *Dowreh* and *Partibazi*

Persons who perceive themselves to be equal and subject to the demands of interaction and exchange obtaining between intimates are most often those who have a significant degree of communality of life-experience. They are most often directly related to each other. They are often the same age and have known each other for a significant period in their lives. At times, the basis for their relationship may consist solely in the fact that they may be thrown into similar circumstances for a period—an occurrence common for Iranian students living broad, who develop binding relationships with persons with whom they would be unlikely to associate at home.

It is difficult for many Americans to appreciate the quality of intimate relationships in Iran. The degree of emotional commitment to a cousin, brother, or close friend can reach levels that for Americans begin to have sexual connotations. To interpret this kind of relationship as sexual is a mistake, however. Besides being generally disapproved, homosexual relationships as practiced in Iran contradict the pattern of equal reciprocity in intimate social relations between equals by demanding that one person be in a subordinate position. A more common sexual activity among male intimates who perceive themselves as equals is the sharing of a prostitute, which may serve partially as a physical release related to the emotional ties obtaining between the two.[4]

Personal relations of equality have their institutional counterparts in Iranian society as well. Arasteh divides traditional Iranian society into three groups characterized by dimensions that correspond to the exchange relationships set up in the last section. I will deal with the first two dimensions he treats, "dominance" and "submission," in the following section. A third group in traditional society has been characterized by Arasteh with the label, "autonomy." According to him, this group

included the creative urban element of craftsmen, artisans, some merchants and an allied group of writers and religious mystics. This independent group was chiefly responsible for maintaining the continuity and expressiveness of Persian culture over a long period of time. The principal mode of conduct within this group was the mechanism of cooperation and the spirit of fellowship. This principle functioned particularly within the social institutions of urban communities. Among the various social and cultural associations were professional, recreational and other groups. The heads of these organizations, often prominent informal leaders customarily cooperated with religious leaders to check the unjust practices of the dominant (Arasteh 1964a: 184).

In contemporary Iran, however, the obligations of intimate, equal relations are best seen embodied and perpetuated in two extraordinarily pervasive institutions: the *dowreh*, or circle of intimates, and *parti* or *partibazi*, the institution of "pull" or inside connections with persons in the position of granting favors or marshaling power on one's behalf. Both of these institutions have been dealt with at great length by political scientists commenting on Iran (Bayne 1968; Bill 1972; Binder 1962; Miller 1969; Nezami-Nav 1968; Zonis 1971). On reading these accounts, one gets the impression that the *dowreh* and the practice of *partibazi* are limited to only the upper classes and political affairs. In sketching these two institutions below, I will try to demonstrate the ways in which they are operative at the village level as well.

The *dowreh* is essentially the institutional embodiment for the first exchange pattern outlined above. It consists of a group of persons, either all men or all women, who feel themselves to be equal and alike in some important way. Any of the following may serve as the basis for formation of a *dowreh*: members may all have attended educational institutions together; they may all have similar cultural interests; they may have common backgrounds of foreign residence, all having lived in France, for instance, or the United States; they may share the same political or religious beliefs (cf. Bill 1972: 44–47; Binder 1962: 258; Miller 1969: 163–65; Zonis 1971: 239). *Dowrehs* generally meet together on a regular basis, ostensibly to socialize and to carry on some common activity, such as listening to music or reading poetry. Within longstanding *dowrehs* there gradually develops the kind of absolute obligation on the part of the *dowreh* members to further the interests of the individual members characterized in the last section as obtaining between perceptual equals. This is, of course, extremely important within the political arena. As Zonis notes, "Without straying beyond the confines of his own *dowreh*, a new prime minister may locate individuals to hold ministerial portfolios, men who have known each other, communicated with each other on a relatively intimate basis, and developed a more or less common outlook together for a number of years. While the premiership is the most vital example, similar opportunities and problems arise when one member of the *dowreh* accedes to any position of administrative responsibility" (Zonis 1971: 240).

As several writers have pointed out, not the least function of the *dowreh* is as a communication link. Political information of consequence is rarely obtained firsthand through the press or other news sources.[5] The network of personal connections members of the press have is their first and foremost link with major developments as they break. Also, since individuals belong to more than one *dowreh*,[6] the flow of information through informal channels of communication is nearly immediate. As Zonis writes, ". . . *dowrehs* . . . frequently cut across social class lines. As a result, the message will fan out not only within a given social class, but also between social classes. No wonder that a message generated at the Imperial Court will reach the most humble *bazaari* within a day or two" (Zonis 1971: 240).

Groups of this sort have existed for centuries. In an important sense, *dowrehs* operating in the political sphere are the secular counterparts of Sufic orders, many of which involve persons who have conventional secular occupations. It is interesting to note in this light that the various bodies of Freemasons in Iran used to constitute a kind of multiunit *dowreh* that involved the royal family and was generally supportive of the regime (cf. Bayne 1968: 89).

At the village level, associations of this sort most definitely exist. Often at stake are land and water rights, wages to be paid to agricultural laborers, management of school affairs, or the establishment of lobbying groups to deal with relations between the village and larger governmental bodies. The bases for such *dowrehs* in the village rest on economic, educational, and land-ownership status, as well as direct kinship ties.

One *dowreh* that was operative during the time I was in Gavaki involved the head of the village association, two of the schoolteachers resident in the village, another man who worked in the office of Tribal Education in Shiraz but was resident in the village on weekends, the brother of the head of the village association, and the secretary of the village association. These men socialized together nearly every Friday and often on other evenings before the evening meal. They marketed crops together, bought animal feed jointly, hired agricultural workers jointly, and generally were responsible in an informal way for decisions regarding the school, development and improvements in the village, and other civic matters, although there existed other persons who were constituted to carry out these functions. In a survey of village heads of households, the names of the persons in this *dowreh* emerged as the most trusted and respected persons in the village, although they were by no means the wealthiest or the largest landholders. One indication of their power to further their interests beyond the limits of the village consisted of their ability to have one of them elected to the provincial village council at every election. They lent each other money, helped each other on labor projects, and to boot lived just a few houses removed from each other in the village. They were a true mutual interest group within the village, one which few could intrude upon. As I will try and show below, this *dowreh* setting was also the most "informal" setting one could find these men involved in, and the language of their interpersonal communication reflected this to a great degree.

In a very real sense, the family itself constitutes a natural *dowreh*. Members of families must be able to further each other's interests and provide for the survival of the family unit as a whole. For this reason it is to the advantage of the family to have great diversity in its membership in terms of occupations, interests, political connections, life styles, and so forth. Indeed, the family of the former shah reflected this diversity. For this reason, too, entrance to a family through marriage is a highly considered operation. Marriages in Iran are predominantly arranged or at least requisite of family approval. This system prevails even among urban, modern families, not so much because children are under the control of socially and religiously conservative parents, but because as a rule people in Iran do not marry people; families marry families. Thus marriage negotiations can approach the complexity of a corporate merger. Moreover, the common Western notion that it is the woman who is treated as chattel in an arranged marriage is dispelled under the realization that both the bride and the groom serve as coin in these negotiations. As was so often the case with European royalty in the sixteenth, seventeenth, and eighteenth centuries, marriages today, particularly in the case of wealthy and powerful families, are often contracted as a matter of expediency rather than as a matter of affection. In such situations, though lifelong marital faithfulness may be required "for public consumption," it is not really anticipated.

Here again, the principles obtaining for the wealthy upper classes are pervasive and operative in smaller towns and villages. In Gavaki, the biggest piece of news during the year I was there was the contracting of marriage between the daughter of one of the claimants to the title *kædkhoda* and the son of the brother of one of the other claimants. This was an extremely astute move politically, and nearly everyone was happy about it. It meant that a major communications rift had been bridged in the village, and that one *kædkhoda*, who represented large landowners in the village, would be under some pressure to represent the needs and desires of villagers identifying with the other *kædkhoda* claimant in a more sympathetic manner. Similarly, large landowners could count on greater cooperation from other villagers for development and economic projects they favored. The marriage did not resolve the *kædkhoda* situation in favor of either claimant, but it did make communication much easier between two major village factions.

If the *dowreh* is the institutionalization of exchange relationships between persons perceiving themselves as equal according to some significant dimension, then the behavior obtaining between such persons is institutionalized in the practice of *parti* or *partibazi*. Binder describes *parti* as a form of lobbying, and indeed it is, in a sense. However, lobbying as we understand it in the United States consists largely of the representation of group interests. *Parti* in Iran deals in the representation of individual interests to persons with the power to grant privileges of various sorts: employment, licenses, exemptions to certain laws, or other favorable acts (Binder 1962: 255). In order for the system to work, it must involve persons linked in a chain-like fashion by bonds of obligations. The crucial links in the chain of obligation that lead to effective action in *partibazi* are most often those that obtain between perceptual equals—individuals who have some degree of absolute claim on others, either through family or through friendship.

Occasionally the crucial link in *partibazi* will be based on petition-request from a subordinate, but this is rarely effective if the ultimate recipient of the favor is several links removed from the potential granter of the request. On the other hand, any request pressed by a close perceptual equal must be granted or must seem to be granted. In order to implement strategies of this sort, adroit operators in Iran go to all sorts of pains to discover what social linkages actually exist between themselves and people in power. James Bill (personal communication) tells of persons who regularly read obituary columns to discover the outlines of networks that they might key into. Similarly, knowledge of another person's close friends and associates becomes prime information in the play for personal advancement and the obtaining of personal privilege.

Here again, the exercise of *parti* need not be restricted to either the urban or the national political arena. In Gavaki, I observed numerous instances of *partibazi*, but on a much lower scale. One principal area concerned secondary school admission. A fairly respected and well-established landowner in the village was friendly with the teachers in the village school. He entertained them often, even those who were not resident in the village. His son, who was something of a dullard, began to get improved marks in school. Finally, the father prevailed on one of his teacher friends to see what he could do about getting his son into a fairly good high school in Shiraz. The teacher went to one of his friends who was in an administrative position in a high school in town, and he admitted the youngster. The boy's grades were good until the administrator left the city to live in Tehran. After the change in administration, the boy promptly failed all of his subjects. The son blamed his father for the failure because the father's *parti* wasn't good enough to sustain the son's satisfactory grades. The whole situation embarrassed the father no end—not so much because his son was not bright, but because what his son had said was true: his *parti* was inadequate to care for his relatives.

Another area where *partibazi* was used in Gavaki concerned dealings with village landowners who had moved to Shiraz, but whose land holdings were fairly substantial. A typical situation came up every spring and fall when one or more of these nonresident landowners would hire a tractor to either plow or harvest grain crops. Often the tractor would be hired for a full day or several days, but would not have enough work to fill the whole time. Persons who had small land holdings were anxious to cut in on the tractor time and pay for the small proportion of the total time they might be able to use the services of the machine. For the small landowners, there was very little alternative if they wanted their land plowed or their crops harvested by tractor. The number of persons who would have to combine forces and agree on a single day to hire a tractor to plow a number of small scattered plots of land would be quite large, and reaching agreement among themselves as to what day and what payment methods would be used would be nearly impossible. Clearly, then, the best way to get one's land plowed by tractor was to become attached to the plowing on the days that large landholdings were being plowed. However, not everyone could have this privilege.

Around plowing time everyone's ears seemed to be pricking to find out when a tractor had been hired to come and who had hired it. When the facts were known, all the landowners would try to find some way to coerce the relatives of a man who had arranged for the tractor to plead their cases before that individual, so they wouldn't be cut off from some tractor time. Of course, the man's own relatives had first call on being included, so they were rarely eager to plead the case of others. This led to a whole secondary level of *partibazi* where friends and relatives of the relatives (usually at this point wives were brought into the picture) would be called on to plead with the relatives of tractor hirers to plead the case of those, with more distant claims, who wanted to be cut in. Though things rarely got much more complicated than this, the village situation here described already begins to resemble the intricacies of the Tehran national government.

Rather than quote still more examples, let it suffice to say that in general people would attempt to obtain any scarce commodity or service in the village through the application of *partibazi* to the person who controlled the scarce commodity. Further, the price to be paid, if there was a price involved, was to be a nominal one. This is to say that when prices were set on scarce commodities they would not fluctuate upward *solely* because the commodities were scarce.[7] The person dispensing the scarce commodity would be content because he was able to continue selling when others were not able. The right to buy something scarce was purchased not with more money but with more human influence.

This situation obtained only within the social network of the village, however. When the nomadic Qashqa'i tribesmen passed through the area and came into the village to make purchases, a true bazaar situation was created, with merchants trying to charge whatever they could get for the goods they were selling. In this case, scarcity of an item definitely would drive up the price, since it was rarely the case that nomads making purchases had the means to apply *parti* with merchants.

Relations of Inequality—Hierarchy and *Tæ'arof*

If a relationship has not been created between two individuals so that they have been able to develop or begin to develop the obligations that obtain between perceptual equals, then the interactions involving those parties must embody a degree of polarity, one's alter being conceived as either superior or inferior to oneself. As I will show below and in the next part of this discussion, it is possible for all persons to demonstrate that they regard their alters as superior or (and this is very rare) inferior. This creates a situation where the perception of one's own superiority or inferiority is very much a relative matter. The highest official is inferior in an interaction with the leader of the nation, and the lowest street sweeper is at least superior to younger street sweepers.[8]

Consequently, adroit individuals in society must be capable of operating at different levels at all times, knowing both the proper and the effective ways that one's actions should be taken. Indeed, Islam itself in demanding fulfillment of the five sacred duties incumbent on believers—pilgrimage, prayer, fasting, tithing, and alms—makes it possible for one to be elevated above one's peers while prostrating oneself before God's will. It may be this quality of the way in which behavior is both projected and interpreted in Iran that has prompted foreign visitors like Lord Curzon to observe that in Iran, "The same individual is at different moments haughty and cringing" (Curzon 1892: 15). Additionally, although positions within society are fairly rigid in their relative "status" markings, individual mobility through and around these positions may be quite rapid. Education, in particular, has elevated many persons to positions in society where they are regarded by their former peers as being far superior.

A young Iranian of my acquaintance was totally dumbfounded when, on his return home after receiving a full college education in the United States on an international scholarship, his father and uncles all tried to kiss his feet (a gesture of sincere and extreme respect). His relatives' perception of themselves as inferior to him as a result of his education became so disconcerting for him that he was unable to stay in his boyhood village for any length of time without feeling uncomfortable.

To review the exchange relationships involved in superior/inferior relationships in interaction, as I have mentioned above in the second section of this chapter, perceptual superiors are bound by an ethic of duty toward perceptual inferiors emanating from the ethic of noblesse oblige, whereas perceptual inferiors are bound by an ethic proceeding from submission, gratitude, obedience, and respect. The "ethics" that I have identified here—noblesse oblige on the one hand and submission, obedience, respect, and gratitude on the other—are perhaps ill-named, but they are the linchpins in a system which keeps social interaction rolling smoothly. Material rewards flow from high to low status, material tribute from low to high. Actions flowing from high to low status are interpreted as favors, whereas actions flowing from low to high are interpreted as service. Stimuli for goods or actions issuing from superior to inferior are labeled as orders, whereas stimuli from inferior to superior are petitions. The actual material, action, or request could be identical in content, whether passing from a perceptual superior to a perceptual inferior or vice versa; what counts in social interaction is not what these activities *are*, but what they are conceived to be.

Perceptual superiority is further characterized by *separation* and *stasis*. Thus the person perceived to be superior is removed from other persons and not allowed to be as mobile as others. An ever-widening circle of greater and greater activity thus centers on the persons perceived as most superior by others in any social gathering, with the persons perceived as most inferior—often servants, young males, and women—engaging in the greatest activity on behalf of the older, higher-status males.

The range of behavior expectations obtaining between persons of unequal status is represented in figure 1. Instances of interpersonal inequality relationships that prove the applicability of the "ethics" cited above are legion and pervade every Iranian institution. Hanessian (1963), for example, cites numerous parallels between the vertical hierarchy differentiating landlord and peasant (before land reform) and the hierarchy separating Shah and commoner.

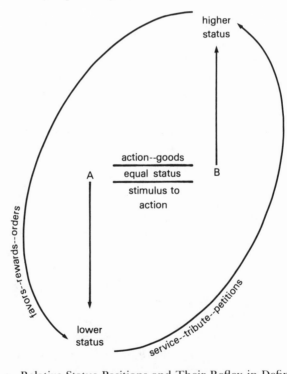

Fig. 1. Relative Status Positions and Their Reflex in Defining
Transfer of Action, Goods, and Stimulus to Action.

A few examples from various social contexts in which my fieldwork was carried out may suffice to establish how the mechanisms of behavior between those in superior/inferior exchange relationships operate in actual reciprocal behavior.

Case 1

An army private assigned to quartermaster duty regularly fills the automobiles of his immediate superiors with army gasoline without noting the fact in his inventories. Any emergency excuse he gives for requesting a special leave is accepted without question.

Case 2

A university professor returns to his rural home district where he is the only university-educated person and the one in the area with the most contacts in the capital. He brings several house guests with him from the city. His neighbors all leave their own work and come to cook and care for his guests for several days. He is perturbed when it is asked whether he might do the same for his neighbors in a similar situation.

Case 3

A worker in a university office is consistently told to run personal errands for his superiors. He will expect a larger-than-usual cash gift at Now Ruz (the Iranian New Year) if his services exceed that of his contemporaries.

Case 4

An agricultural laborer helps recruit other workers during harvest time for a large landowner. The landowner attends the wedding of the man's son personally and makes a large cash gift.

Case 5

The former empress makes a tour of a rural province. Upon returning, she sets up a temporary office staff to answer the thousands of written petitions she has received from people who may have traveled two or three days overland to deliver them into her hands, throw them into her car, etc. She says in a press conference that one woman presented her with a piece of her own handiwork as a token of her esteem and it was noteworthy that she had no petition to make, "although I would have gladly granted any request she might have asked."

Case 6

A government ministry employee consistently informs the divisional head of departmental developments, rumors and gossip, often to the detriment of his colleagues. He is assigned by the head of the ministry to extremely lucrative and desirable temporary foreign employment.

Case 7

Two workers in a government research bureau submit a report to their superiors. The report is subsequently translated and published in a foreign journal under the name of the superior. One researcher complains and is soon fired under some pretext. The other remains silent and is soon promoted.

Case 8

A man stands on a street in any Iranian city next to a line of parked cars. When the owner approaches he quickly wipes the windshield with a rag and opens the car door. He receives a gratuity.

Case 9

A man wants something in a government office, but the official he is dealing with is recalcitrant. The man finally begins to plead and breaks down crying. He immediately gets what he wants.

Case 10

A man gives out very large New Year's gratuities to the tea-servers and errand runners in his office. The next day, one of the tea-servers asks the man to find employment for his brother.

Case 11

The village's headman, schoolteachers, and large landowners are all seated at the head of the room for a village wedding. They do not move as the father and bridegroom, with members of their family, bring them tea and cigarettes and serve them food.

Case 12

Before land reform, villagers would always invite the landlord's representative to weddings and religious events and would entertain him, either in a separate room or at the head of the room on a raised platform. After land reform he is no longer treated in this manner and stops attending weddings, except those of his immediate family.

Case 13

At a tribal wedding, guests are separated into distinct groups for eating. All women are in one group. Khans and their male relatives are in another group. Non-Khans and their male relatives are in another group, and urban governmental dignitaries with their whole families, both male and female, are in another. Liquor is served to the foreign guests and the khans' families. The urban guests and the khans themselves are served chicken; everyone else eats rice and stewed lamb with carrots or eggplant. Khans and their families plus urban guests are given forks, individual plates, and spoons, although some eat, out of preference, with their hands. Nonkhan tribesmen are given no utensils and eat from common platters.

Cases 1–13 involve, for the most part, clear exchanges where the perceptual inferior provides a service, renders tribute, or makes a petition, whereas it is incumbent on the perceptual superior to provide favors, give rewards, or issue orders. Case 9 is interesting in that it shows a move on the part of the man confronting the official to place himself in a more and more abject position relative to the official. Weeping constitutes a truly abject petition, making it virtually mandatory that the official respond in kind with the proper favor. Case 10 represents a mistake on the part of a man toward persons who are perceived as inferiors. By giving out larger gratuities than expected, he sets up an exchange relationship that is marked by workers in his office as special. Because he has bestowed a greater favor, he can expect petitions and requests for aid more often.

The final three cases illustrate the principles of separation and status that distinguish superior positions from inferior positions in social situations. Cases 11 and 12 both involve status and separation at the "head of the room." Case 13 demonstrates various means that can be used to separate and differentiate different strata of individuals in a large and complex social situation.

The relationships here are reciprocal, but not necessarily so. It would be better to say that the potential for reciprocity exists when the polarized inequality relationship becomes established in interaction. Perhaps a better way of describing the situation is in terms of role expectations. Case 10, already mentioned, points this up well. The office worker, in giving large amounts of money, places himself in a position to be petitioned for other favors as well.

At this point, I would like to interject a brief statement on a theme I will return to: the motivation of behavioral choice in interaction. The schools of thought current today in the study of social behavior seem to represent polar views on the idea of this point. One school, which I might label "Parsonian," views action as basically reflexive, based on an assessment of the factors that an individual sees as encompassing him at the moment of action. The second choice might be labeled "Goffmanian." According to it, the most adroit individuals are seen as able to impose on others the definition of a given situation that most suits their purposes, through (symbolic) impression management.

The Iranian interaction situation could be described only by using both lines of thinking about human action. Individuals in interaction do gear their actions to reflect that which they know is proper according to the norms and ethics of the situation they find themselves in. At the same time, the most adroit individuals are able to cause their own actions to be defined in such a way as to impose these societal norms, ethics, and social pressures on others, making them work in their own favor.

The interplay of strategic and reflexive action in Iranian unequal status situations is brought to light extremely well in situations that highlight the perceptions of relative superiority and inferiority of a number of individuals involved in the same realm of activity, such as eating, drinking, or engaging in discussion or ceremony. When some unanimity about hierarchy of perceptions exists in interaction situations of this sort, acting according to the ethic implied by one's role is rewarded, as Laurence Loeb (1969) points out in his study of the Jewish community in the city of Shiraz through an analysis of *tæ'arof* behavior in the Jewish *knissa* (temple).[9]

Tæ'arof, which Loeb glosses as "compliment, ceremony, offer, present," is an extraordinarily difficult concept encompassing a broad complex of behaviors that mark and underscore differences in social status. Indeed, I would maintain that *tæ'arof* is the active, ritualized realization of differential perceptions of superiority and inferiority in interaction. It underscores and preserves the integrity of culturally defined roles as it is carried out in the life of every Iranian, every day, in thousands of different ways. Iranian youth cry in despair at its pervasiveness, but they are powerless against it and practice it themselves even while complaining about it.

Loeb, in speaking about the social ritual of the *knissa*, maintains that members of the community are able to accrue honor through the use of *tæ'arof* in offering the right to other members of the *knissa* to lead the community worship services. The ground rules are simple. The chief *Shaliah Shibbur* offers the *xavod* or "honor" to whomever he chooses. On high holidays all must defer to him by not accepting the *xavod* themselves. Otherwise the *xavod* may be pressed on any member by any other literate member of the community. As Loeb maintains, "One 'scores' by: 1. accepting the offer after much protestation. 2. deferring the honor upward to the individual who accepts it. 3. magnanimously bestowing it on someone lower in rank. 4. pressing it on a near equal" (Loeb 1969: 6).

I would maintain that accruing honor in this situation is simply ritual statement and maintenance of one's own hierarchical position *in that momentary situation*. One must first of all be adroit and astute enough to know how one is perceived within *that social setting*. One then (a) defers to superiors (tribute, although nonmaterial), (b) confers on inferiors (favor), (c) accepts after protest, or (d) presses it on an equal (neither tribute nor favor), and thereby "wins." The honor that one receives thereby is community approbation for maintaining social order by verifying everyone's perceptions in that particular interaction.

Loeb does not go into the detail about the interaction, but I would suspect that, aside from the ultimate deference to the chief *shaliah shibbur*, an ultimate acceptance is preceded by insistence from one's perceptual equals that the honor be accepted. This is facilitated by the device allowing the offer to be made by any member of the community. In this way, an offer need not have any of the implications of the reciprocity inherent in other hierarchical situations and allows one to accept.

Loeb goes on to describe what one would expect, given the situation—namely that one may not "accept an offer made by someone very much higher in rank" since acceptance would imply that the recipient is being mocked. "One may accept an honor offered from below, since such is one's due" (Loeb 1969: 7). Thus the honor of leading the service may be pressed on one by one's equals or accepted as one's due from one's inferiors. Upward mobility within the system involves stepwise gradual progression into higher and higher groups of "equals" who can confirm one's higher standing by pressing the honor of leading the service on him.

The ritual described by Loeb is repeated throughout Iran at every turn. Every time tea is offered to a group, every time several persons wish to proceed through one door, every time friends meet on the street, every time guests proceed to the dinner table at a party, the constant unceasing ritualization of the assessment of climate of relative superiority and inferiority occurs and recurs. It is this more than any other factor that gives social life in Iran its unique flavor compared to that in other oriental societies. The fact that "status" is *relative* for individuals in different interaction situations and the fact that, as a result of this relativity, rights and obligations shift constantly with changes in one's social environment, make these constant social gestures important tools in everyday social relations.

So far, I have been discussing the indexical use of behavior to indicate status in interaction. This involves questions of propriety and correctness. If one fails to perceive elements of an interaction properly, one cannot respond with behavior that is a correct index of a correct perception of the situation. Inappropriate behavior signals either that one cannot perceive social situations correctly or that he does not know how to manage one's own behavioral repertoire to produce appropriate behavior. In either case, one is judged as socially inept.

The Strategic Use of *Tæ'arof*—Getting the Lower Hand

In the sense, then, that *tæ'arof* constitutes in all social interaction the broad ritualization of behavioral expectations that result from status differentiation in interaction, instances of *tæ'arof* are always to a degree reflexive, or indexical, of an interaction situation. However, as I have stated earlier, one might expect that the use of *tæ'arof* can also be strategic or conative in interaction.

The system within the *knissa* as described by Loeb points out the essential point in struggles between individuals for social advancement in Iran. This is, if the issue is status or power, one cannot win in direct confrontation with another, even though he can be perceived as superior only relative to another. One only wins when that superiority is acknowledged by a third party. If acknowledgment of his superiority is made in the presence of his rival or rivals, then the victory is a smashing one.

To reiterate, one cannot accept the honor in the *knissa* from a superior. One must defer upwards, rendering to superiors their tribute in an act of service, or bestowing on inferiors a reward in an act of favor. All three actions—the offer, its denial, and the redirection of the offer—are the three stages of *tæ'arof*. The redirection of an offer in hopes that it will eventually devolve on oneself constitutes one principal strategic use of *tæ'arof*.

However, the most effective and widely used strategic formula in the use of *tæ'arof* is to aim for a lower relative status position and defer to another person. In doing this, one has either shown virtue by acting modestly in accordance with one's proper relative status or been extraordinarily magnanimous in granting a favor to an underling (who then becomes a boor if he accepts).

Thus, one cannot lose by deferring conferment of an honor, gift, status-marked prerogative, or compliment. One can lose by accepting, however. In Loeb's Jewish community situation, one can really only safely accept the honor of leading worship from an equal, and this applies generally for all *tæ'arof* situations (tea drinking, going through doors, etc.). It may be noted that some people will not visit exalted and powerful persons socially, even when offered the opportunity, in a situation where they might have to take the role of guest, since it would be too humiliating to have to be placed in a superior position one does not deserve.

Thus far, the instances of social interaction we have been dealing with have all involved cases where relative rank is known and fairly well fixed within the arena of social interaction. Another kind of social situation also exists in Iranian interaction, one in which the elements of the relative superiority and inferiority of individuals are ambiguous or at best vague. This allows a clever person to employ behavioral forms in a strategic manner to define the situation and the elements contained in it for the other persons involved, presumably for his own ends. In this situation, it turns out that taking an inferior position offers the greatest advantage once again.

There are various reasons for an individual in any social relationship where his own status is unknown to opt for using behavioral forms that indicate that he is lower in status than the other party. I have noted in the last chapter that the highest cultural admiration is given to the person who can be *zeræng* (wily, clever) in his dealings with other people. Defining oneself as an inferior in face-to-face social situations gives one a tactical advantage in dealing with his interaction partner by giving one more maneuverability. This is explained as follows. First, in defining the status relationship behaviorally *after* the interaction has begun, the person in inferior position has automatically removed one of the stratagems of the person in superior position, namely the right to choose to interact at all or not. This is no small matter; in clearly defined status relationships a high-status person can avoid petitioners, in particular, by simply not seeing or acknowledging them. As I mentioned in an earlier paper (Beeman 1976b), this prerogative carries over to such routine matters as the ordering of interaction in telephone conversations.[10] Second, the inferior person can fine tune the relationship by systematically using behavioral stylistic forms that indicate even lower status for himself or herself that indicate even higher status for the person in the high-status position.

In any case, the effect of this strategic use of behavior is to make incumbent on one's interaction partner the role expectations attached to a particular relative status. If another person can be led to accept a superior position, it becomes incumbent upon that person to grant favors, give presents or gratuities, practice noblesse oblige (thus be noble, tolerant, generous, forgiving, charitable, etc.), and occasionally issue commands on the behalf of someone. Occasionally one will cast *oneself* in a superior position to try and exact obedience and service out of an inferior or a subordinate. This occasionally works if particularly serious threats can be made convincingly. However, a person cast in an inferior status position has many more exit channels open, among them disability by virtue of thus acknowledged inferiority: "If you yourself acknowledge that I'm a poor slob, how can you expect anything of me?"

Partibazi and *Tæ'arof*: Some Final Comparisons

I have described the two behavioral practices, *partibazi* and *tæ'arof*, as the institutionalized behavioral realizations of two basic social patterns in Iran, one involving perceptual equals, the other perceptual nonequals. That the two practices do indeed correspond to these two modes of social relations in interaction is witnessed by the inappropriateness of the use of *tæ'arof* with intimates and the impossibility of the application of *partibazi* with hierarchical superiors.

Partibazi, as I have characterized it, is a series of links of intimate relationships that lead eventually to a person in a position to do a favor. If any of these links involve communication between a designated or perceptual superior and a perceptual inferior, that communication link must mark the hierarchical difference between the two parties. That marking of difference must be an instance of *tæ'arof*, and the effectiveness of that communication is no longer based on the absolute claims of intimacy, equality, and friendship, but rather on the degree to which the ethics involved in superior/inferior relationships can be made incumbent on the parties involved. Communication occurring from superior to inferior in the process of *partibazi* is already in a sense "post-*parti*." That is, when a communication made to an inferior affects the state of the originating individual, the act is already in the process of being consummated; the *partibazi* has been effective, and the orders are then on their way down. From this point there is little chance for return to the top. Therefore, a person in power who wants to satisfy duties to persons pressing equality claims will give the order that such and such a request be carried out, but will purposely not see the action through to its conclusion or will cause the consummation of the action to be slowed down or stopped after the order has been given. In this way, individuals are able to protect themselves from having to carry out acts that would be disapproved of by their superiors and at the same time meet the demands of their intimates and equals. For this reason, persons who intend to use *partibazi* to gain a concession, advantage, or favor will often choose several routes to press their claim. As one of my Iranian friends so aptly stated, "Doing business in Tehran is like trying to unravel a ball of string that has a lot of loose ends. You grab for any and all of the ends you see, and try to work at unraveling the ball from all sides."

On the other hand, one does not practice *tæ'arof* with intimates; one interprets or should interpret respectful code forms as conveying the message that genuine respect prompts their use. Of course, among nonintimates no such feeling is implied *per se* (this fact suggests, and I think correctly, that a clear show of respect is not *tæ'arof*).

Tæ'arof and *partibazi* as institutionalized communication techniques are unified by their opposition in many other ways as well. *Tæ'arof*, in embodying relative perceptions about superiority and inferiority, is an interpersonal operation. One cannot *tæ'arof* a collective group, only individuals within that group. The end result of the application of *tæ'arof* in any given situation is, however, a clear status ranking of everyone participating. This is to say that in the application of *tæ'arof* one builds temporary group hierarchical structures from the sum of the perceptions of individual dyads about superiority and inferiority.

If the social composition in the interaction changes, so does the structure of the hierarchy obtaining for that interaction. Thus the movement in the application of *tæ'arof* is from the individual to the collective, from fixed perception about one's own status vis-à-vis other individuals to the construction of a temporary collective hierarchical structure.

Partibazi, on the other hand, starts with a permanent and enduring series of group structures that involve individuals who have absolute relationships to each other and moves toward forming temporary links with individuals for a single occasional purpose. Thus the movement in *partibazi* is precisely the opposite: from the collective to the individual, from a permanent collective structure to a series of temporary individual relationships.

Just as Sufistic tradition provides a counter-structure to the interpersonal relationships outlined earlier, in the ultimate unification with the exalted Beloved on the one hand, and with all living things with whom one is on an equal plane on the other, so does Sufism offer a process in social conduct that constitutes a counterprocess in many senses to those outlined above. This consists of the dual process of *tæjrid*, or outer detachment, and perception of, and absolute devotion to, the beauty of the inner essence of being (*dhat*) and conjointly, the inner truth (*hæqiqæt*) that is perceptible in that essence.[11]

This is a direct counter to the intense worldly involvement shown in the practice of *tæ'arof* and *partibazi*. More importantly, it denies directly the importance placed in those two processes on external attributes and characteristics in the pursuit of external gains and goals. As Rahman points out, such a system poses a direct counter to the established social order: "A thoroughly monistic system, no matter how pious and conscientious it may claim to be, cannot, by its very nature take seriously the objective validity of moral standards" (Rahman 1968: 176).

The best contemporary treatment of the role of detachment and the need to seek a kind of inner purity in daily life is contained in a remarkable essay written by an international group of scholars meeting regularly in a *dowreh* to discuss core aspects of Iranian culture. The essay, "Sæfa-yi Batin" ("Inner Purity") (Bateson, Catherine, et al. 1977), shows how desirable it is for individuals in Iran to discard the outer structure of social interaction and seek the integrity of inner truth. It features two ideal figures, the *darviš*, a mendicant seer figure, and the *luti*, a strong-willed, strong-bodied person charged with the personal responsibility for public morality. Both must see good and evil for what they are, not merely for what they appear to be, and act accordingly. Both are ideals and have rejected the superficiality of the *zaher* (external) for the purity of the *baten* (internal—*batin* in the transliteration of the article).

In exhortation of individuals to seek detachment from the external world and to pursue the beauty of the inner essence of being as a means for unification with the Deity—the All—the Sufistic counter to essential social processes also obliterates the social base for those processes. In a state of true enlightenment, one perceives the essential truth in all beings. Therefore, humanity in all its variety and differentiations becomes a manifestation of the same Absolute. As Jami, the mystic poet (b. 817/1414—d. 898/1492) wrote:

> the companion, comrade and co-traveller, All is He!
> In the mendicant's tattered robe and in the brocade of the
>   regal dress, All is He!
> Whether in the display of variety or the privacy of unity—
> By God All is He! Again, by God All is He!
>
> (Rahman 1968: 176)

IV

THE MARKING OF PARAMETERS
EVENTS

The Problem of Context

The notion that language must be analyzed according to social context of occurrence is associated primarily with Malinowski and the "London school" of linguistics, which followed through the teaching and writing of J. R. Firth. This context-centered line of thinking was seen by Firth as a direct counter to both the linguistic separatism of Saussure and the behavioralism of Bloomfield.

The idea of context of presentation itself has been an extraordinarily difficult one to delineate with much precision as a separable component in the analysis of speech events. The difficulties that arise are of much the same sort as difficulties that arise in the vain attempt at specifying all possible attributes of potential participants in conversation. To specify all possible contexts of presentation in the social life of members of any society is likewise literally impossible, particularly without some criterion for distinguishing meaningful from non-meaningful shifts in the components that comprise contexts.

Technically, the broad notion of context of interaction encompasses the persons participating in interaction, as well as the two elements that Hymes identifies as "setting" and "scene." "Setting" consists of the "time and place of a speech act and, in general, to the physical circumstances" (Hymes 1974: 55). "Scene" is a far more culturally marked concept and implies as well a cognitive dimension which helps in determining how participants distinguish between meaningful and non-meaningful contexts.

> In daily life the same persons in the same setting may redefine their interactions as a changed type of scene, say, from formal to informal, serious to festive, or the like. . . . Speech acts frequently are used to

64

define scenes, and also frequently judged as appropriate or inappropriate in relation to scenes. Settings and scenes themselves, of course, may be judged as appropriate or inappropriate, happy or unhappy, in relation to each other, from the level of complaint about the weather to that of dramatic irony. (Hymes 1974: 55–56)

The role of context in the determination of meaning has been explored at some length by Halliday in an elaboration of the basic principles established by Firth. Halliday elaborates first on Malinowskian and Firthian concepts of the "context of culture" and the "content of situation": "Language . . . is a range of possibilities, an open ended set of options in behavior that are available to the individual in his existence as social man. The context of culture is the environment of any particular selection that is made from within them. . . . The context of culture defines the potential, the range of possibilities that are open. The actual choice among these possibilities takes place within a given context of situation" (Halliday 1973: 49). However, all contexts are thought to have "meaning potential." According to Halliday, a treatment of language as social behavior is to regard it as behavioral potential: "it is what the speaker can do" (Halliday 1973: 51). The relationship between language and behavior in social context is expressed in the conversion from behavioral potential to linguistic potential: "The potential of language is a meaning potential. This meaning potential is the linguistic realization of the behavior potential; 'can mean' is 'can do' when translated into language. The meaning potential is in turn realized in the language system as lexicogrammatical potential, which is what the speaker 'can say' " (Halliday 1973: 51).

Halliday's view of contexts as embodying meaning potential makes it difficult to talk about them separately from consideration of people, messages, and ends. In a real sense, the scene in interaction can potentially shift any time one of these elements changes. For example, almost everyone has had the experience of carrying on a conversation with an intimate friend on a private topic only to have that interaction interrupted by the arrival of a third person who makes it impossible for the original participants to continue to define the scene in the same way. As a result, the topic of conversation will likely shift, as will the manner of speaking, body positions, voice volume, and a host of other possible variables. In a sense then, sensing that there has been a shift in scene is to register a shift in the meaning potential of the context—i.e., the *total pattern* of the interrelationships of potentially meaningful elements involved in the interaction event. It is, to return to Bateson's apt phrase, the registration of the result of the occurrence of a "difference which makes a difference." It is not surprising, moreover, that shifts in single significant elements should radically alter perception and identification of the scene.

Individual elements in interaction can be thought of as not interacting with each other in a simple additive fashion, but rather in an interference pattern, much as the way complex acoustic waves are created from the interference of simple waves with each other. Therefore, with the addition or subtraction of a single significant element, the entire complex pattern resonates with a different "frequency" and "amplitude." Communicators within interaction situations can be thought of as possessing culturally established mental "tuning forks" that resonate to contexts and aim them in their negotiation of the interaction. Naturally, there are adroit and maladroit operators in any society, and the ability to identify and understand the ramifications of the contexts in which one finds oneself is a measure of that adroitness.

Furthermore, adroit individuals should be able to know how to *supply* those elements that create the scenes that they wish to have operative in their interaction with others. The art of counseling, the ability to be an adequate hostess, the developing of a good bedside manner for a doctor, all require communication skills that contribute to the establishment of believable and effective scenes.

The creation of scenes is a process that Goffman has termed "framing" (Goffman 1974), a term he borrows from Gregory Bateson's influential essay, "A Theory of Play and Fantasy" (Bateson 1956a). Goffman's analysis (treated at greater length below) deals not only with normal contexts but with transformations of those contexts, the establishment of false contexts, the mechanisms of fine-tuning the perceptions of individuals to particular interpretations of "reality," and much more. His discussion is both rich and suggestive, and it should be consulted in its entirety. However, a brief review of some of his central concepts is in order for this discussion.

According to Goffman, the process whereby specific frames are established and identified in interaction is one that he terms "keying." He describes the concept as ". . . the set convention by which a given activity, one already meaningful in terms of some primary framework, is transformed into something patterned on this activity but seen by the participants to be something quite else" (Goffman 1974: 43–44). Goffman's notion of keying implies that there are definite signals, to which all are party, by which the new "key" is established in the context of basic, unmarked ongoing reality:

> Participants in the activity are meant to know and to openly ac-
> knowledge that a systematic alteration is involved, one that will radically
> reconstitute what it is for them that is going on. . . .
>   Cues will be available for establishing when the transformation is to
> begin and when it is to end, namely, brackets in time, within which
> and to which the transformation is to be restricted. Similarly, spatial
> brackets will commonly indicate everywhere within which and nowhere
> outside of which the keying applies. (Goffman 1974: 45)

Thus Goffman's use of the concept of keying involves fairly bounded
and rigid cognitive definitions of context that become imposed on the
situation through common knowledge, on the part of participants, of
the procedures needed to establish those particular keyings. Examples
of keyings in Goffman's scheme include make-believe, including play-
fulness and daydreaming; contests; ceremonials; technical redoings,
including practicing, demonstrations, and replication of events through
documentation; and regroundings, which involve "the performance
of an activity more or less openly for reasons or motives radically
different from those motivating ordinary actors, such as society women
performing sales work for charity, or apprentices in craft industries
performing a craft not primarily for profit, but to learn to become
expert" (Goffman 1974: 47–48).

In all of these cases, behavior performed within the keyed event is
distinct from behavior performed outside of it. All parties are aware of
the internal logic that governs keyed activities and are able to mark clearly
the beginning, ending, and transition points within the keyed activity.

Dell Hymes refers to a very similar notion that he also terms "key,"
but which is much looser than the notion as used by Goffman. Hymes
describes it thus:

> Key . . . provide[s] for the tone, manner, or spirit in which an act is
> done. It corresponds roughly to modality among grammatical cate-
> gories. Acts otherwise the same as regards setting, participants, message
> form, and the like, may differ in key, as e.g., between *mock: serious* or
> *perfunctory: painstaking*. . . .
>   . . . The significance of key is underlined by the fact that when it is
> in conflict with the overt content of an act, it often overrides the latter
> (as in sarcasm). The signaling of key may be nonverbal, as with a wink,
> gesture, posture, style of dress, musical accompaniment, but it also
> commonly involves conventional units of speech too often disregarded
> in linguistic analysis. . . . (Hymes 1974: 58–59)

In both Goffman's and Hymes's uses of the term keying, the element
of purposiveness is involved. That is to say, when an event is estab-

lished as a keyed event, i.e., when participants realize that a keyed event is in progress or determine that a keyed event shall be in progress, one must give some thought to the individual actions he carries out within such an event: his actions become subject to appropriateness criteria that themselves adhere in the keyed situation and can only be interpreted when he understands the nature of the keyed situation. Thus, cheating in a game is only interpretable as such when one knows the behavioral appropriateness criteria that we call "rules" for that game. Reflections of such appropriateness criteria are seen in such everyday statements as, "That is no way to behave at a wedding," "A real sportsman would never behave that way on the court," and "I just couldn't seem to say the right thing; I was so embarrassed."

A major problem in considering the notion of keying arises from the difference between observer and participant in interaction. From an observer's standpoint, there are no unkeyed situations—every interaction situation can be described contrastively with regard to every other interaction situation. For participants, however, some situations demand less attention than others: there is less likelihood that one will make a behavioral "mistake" in some events.

Goffman tries to get at the feeling that underlies the sort of basic steady state of social affairs where activity is not "marked" for participants in his discussion of the "basic schemata" or basic frames of reference that individuals use to "make sense" of ongoing reality—of the "everyday world" (Goffman 1974: 23–24). In Goffman's treatment, keyings involve stateable transformations of the basic schema; that is, there is a direct relationship between the basic schemata that people use to interpret their ongoing existence and the keyings that are set aside as special and "marked." Unkeyed activity is treated thus: "Whenever individuals restrict themselves to the use of basic schemata in coming to an understanding of the events around them and in responding to these events, I shall speak of them as being lodged in 'literal' activity, this participation generating one sense, but only one sense, of what is taken to be 'real' " (Goffman, 1974: 30).

In taking a phenomenological and pragmatic approach to the study of interaction context in Iran, I am attempting to demonstrate principles whereby the nature of the interaction scene is identified and the "meaning potential" of the particular scene becomes activated and interpretable to those who are participating. The concept of keying that I use in my discussion attempts to encompass both Hymes's and Goffman's notions under a single rubric. As will be seen below, this is a "large net" approach in which are caught a wide variety of diverse phenomena.

Goffman has said (and he may be right) that to carry out this kind of analysis for a culture other than one's own is impossible (personal communication). There is no question that the richness of Goffman's own extensive work on American society probably cannot be duplicated for the Iranian scene by an outsider, such as I. Nonetheless, I hope here to sketch in a highly general manner the classificatory dimensions whereby scenes are evaluated, created, and managed in everyday Iranian interaction.

Dimensions of Iranian Contextualization

Throughout the history of Iranian culture, a major theme has been the advancement of philosophies of dualism. The prime example, of course, is Zoroastrianism, which revolves around the central polarity of good and evil. Zoroastrianism eventually yielded to Islam in the Middle East and Christianity in Europe, where it had spread and gained tremendous ground in both the Roman and Byzantine empires in the form of Manicheanism. However, Sufistic doctrine in Shi'a Islam continued to reflect dualism in the dichotomy seen between undesirable external physical desires and needs and internal spiritual needs.

In classic Sufistic tradition, man is torn between his *næfs* (animalistic and materialistic tendencies) on the one hand and reason on the other. *Næfs* is described by Arasteh in this way: "All the Sufis describe *næfs* as being artful, cunning, and motivated by evil and possessing a passion-producing nature. In the form of lust it robs the mind of intelligence, the heart of reverence. It is the mother-idol which compels man to seek material aims in life and deprives him of growth, or it may even create in the mind such idols as greed, lust, and love of power per se" (Arasteh 1964a: 72).

It is through the application of reason that one becomes free of *næfs* and is able to begin the long and difficult road to enlightenment, perfect love, and union with the absolute. The application of reason is difficult, for it is opposed by the tendencies of *næfs* at every turn: "The dominance of *næfs* in man's situation increases his rational insecurity. Relating one's self to immediate pleasures encourages regressive tendencies. *Næfs* gains its dominance by opposing reason, for in the ontogenetic development of the individual and the history of mankind, reason appears when impulses have held the controlling power. Therefore, the path of *næfs* is initially the one of least resistance" (Arasteh 1964a: 72).

It is because of *næfs*, according to this doctrine, that men abandon their human qualities and do evil to each other, commit crimes, and abandon God. This is a doctrine of dualism that is projected equally on the universe and on individuals. The individual in the face of Islam is charged with responsibility for right actions precisely because he possesses free will.

The relationship between the needs of the real, internal self and those of the outward-oriented, *næfs*-dominated self creates a parallel structure between the environments toward which these energies are directed. Thus the internal (*baten*) is opposed to the external (*zaher*), the former carrying a more positive connotation.

The juxtaposition of the internal and the external is a dominant theme in Iranian life today. Sufistic practice, with its doctrine of detachment, specifically rejects the *zaher* in favor of the *baten*. Both religious doctrine and poetic expression demand knowledge of the internal meanings of texts as derived from the external.[1] Moreover, the two concepts are the subject of many common maxims and much everyday discourse, from *"xᵛahi rosva næšævi, hæm ræng-e jæma'æt šo"* ["If you don't want to be found out (lit. "a public scandal, infamous"), be the same color as those around you"] to the comment of a woman in Gavaki about her son-in-law of some ten years: "Well, he's been a good son-in-law so far, but we don't know his insides and outsides yet."

Because the *baten* of any individual is a deep, dark, and secret well, it must have special routes of access. Music, poetry, and religious ceremony are common paths that lead to overt expression of inner emotion. As one amateur violinist of my acquaintance told me, "I don't know what I would do without my violin. If I am sad, I can come and play *šur* [a mode in Persian music] and cry and release my sadness." Similarly, another friend would regularly repair to a cabin in the mountains to read Hafez and purge himself.

Group expressions of mourning, during the month of Moharram, for the martyrdom of Imam Hosein, which constitutes in many ways the central "myth"[2] of Shi'a Islam, wrenches emotional expression, self-flagellation, and weeping from the populace through a variety of visual displays, rhetoric, and musical chanting.[3] The single great piece of traditional Persian drama is the *tæ'ziyeh* or passion play, which combines music, poetry, drama, public ceremony, and group participation into a week-long spectacle that at times has caused spectators to become so involved that they have injured actors playing villainous roles. The relation of these expressions of mourning to individuals was clearly expressed in a remarkable sermon given by a clergyman to his assembled congregation one Friday when I was in attendance.[4] On this occasion, the clergyman launched into the recitation of the martyrdom, exhorting the congregation to cry and express their grief. Then he stopped and fairly yelled, "Cry, weep, all of you! But don't cry for Hosein—he's dead! Cry for yourselves, for your misery, for your sins and evil ways."

Imam Hosein is perhaps the most powerful symbolic representation of the struggle between *baten* and *zaher*. As true leader of the faith and the most powerful guardian of the inner truth of Islam as transmitted from the prophet through his bloodline, Hosein's personal inner purity is equated with the inner purity of Shi'a Islam itself. In his death at the hand of Yazid, Hosein is further defending his inner purity from an external corrupting force—a force that has no legitimacy, but will readily destroy him. Hosein's death is a triumph for the forces of internal truth, for though he dies, he does not compromise with the external usurper.

The success of Ayatollah Ruhollah Khomeini in bringing down the regime of Mohammad Reza Pahlavi in 1978–1979 is due in part to Ayatollah Khomeini's having been able to use the symbolism of the martyrdom of Hosein and project it onto the struggle between the throne and the people. The former shah was placed in the role of the agent of an external, illegitimate force (the West—more specifically, the United States) and could be shown to be fulfilling that role perfectly as thousands of unarmed persons were shot in the streets of Tehran and became "martyrs." Ayatollah Khomeini's unwillingness to compromise with the United States on any matter, even the release of fifty-three United States diplomatic hostages, held for an extraordinary length of time, is in part a reemphasis of the need to protect the inner truth of the faith by not compromising with the enemy.

Conversations with Iranians about the realm of the personal *baten* reveal it as the seat of the strongest personal feelings one has. The inner peace and joy of the enlightened Sufi contrasts with the inner turmoil and conflict felt to exist in the *baten* of most individuals. One term which is commonly used for this feeling is *'oghdeh*. This is a black emotional feeling, indeed. It is the term that Iranian psychiatrists have taken over to use for "complex," as in "inferiority complex." Another kind of strong internal feeling is labeled *gheiræt*. This might be labeled "sense of indignation at a personal affront." It is the violent angry outburst that comes when a man's name is taken in vain, or if he is being cheated or wrongly accused. On the more positive side, internal feelings include deep romantic passion and longing—also barely controllable. Romantic passion, like anger, seethes and may be kindled at a moment's notice. Thus the *baten* is the seat of internal turmoil and passions that are difficult to control.

Despite the rather unsettling geography of the *baten*, the emotions contained therein are positively regarded. A man must express his *gheiræt* when he is wronged. *'Oghdeh* is often the attributed source of inappropriate social behavior, such as moroseness or surliness, but it is also a creative source, as the black writings of the great modern novelist, Sadeq-e Hedayat, attest. Finally, romantic passion is glorified in literature and in everyday life. I knew three students at Pahlavi University who spent a great deal of their spare time on particular street corners waiting to catch a glimpse of their particular *inamoratae*. One student had been at this for three years without the woman who was the object of his passion ever overtly seeming to detect his presence. The seat of passion lay in the attachment to the unattainable.

The realm of the *zaher*, on the other hand, is a realm of controlled expression. It is the realm of politesse and of proper expression and behavior, where social relationships are carefully marked and regarded. The *zaher* is the area of personal manipulation—of the exercise of *zeræugi*. It is also the arena for the use of *tæ'arof.*[5]

Despite its importance, the *zaher* is nonetheless denigrated. It is the realm of artificial behavior and mundane expression. Superficial by definition, there is little that occurs under its rubric that can have strong personal meaning for individuals. It is the arena of materialism, of success in worldly terms—highly necessary, but disdained.

The notions of *baten* and *zaher* as applied to individuals have their counterparts in contrasting physical contexts. The *birun* or *biruni*, the external or outside, has its counterpart in the *ændærun* or *ændæruni*, the internal or middle. Traditionally the *ændæruni* was the most private, secluded place of a man's residence—the women's quarters. The term *ændærun* also is used to indicate the viscera or heart—the seat of internal emotions.

The internal and external are not just physical locations but states of mind as well. The importance of being able to move throughout the country and be assured of always being able to find a hospitable *ændærun* in the house of a relative or close friend is very great for Iranians. This is one reason why the internal hotel and restaurant industry remained undeveloped in Iran for many years. Cousins and in-laws, even distant ones, are routinely expected to visit and be provided hospitality by their relatives. Houses are set up to be able to do this. Moreover, it becomes vital that at least one set of social considerations in marriage be assurance of the fact that members of one family can indeed become admittees to the *ændærun* of the other family.

Before proceeding with a discussion of the ways in which the notions of *birun* and *ændærun*, *baten* and *zaher* play in the contextualization of communication behavior, I would like to digress briefly to introduce a set of related terms: Mary Douglas's notions of grid and group.

Mary Douglas, in her recent theoretical essay, *Natural Symbols*, proposes a methodological principle for the classification of social relations based on the intersection of two dimensions that she labels "grid" and "group." Douglas describes the use of grid and group through its application to describing the family and its operations: "To the extent that the family is a bounded unit, contained in a set of rooms, known by a common name, sharing a common interest in some property, it is a group, however ephemeral. To the extent that roles within it are allocated on principles of sex, age, and seniority, there is a grid controlling the flow of behavior" (Douglas 1970: 57).

These two variables may be seen in a different way, however: not as typologies, but as reflections of different perceptual modes by which individuals in society classify contexts in which social interactions take place. In Iranian society, as I have pointed out in the previous two chapters, considerations of perceptual relationships to others in hierarchies (grid) and in equality relationships (groups) are both active in governing individual interaction behavior. These same considerations can be thought of as providing the basis for the identification of the total context within which interaction takes place, and as forming the basis for the establishment of principles of communication for dealing with eventualities as they may arise.

A simple example of how perceptions of human relations and principles that are operative in human interaction can be generalized to perceptions of interaction contexts can be seen in the phenomenon of dressing for an occasion. The interactions one anticipates in some specifiable future context cause one to consider how to identify that context and what to do about one's outward appearance to meet the principles of interaction and environment operative in that context. Here as in all interactions, adroitness involves skill in identification and prediction of the circumstances involved in a particular interaction context. The person who continually underdresses or overdresses either is maladroit or does so for a particular purpose.

Rehearsing a formal speech can likewise be seen as reflective of an expectation others will have of a particular level of speaking competence. That is to say, the context is identified by the person rehearsing the speech as one where performance according to certain criteria is expected. The speaker therefore prepares accordingly.

In general, situations that in Iran are perceived as more *birun* are seen as subjecting individuals to the ethics of interaction obtaining between individuals interacting in the "grid" context. Situations perceived more as *ændærun* subject individuals to the ethics of interaction obtaining between individuals acting in the "group" context.

Yet one other factor that bears on the individual's conduct in different interaction contexts concerns feelings about *ability* to operate within different contexts—the degree of "freedom" felt in personal expression in interaction. An individual who feels able to deal with people freely in social situations, to the point of being brash, is labeled as *por-ru* (lit. full-face).[6] Though the term *por-ru* has a slight pejorative quality to it, it comes closest to representing one pole of the individual behavioral ethic dominant in interaction. *Por-ru'i* can be valuable in high-grid *birun* situations, as immortalized in a saying I ran across in Tehran: "One needs three P's to achieve success: *pul* (money), *parti* (pull), and *por-ru'i*."[7] Although it is tempting to think of *por-ru'i* as a personal quality, it is more accurately a measure of an individual's feeling about one's own communication ability as measured against the contexts one feels he or she will be involved in. The sort of behavior one would label as audacious, brusque, or rude in a public context with superiors or strangers is normal and expected in a social situation with one's peers. "Intermediate" contexts, such as the classroom, provide the context where *por-ru* behavior could begin to be considered inappropriate. However, the brashest students I knew in the classroom would decline with embarrassment a second-hand invitation to a social event in the home of a high-status person they did not know; their *por-ru'i* would thus vanish in the face of an intimidating context in which they felt they could not operate.

The opposite of *por-ru'i* is *kæm-ru'i* (lit. little face), or *forutæni* (lit. lowering of the body)—humility, reticence, and bashfulness. Although these terms are also slightly pejorative, this mode of behavior can be nonetheless attractive in high-grid *"birun"* situations, especially when there is a great disparity in hierarchical positions. A man who is properly *forutæn* in the presence of his superiors may feel quite rightly that he is likely to be remembered for that quality. In any case, *forutæni* is a mode of communication that reflects an individual's lack of ability or desire to exert a positive and direct effect on an interaction situation.

Por-ru'i and *forutæni*, or *kæm-ru'i*, are the natural expressions of high-group internal and high-grid external contexts, respectively. They are, in fact, expected behavior in their natural context of occurrence. A person who is *kæm-ru* or *forutæn* with same-age cousins and school-mates in contexts that would be classified as internal, or *ændæruni*, such as in one or another's own home, or garden, or out engaging in some social activity together, would be behaving in a very odd manner. Similarly, *por-ru'i* must be used with discretion in high-grid, external contexts, since it can arouse anger, which could be damaging. Indeed, as we will see in the next part of this discussion, the remedy for anger aroused in high-grid situations is to immediately practice *forutæni* until that anger is abated. To allow one to take liberties in being *por-ru* is indeed to *confer* face on that individual (*ru dadæn*), thus altering his condition from the expected normal state of *kæm-ru'i* (little face). The fact that the expressions in Persian that have evolved for these two modes of interaction behavior are slightly pejorative is explainable in that the only time that a person's behavior in one or another direction would be cause for comment would be when he was developing in-appropriately for the context of interaction.

I have thus far elucidated three dimensions of elements on which are based the ways in which perceptions of the context of interaction can serve as the foundation for principles of communicative behavior. The first dimension involves the juxtaposition of the internal with the external. The second involves perceptions of grid, i.e., hierarchically dominated situations, versus perceptions of group, i.e., equality-dominated situations. Finally, we see the indexical expression of overt individual control and contact across contexts of interaction in the notion of *por-ru'i* and *kæm-ru'i* or *forutæni*.

The Iranian Basic Schema

I have suggested that the basic social pattern in Iranian interaction consists of a correspondence between the three dimensions I have mentioned above: (1) the controlling arena of activity—*baten/ændærun* versus *zaher/birun*; (2) the controlling social ethic—group versus grid dominance; and (3) the controlling individual ethic represented in this discussion by the notions *por-ru'i* versus *kæm-ru'i* or *forutæni*. In

general, the normal expectation in interaction is that these three dimensions will correspond to and co-vary with each other. That is, one
will find two poles in interaction behavior, which I will label "Pole A"
and "Pole B" for convenience.

Pole A	Pole B
zaher/birun	*baten/ændærun*
grid/dominance	group dominance
kæm-ru'i (restricted expression)	*por-ru'i* (free expression)

Without for the moment considering exceptions to this schema or
the transformations that occur when factors are altered, I wish to
characterize the two polar positions in their "pure" state. First, it is
the expectation of individuals that in *normal, unmarked* interaction
situations, the three dimensions mentioned above remain roughly in
proportion with each other. Thus normal interaction is seen not as a
single state, but as a dynamic continuum. This means that in establishing normal interaction, it is incumbent on participants to demonstrate that these factors are in fact in proportion with each other.

One cannot, for example, entertain a stranger in one's home in
pajamas. Most households maintain a guest room where outsiders are
received. In the cities, Western furniture is kept in this room, in
contrast to the family sitting room, where persons relax on the floor.
In the village, even if one room is all there is in the house, it can be
quickly transformed from an internal family room to an external guest
room, by having the household head stand in greeting guests (and
put on his trousers if he wasn't already wearing them), bringing something special for the visitor to sit on, and having the women leave the
room. In each case the new context that is established is one that
conforms to the changed circumstances of the interaction: participants
must carry themselves differently, they dress in more constricting
clothing, they sit on more constricting furniture, and their verbal
expressions become correspondingly less free. To do otherwise would
be to violate normal expectations.

The reverse procedure occurs in intimate surroundings. The intimate male visitor may proceed unannounced into the inner quarters
of the household, he may be offered a pair of pajamas (which most
urban families keep on hand), and, though he may be offered re-
freshment, it will likely not be pressed on him to the degree that it

would be pressed on a person more outside the intimate circle of the household.

Not only does the quality of behavior change, but there is also an increase in redundancy in behavior as one moves from Pole B toward Pole A. Thus gestures become exaggerated, speech more distinct, and repetition of subject matter more frequent. More behavior is devoted to establishing and reaffirming communication parameters than in conveying novel content between participants.

Whereas a man will greet an official in an urban office differently from the way he will greet, say, his brother-in-law in his own village, not only will his greetings to the official mark that official's relative superiority linguistically, but by bowing, standing until asked to sit (probably never), folding his hands in front of him, casting his eyes down as the encounter continues, refusing to drink tea if it is offered him, showing reluctance to speak unless exhorted to, lowering his voice, and using standard urban speech along with numerous linguistic qualifications in prefacing his remarks and in addressing the official directly, the villager will demonstrate that he defines the scene as a Pole A context. The context is characterized not only by the presence of one or more of these characteristics, but also by the fact that they co-occur and are repeated in combination again and again throughout the encounter—tending to reinforce the nature of the scene over and over. The number of redundant features on many behavioral levels seems to increase almost geometrically, until in formal court settings where the shah is present, there seems to be virtually no "content" to the encounters at all[8]—every piece of behavior reinforces and reaffirms the context. It is small wonder that official pronouncements in such contexts have an empty ring.

An example of a consideration of basic schemata in social behavior as a continuum of correspondences of social dimensions can be seen in Edward Hall's work on proxemics (1959, 1966). Hall has demonstrated that a correspondence exists between a continuum of spatial distance between interaction participants and a variable set of associated activities. The correspondence between the activity set and the continuum of proxemic distance constitutes one vital aspect of the basic schema of social activity. To behave in a way that reflects other correspondences is to perform in a way that is slightly odd or makes others uncomfortable. One does not, for example, pronounce endearments at fourteen feet or discuss a business transaction at a distance of three inches. In communication systems, such as in Iran, where there is a strong correspondence between several continua of interaction dimensions, it is the variation from that set that constitutes a marked activity, not stages along the continuum. Thus, whereas it is within the realm of normal behavior to compliment one's superior in public and damn him in private, to do the reverse might not only be personally dangerous, but it would confuse people—it would be uninterpretable. It would probably also be difficult to bring oneself to do such a thing; to be insulting to one's superior in public is as difficult in Iran as delivering a sermon at six inches in the United States.

Still, the unthinkable sometimes does occur. As an apocryphal story has it, the former shah was in Los Angeles and was confronted by an American news reporter who had spent some time in World War II in Iran and had picked up a little colloquial Persian. Approaching the shah, the man said, in Persian, the equivalent of, "Hi, Mr. Pahlavi, how 'ya doin'." ("*Sælæm agha-ye Pæhlævi, halet četour-e*".) The shah was reportedly taken aback and could only sputter, "*Væ to ki hæsti*" ["Who are *you* (second person singular) anyway?"], as he might speak to the lowest underling. I interpret this not as rudeness on the part of the former shah but rather an attempt on his part to maintain the proper social interactional distance, as the situation demanded, between himself and the other man. The reporter had addressed the shah in a form used between intimate equals. It was thus up to the shah to reestablish the proper social distance. Of course, had he not been taken by surprise, the shah might have remembered that he was not in an Iranian context and was not speaking to persons operating under Iranian interaction conventions.

One can approximate the point on the continuum of the basic interaction schema people are operating at by attending to linguistic and behavioral variants that are also scalar. I will deal with the variations in linguistic style in the last chapters of this study.

An important nonlinguistic index of the contextual mode of interaction has to do with body carriage, proximity, and orientation to other individuals. In general, as one moves from Pole B to Pole A, carriage tends to become more rigid. Arms are kept at the sides, weight is distributed evenly on two feet. If seated, persons tend to slouch less, even in village situations. Extending the feet while seated on the floor becomes more permissible as one tends toward Pole B, and forbidden as one approaches Pole A, where one bows or inclines the head to acknowledge the presence of those entering the room, and stands to greet eminent persons. As one moves toward Pole A, more and more persons come under the rubric of those who must be stood for. Though status differences are still marked by the formality of verbal greeting and the juxtaposition of bows, half-bows, full standing from a sitting position, or half-raising of the body from a sitting position, in general a movement toward Pole A increases the frequency of activity and the number of people it is applied to, as these examples will illustrate:

Case 1

In Gavaki, two fairly large landowners live at a short distance from each other. They are, furthermore, matrilineal second cousins. One is older than the other. When I would be sitting with one or the other of the two in his own home, and the other would enter the room, the one seated would make no move to rise and the one entering would sit with no invitation to do so. There would be no greeting between the two on such occasions, but one or the other would begin the interaction with a substantive remark such as, on one occasion, "When do you want to prune the grapevines?" or, "Is your son going to come and help me or not?" The elder would not object to my standing when he entered the room, though his cousin did not, and would go through an extended greeting routine with me. The younger would not allow me to stand when he entered the room nor occasionally even when his cousin would enter, saying, "Sit, sit, stay in your place," although he would not cut off the extended greeting between myself and his cousin. Since I rarely visited one without the other's stopping in, this whole situation became routinized, something I could expect when visiting these two.

Some time later, a wedding was held in the house of the brother of the younger cousin, and the elder cousin, while his wife helped with the cooking for the wedding dinner, didn't participate in the preparations, but came as a guest. On this occasion, when he entered the room, the younger cousin who was host for the occasion rose, crossed the room, grasped the hands of his cousin with both of his hands, and with a bow pulled him across the room into a position of honor at the head of the assembly, muttering greetings all of the time. This same pattern was repeated when the younger cousin held a holiday meal and sermon (see *rowzeh*, above) that the elder attended, and again in reverse when the elder cousin was hosting some visitors from Shiraz for a Friday noon meal. In all cases the greetings, bows, and bodily attitudes were reciprocated by the other cousin.

Case 2

The head of the Department of National Development at Pahlavi University never stood when individuals came into his office singly on business of various sorts. On the other hand, at regular weekly meetings of the department he stood when the first person arrived and ushered the first and subsequent arrivees to their seats in his office with a wave of his hand.

On two occasions, members of the department along with the head all had occasion to meet with a higher official in the university. In this situation, too, the department head remained standing for department members as they arrived, greeting them extensively as they entered the room of the superior official.

Case 3

I had had some dealings with the head of a section of the Iranian Plan Organization, who had been involved with some consultation I was doing for the Institute for Social Studies and Research in Tehran. When I first entered his office, I waited some time before he looked up from his work and finally motioned me to sit down.

Later I encountered this same individual in the office of the head of a charitable organization connected with the royal family. On this occasion he rose, shook my hand, and carried out an extended greeting, bowing as he talked. He then offered me his own seat.

Case 4

In 1969 I had lived for approximately a month with a Teherani family. The head of the household was a musician and sang with a small group in a locale near his home. In his home I was able to operate freely—come and go as I wished and not be greeted extensively when I came in nor exhorted to eat more than I wished at meals.

Where the man worked, this pattern was reversed. When I would enter the door, he would leave his place, order me a seat, bow, and provide an extended greeting. I soon learned not to come to the locale after having eaten, as I would have a full meal ordered for me without my asking.

Case 5

Service personnel in university offices were generally asked to do the most routine work, such as bringing a glass of water, sweeping spilled refuse, and going on personal errands for office workers. In all cases within the office, orders were given without ceremony and without preface.

The pattern changed when such persons were consulted in the presence of a person from outside the office. When a Tehran official was inspecting university facilities for possible use as a training center for U.S. volunteers, the service personnel would be consulted, since they would often be the only ones who had certain information at hand. In such situations, the general dimensions of interaction with them would change. They would be addressed with second person plural personal pronouns instead of the second person singular; they would emulate, or be invited to emulate, the bodily position of their interviewers—sitting or standing as the interviewers did; they would be offered tea if others were (though I never saw one actually drink tea in such a situation).

Case 6

On accompanying a group of foreign visitors through one of the hotels in Shiraz, the manager and maintenance staff established similar relations to each other as the visiting group raised questions about the hotel operations. When I asked an acquaintance in the hotel about this situation after the tour, he declared that the manager's attitude was assumed for our benefit, as he was notorious for his bad treatment and bad language with the maids, cooks, waiters, and other service persons.

Another important shift in behavior that occurs in the movement from Pole B to Pole A consists of the shift in the orientation of group members as the context changes around them. Another example from Gavaki will serve to illustrate.

Case 7

All of the heads of the work/landholding groups of the village had assembled at the house of the head of the village association to discuss the appropriation of funds for sanding the often muddy village streets. As each entered and was greeted by the head of the village association, he removed his shoes and seated himself against one of the walls of the room. The large carpets, which were normally rolled up in the corner of the room, were now spread on the floor for the guests to sit on. The small sons of the household brought in a charcoal brazier with a small basin of water, several cups, and a teapot full of hot tea, which was then set on the brazier. The head of the village association poured tea and passed it to all in turn, starting on his right and moving around the room counterclockwise. As he poured, he joked with the persons on his immediate right and left.

The room was broken up into several conversation groups of two and three speakers. Topics were disparate, but all spoke animatedly, with much laughter, and in village dialect. No person spoke louder than any other.

When all had been served tea, the head of the village association addressed one of the men at the far end of the room with a humorous remark, still in village dialect. He then addressed the secretary of the village association at the same vocal level he had used to speak to the man at the other end of the room, but this time in standard urban Persian. He asked if the accounts of the organization were at hand. On receiving an affirmative reply, he addressed all of the men in standard urban Persian with a rhetorical question, still at the same voice level, prefacing his remark with an introductory phrase used in addressing equal or higher-status persons in informal situations or anyone in formal situations. At this point, all the groups of conversants broke up, and all focused on the head of the village association. From then on, all conversation proceeded in standard urban Persian, with occasional lapses into dialect at points of animated conversation. Individuals spoke one at a time, lower-status persons deferring to higher-status ones.

In Case 7 it is possible to "read" a good deal of communicative behavioral action that does not consist entirely of verbal performance. The fact that the meeting was held at the house of the head of the village association was significant in setting off the event as one where business would be conducted. The individuals who attended never saw each other together except at business meetings, at weddings, or during Moharram, the Shi'a Islamic month of mourning, when all would assemble together at the mosque or in the fields. Some, not being kin or neighbors of the head of the village association, would never have had occasion to speak to him except on these occasions, or if they passed him in the street and greeted him casually. Still, in many ways the head of the village association was able to maintain his authority and influence in the village by having reason and occasion to interact with more persons on a day-to-day basis than did any other individual.

Rugs spread on the floor served as another indication that the event in which all were participating would not remain a Pole B gathering. Since two rugs were spread, it was indicated that many persons were expected rather than just a few. Had the persons attending been issued an invitation to come, as to a wedding or during a religious celebration, the sons of the head of the village association would have brought cups of tea to each guest individually, and sweets of some sort would have been served. Sweets might also have been served had a stranger of some importance been present.

The conversation pattern among the individuals in the room was typical of an informal gathering of equal- or near-status persons. The shift to a situation where one person assumed a higher-status position was marked by his rise in vocal level, effected by a very smooth and natural transition via his addressing a person at the other end of the room in a slightly louder voice to adjust for distance, and then addressing the entire room at the same vocal level to assume his authority in the meeting. The shift from a Pole B to a Pole A situation was effected by the shift from village dialect to standard urban Persian and the consequent shift in conversation patterns from simultaneous speech among members of several scattered groups to ordered turn-taking in speaking. The use of standard urban Persian was reinforced by the return to it following animated lapses into village dialect, and the conversational structuring was reinforced by the head of the village association, who would frequently tell people to be silent if they were violating status-marked speaking order or if he didn't like what they were saying.

The shift from small independent conversation groups to focus on a single leader was a major interaction principle functioning in a series of meetings I attended in the office of the provincial governor. As I have mentioned above, the series of meetings was held regarding a development project and involved persons from several government departments. Before the governor would enter the room, the group would be split into separate circles of interaction, each circle oriented toward the highest-ranking individual within each group. When the governor would enter, all would stand, the separate groups would break up, and attention would be focused on the governor. He would then be called away from the meeting, and the large group would again break into smaller ones, even though the general group meeting was still in progress. On the governor's return, the small groups would again break up, and focus would center on him again.

Transformations of the Basic Schema

As I have suggested throughout this discussion, it is incumbent on participants in interaction everywhere to demonstrate not only what they are doing, but also that they are doing what they are doing. This is no less true of normal, routine behavior; individuals must demonstrate that the behavior they are carrying out is interpretable and congruous with the phenomenal elements that co-occur with that behavior.

A transformation of the basic schema of interaction involves a redefinition of the principles of account for one's behavior and/or the behavior of others and demonstrating that such a redefinition has occurred. It is one of the ways of dealing with systematic violations of the pattern of congruity of phenomenal elements that is exhibited in the basic schema.

Some of these transformations can be thought of as accounting procedures that allow people to deal with anomalous or unexplained phenomena after the fact by categorizing those phenomena in various ways as, for instance, accidental, lucky, or coincidental.[9] We would expect that all societies have a different set of such accounting procedures and different criteria for their application. Though all such procedures may not involve transformations of basic schemata, all do consist of procedures for bringing incongruous phenomena in line with the basic schema.[10]

Some accounting procedures involve the labeling of people and their actions with generalized attributes that mark the incongruity of the behavior of those persons with the basic schema but still reaffirm one's own expectations of how things normally proceed—the pragmatics of one's view of the principles and processes of social interaction. Ironically, the notion of appropriateness, which has been used implicitly and explicitly throughout this discussion, constitutes a judgment criterion in such a procedure. To make a judgment that an action is inappropriate is to account for it in a way that reaffirms one's feelings about the way appropriate actions proceed.

"Insanity" is an extremely important category in this respect and even more important in cross-cultural comparison. Though psychiatrists staunchly maintain that there is cross-cultural uniformity for a good deal of mental illness (i.e., true psychotics will be recognizable anywhere), not all communication on the part of medically certifiable psychotics will be labeled as insane.

Old Iran hands would generally agree that every village in Iran seems to have its own idiot/crazy man; the attributes, *divaneh* and *xol*, which are most often applied to village residents who regularly exhibit behavior incongruous with the events around them have strong religious and mystical overtones. Such persons seem not to be ostracized but, being allowed to roam at will, are cared for and given food by their families and neighbors.

The person in Gavaki who fit this description was notable in that he regularly violated interaction and other general behavioral principles. He was responsive to children's requests and orders and would sing or perform for them as long as they didn't tease him too much. On the other hand, he would regularly rant and rave at village elders, much to everyone's amusement. He would wander about during dinners at weddings and religious holidays and could be found sleeping during the day almost anywhere—the mosque, on someone's roof, on the school steps, once even in the back of my car.

The concept of rudeness or impoliteness (*bi-'ædæbi*) serves likewise as a post facto accounting device for linguistic and other behavior that does not conform to expected congruence patterns. Persons whose actions leave them open to being labeled *bi-'ædæb* are most often applying behavior appropriate to contexts grouped in the direction of Pole B to contexts that others define as being grouped in the direction of Pole A. Thus, persons who do not stand, bow, or use proper linguistic forms, or whose posture is not properly oriented are seen as failing to demonstrate that they are behaving according to normally expected patterns of congruence of behavior and context.

The relationship between "crazy" behavior and reality is one of disjunction. The person labeled as *divaneh* often does the opposite of what one expects in any context whatsoever or performs some action uninterpretable in terms of any conceptual framework. The individual who is rude performs actions that might be judged appropriate in *some* context, but not in the context within which he is being labeled as *bi-'ædæb*.

The notion of rudeness can serve as a much more potent social control in Iran than in the United States. The word *bi-'ædæb* connotes not only social inappropriateness but also a lack of all of those refinements that separate humans from animals. Another term that is often used synonymously with *bi-'ædæb* is *bi-šæræf*, which connotes a lack of honor and respect for one's own family. This is confirmed by yet a third synonymous expression, *bi pedær væ madær* (without a father and mother). All three expressions suggest that a person who is judged to be incapable of carrying out appropriate behavior in society has himself no basic social orientation and no basic social unit within which he has been trained. The outward response to any offensive act from within one's equality-oriented reference groups—the family friendship circles or the *dowreh*—is often withdrawal from any interaction whatsoever. To initiate a state of noninteraction, *gæhr shodæn* constitutes an extreme expression of anger with someone with whom one has equality ties for something they have done. Symbolically, the verbal sanctions voiced against individuals by other members of society, such as *bi-šæræf*, *bi-'ædæb*, or *bi-pedær væ madær*, which deny the individual's closest social ties, are replicated in the noninteraction sanctions exercised by the members of equality-based groups against their own members.

Thus the categorization of rude behavior through association with the denial of social ties serves to reintroduce the basic schema of interaction in a preventative way. The warning might be paraphrased thus: one performs actions that can be seen to be incongruous with basic expectations about correlation of action and context at the risk of having those actions accounted for by others in a manner that denies one's connections with the rest of society and social life. To have one's actions "framed" or "keyed" as *bi-'ædæb* in after-the-fact accounting is to be declared nonhuman by virtue of being nonsocial. Similarly, to have one's actions keyed as *divaneh* is to be declared nonhuman by virtue of being unnaturally constituted. In both cases, however, the transformed behavior is directly anchored to the basic schema of contextual-behavioral congruence discussed above.

A third framework that allows individuals to account for the unexpected actions of others is anger (*æsæbani'æt*). It is interesting that, whereas the expression of strong emotion, such as weeping, is expected in certain contexts, strong expression of anger must be justified by one's demonstration in the act of becoming angry that an affront to one's personal integrity or the integrity of one's family or friends is being defended. One aims for a judgment by others that *gheirætesh suxt*, his sense of honor was inflamed. To return to an earlier statement on this same point (Chapter 2), the individual himself demonstrates the justification for his anger by turning red, invoking religious oaths, proclaiming his injustices for all to hear, trying to fight, and allowing himself to be held back. Linguistically, expression of anger of this type involves paralinguistic phenomena such as volume, exaggerated accentuation of words, and elongation and lengthening of the vowels of some key words, such as *xoda* (God) or *qor'an* (The Qur'an), conjoined with a statement that serves as a truncated version of the injured person's complaint.

An incident that occurred at one point during my stay in Gavaki will serve to illustrate. I was sitting at the home of a friend, one of my chief informants, when I heard a great commotion, shouting and yelling. Wandering over to the scene with my friend, I saw that the manager of a small bank office in the village was fighting with the father of a boy he had accused of throwing a rock through the bank office's window. In a fashion typical of fights of this sort, each was livid, swearing great oaths, and threatening physical violence while being held back by others in the crowd.

The bank manager kept repeating "*čera feressadi bæčče-ye to mæna 'æziæt kone?*" ("Why did you send your kid to give me trouble?"). The answer was "*ay pedærsæg* [or another invective] *ba xoda* [or another oath] *dorugh migi!*" ("You son of a dog, by God, you are lying!"). This and similar formulae were repeated again and again, with asides to the assembled people by each party concerning the justice of his position. The argument escalated with the inclusion of more and more serious oaths and invectives. Spectators coming late could not understand the reason for the beginning of the argument by watching the two parties themselves, but would be filled in by other spectators. Thus, the outer fringes of the circle that formed around the arguing parties contained the least knowledgeable persons. They would be getting the story gradually from those closer to the center of the circle, who would, of course, explain the event as they themselves had been persuaded that it had proceeded, taking one side or the other. In this way, all spectators became involved in the process of establishing the argument situation as a justifiable display of anger.

Honorable display of anger occurs in contextual situations that tend toward the direction of Pole A as described above, and if properly justified they can serve to sanction behavior that would be outrageous otherwise. I witnessed instances of the principle of justified display of anger again and again in the university as students and their instructors came into conflict. In the office where I was established, one could count on occasional disputes breaking out between faculty and students. At times parties would come close to physical blows over academic matters, principally grades and student dishonesty of various sorts. In such confrontations, justifiable anger became an acceptable way to demonstrate strength in a hierarchical situation. When one's sense of honor or zeal (*gheiræt*) was inflamed, one was not expected to be able to control it. A student accused of cheating could often reverse a disadvantageous situation by claiming to have been wronged through an unjust slur against his honor. *Gheiræt* is an element of the personal *baten*. Thus its expression primarily in situations characterized as tending toward Pole B constitutes a basic pattern incongruity that is nonetheless justified and justifiable as a transformed keying of the basic social schema.

As mentioned above, anger in Pole B-oriented situations tends to be characterized not by angry outbursts but by an opposing action: withdrawal. Occasionally anger is expressed openly between friends or within the family. The pattern of such expression within the family is indicative of the very special status that that institution has in Iranian life. The family is an institution that must be internally as well as externally oriented; inwardly hierarchically or grid-dominated, but group-dominated in its orientation toward the outside world; and, finally, both free and restricted in expressing its internal and external relations. Thus, in many ways, the family setting constitutes an important context in its own right where elements of the basic schema are not juxtaposed from orientation toward one pole or the other, but rather where all of the elements of both polar orientations are *combined* in a single institutionally ordained complex of contexts for interaction.

Whereas anger of a violent sort should not be expressed between friends and intimate companions, anger is freely expressed in the family situation, but only in certain directions. In Gavaki, in arguments I witnessed, husband and wife often argued, but the wife was restricted in her reply to her husband's anger. She might reproach him but not initiate violent argument. The husband might beat his wife. Older sons might also strike both their mothers and their sisters. Such actions would arouse everyone's consternation, but no one would deny the sons' right to do this if the father himself did not object. The strictest taboos are placed on the expression of anger by children toward their father. The kind of expression of pique that children in the United States direct toward their elders, and in particular their fathers, constitutes an outrageous act in the Iranian family.

A seven-year-old child in a family of my acquaintance struck his father in anger over something. His father was so shocked he could only stare in disbelief. His mother began to weep and wail, and the child was so remorseful that he locked himself in the toilet and wouldn't come out even for dinner. Even at that age, the child was expected to contain his anger toward his father and give it no expression whatsoever. In a more extreme case, I was witness to one young man's hysteric convulsions brought on by suppressed anger toward his father during a discussion of the father's desires in the choice of his son's future bride.

Contextual keyings we have discussed thus far are representative of transformations of the basic interaction schema that involve the imposition of elements from Pole B situations onto Pole A situations. The contextuality of interaction within the family situation represents a conjunction of the elements of Pole A and Pole B. The imposition of elements from Pole A onto Pole B situations is also a possibility and can be represented in yet another range of keyings.

One of the commonest social situations in Iran involves the relationship between guest and host. Being a good host is a matter of pride, and the willingness and desire to extend hospitality—*mehman-nœvazi*—is as close to being recognized as a national trait by Iranians themselves as any social attitude could be. However, the guest-host situation is a highly contextualized one. It is framed by an invitation and has a definite beginning, ending, verbal and behavioral formulae, and transition points. In terms of the contextual orientations we have been dealing with, it comes close to an imposition of the elements from Pole A onto Pole B situations.

The host may be thought of as inferior, equal, or perhaps superior to the guests in other contexts. However, for the duration of the guest-host keying, the host is inferior to the guests and provides for them as a matter of tribute by virtue of their status as guests. This keying involves the bringing of persons outside the immediate family circle into a region that is more *œndœrun* or interior than a public place, although it may not be the most private area of the host's physical and behavioral quarters. To have the guest contribute to his or her own welfare in the way of money or labor is bad form, so the host will often anticipate the guest's desires. In this regard the Persian word *mehmani*, which is sometimes translated as "party" in English, indicates the focus of such an event on the guest (*mehman*). I myself have been surprised by being provided with such personal items as medicine, socks, bus fare, postage stamps, and camera film by solicitous hosts who noticed that I needed these things. The first time I genuinely gave offense in an Iranian household was when I suggested that a present I had brought to my hosts was "in repayment for all of their kindness." Though one in fact reciprocates in guest-host situations, one doesn't draw attention to those actions.

In this respect, it was not uncommon, even in 1972, in Tehran to have a congenial conversation with a taxi driver during a trip and have him refuse payment. Though in some cases this was a pleasant but empty gesture, one would occasionally run into a situation where the driver really would not take money even when pressed. The taxi was, for the moment, his own *ændærun,* and the rider had been his guest for a pleasant interlude in the day. That the taxi delineates a personal internal space for its driver can be seen in the amazing touches that some drivers use in decorating their cabs inside and outside. Colored lights, paint, decals, record players, and curtains make some taxicabs into projections of rooms within the driver's own home. It is thus not surprising that drivers will often pick up their own friends and "entertain" them in the cab while picking up fares.

Storekeepers also work extremely long hours during the day. For them the store is not only a place of business but a secondary setting for entertaining guests in an informal way. Every neighborhood in a city has a whole range of shops that cater tea, flavored ices, soft drinks, and food for the members of the surrounding business community and their guests.

Some persons are by definition not available to be guests on all occasions, because they are too close to the *ændærun* by virtue of their kinship or marriage connections with the family unit. In Gavaki, there seem to be degrees of participation in wedding celebrations. A man, his wife, and his children are considered separately for purposes of attendance and participation in the celebration. If a person participates in the preparations for the wedding, he or she belongs to the group of hosts. The closer one's kinship relationship to the bride or groom, the greater the expectation that one will actually lend labor and yet also be a guest, by sending a child to help with the preparations for weddings of persons who are not immediate relatives. Also, since the family of the bride and the family of the groom have separate celebrations, and because the women are separated from the men in each case, the husband and wife can attend separately and participate to different degrees. Thus the wife may be closely related to the groom and will thus be part of the host group for the women of the groom's family, while her husband, who may be distantly related to the bride, is a guest of the men in the bride's family.

Being obliged or expected to take the role of host in the context of the home of another constitutes a part of the transformed interactional principles that become operative in the guest-host keying of reality. Another principle that operates as a transformation of the basic Iranian interactional schema consists of the extension of hospitality context from one physical setting to another. By this principle, relatives of persons who extend hospitality to guests can also become obligated to extend such hospitality, though their guests may be totally unknown to them.

Friends in Gavaki often urged me to visit "their homes" in Shiraz. When I inquired more closely, I found that these residences were owned by brothers, uncles, and cousins of those I knew in the village. This pattern was familiar to me, as I had been invited many times to stay in the homes of immediate relatives of friends whom I had never met, even though those relatives lived in distant cities. Such invitations are often polite gestures but are nonetheless potentially activatable without censure. On a trip to the Bakhtiari tribal region, my companions and I were shunted from one group of relatives to another in a continuing chain of hospitality, though the hospitality given was begrudged in some cases.

Yet another transformation of the basic schema of correspondence in interaction dimensions involving the imposition of elements of Pole A onto Pole B situations entails the use of incongruous verbal behavior and actions for humorous, ironic, or sarcastic effect—for example, according intimates or family members the kind of behavior one would accord either perceptual inferiors or perceptual superiors in Pole A situations. Thus, using deferential linguistic forms to a servant within one's home is interpreted as a keying of the situation whereby the remark will be taken as humorous, sarcastic, or ironic, depending on additional paralinguistic features such as stress, tone, and volume. The same would apply for similar behavior with close friends, same-age cousins, and siblings. This is, of course, not the only kind of humor, sarcasm, or irony in interaction, but it is one form that plays on a regular transformation of persons' expectations of that social interaction conceived as being normal.

Throughout this brief discussion of keyings within normal interaction sequences, it may seem as if several different levels of explanation have been mixed. One source of ambiguity in trying to talk about framing or keying in ongoing reality is the distinction between the labels we as analysts are able to give keyings or frames, and the kinds of special understandings and interpretations that persons operating within those frames give to the actions they observe and make sense of. In a real sense, there is only one important basic fact about a frame or keying that we may label as, say, play. This is that persons engaged in that particular activity interpret the actions they are participating in or observing as playful rather than serious and apply criteria to that event that are different from the criteria they apply to mundane existence. Thus, a bad host is not judged in the same way as a bad employee, and criteria applied to a party are different from those applied to a bank transaction. Nonetheless, such keyings of basic schemata of reality are interpretable because they are relatable to the basic schema—they are seen as composed of the recognizable elements that comprise normal existence arranged in a variation of the normal pattern one expects them to be seen in.

The transition from keying to keying must be an accomplishment of individuals engaged in interaction, just as they must accomplish a demonstration of the orientation with which they are operating within the basic schema, even though the contextual dimensions are largely supplied. Stylistic variation in language is one of the ways that such demonstrations are made. An individual in Iran shows orientation toward Pole A or Pole B contexts through a total pattern of behavior, including use of particular linguistic variants. In the chapter that follows, the pattern of that verbal linguistic variation will be treated in detail and related to some of the broad principles operative in Iranian interpersonal communication.

V

PERSIAN SOCIO-PHONOLOGY

The Persian Phonemic System: Standard Style

To posit a uniform sound system for a uniform dialect of "standard Persian" is to espouse a fiction, because there is no speaker in any language who confines his sound production in actual speech on all occasions to an invariant closed corpus of sounds (cf. Labov 1972, 1973). The positing of such sound systems for analytical purposes has continued as standard practice in linguistics because variation in speech has rarely been a central concern in the description of language until recent years.

Single phonemic systems for Persian have been delineated by several authors (Hodge 1957, 1960; Krámský 1939; Lazard 1957; Matthews 1956; Nye 1955; Oblensky 1963; Rastorgueva 1964; Vogelin and Vogelin 1965; Yarmohammadi 1962). In addition, the following special topics relating to the phonology of the language have been treated: syllable structure (Scott 1964); vocalic length (Krámský 1966; Shaki 1957); stress, accent, and intonation (Bausani 1947; Ferguson 1957; Hamp 1958; Hillman 1970; Lucidi 1951; Oblensky 1963). Additional sources in Russian currently unavailable to me are cited by Lazard (1970).

It has been the practice of the above authors to base their phonologies on standard Tehrani Persian. In present-day Iran the speech patterns of Tehran have with few exceptions been adopted by educated individuals of middle age and younger in all urban areas of the country. The rapidly expanding television and radio network in Iran uses this speech variety as its standard, thus spreading its currency among educated persons. Regional urban standard colloquial varieties, such as those of Isfahan, Yazd, Mashhad, Shiraz, etc., although much made light of throughout the country, have sound systems that vary from standard Tehrani principally in stress and intonation pat-

terns with a few chacteristic and highly standardized vowel and consonant shift differences. Rural speech varieties vary considerably from
the urban standard, however, to the point where they are unintelligible
to speakers of standard Tehrani. Despite a large Orientalist literature
describing these rural speech varieties, they are in need of much
further study to determine their precise relationship to urban varieties
of Persian.

The present study is based on the standard speech varieties found
in urban areas and their stylistic variations. Standard urban Persian
is generally described as containing the phonemes listed in table 1.

Hodge (1957, 1960) recognizes four levels of pitch (1, 2, 3, 4) and
two levels of stress (primary and weak).[1] Oblensky, on the other hand,
recognizes only three pitch levels, but increases Hodge's stress levels
to three. It is my own opinion that four pitch levels and three stress
levels exist in standard urban Persian (hereinafter standard Persian)
phonetically, but that only two stress levels and three pitch levels are
truly phonemic.[2]

Juncture, which informs stress and pitch contours, occurs at period,
comma, and question mark, in agreement with Hodge. Phase final
length is also phonemic in distinguishing declarative sentences from
questions in some cases:

$$\overset{2\quad 1\quad 1}{\text{/næræfti/}}$$ "You (sg.) didn't go."

$$\overset{2\quad 1\quad 1}{\text{/næræfti:/}}$$ "Didn't you (sg.) go?"

The question of vowel length and vowel quantity is complicated
and will be treated at greater length below. In standard Persian, how-

TABLE 1

The Phonemes of Persian

	Consonants	Vowels
	p t č k q	i e
	b d j g	u o
	f s š x h	a æ
	v z ž	
	m n	
	w* r l y '	

*Some commentators treat w as a variant of v or of the vowel u. In Persian script v, w,
and u are all indicated by the same letter.

ever, it may be said that vowel length differentiation is a phonetic feature, but that it is predictable from other features and from the position of the vowel in a given word.

Allophones and their distributions for standard Persian are presented in table 2. Data are based on Vogelin and Vogelin (1965), Shaki (1957), and my own field investigation.

Allophonic variations of consonants seem to be conditioned by the presence of juncture of syllable boundary. All liquids and nasals ([+ sonorant]) are devoiced when they are the second element in a final consonant cluster:

/jæšn/ "celebration" [jæ:šN]
/mesl/ "like" [me:sL]
/æbr/ "cloud" [æ:bR]

Vowels follow the following pattern as observed above. "Long" vowels (/a i u/) retain their long quality except before /'/, final /h/, and final /n/. "Short" vowels (/æ e o/) are lengthened before final consonant clusters. Long vowels append a consonantal glide preceding other vowels:

/ahu/ "deer" [a:huwan] "deer" (pl.)
/širazi/ "native of Shiraz" [ši:ra:ziyan] "natives of Shiraz"

Stylistic Differences in Standard Persian

As a working definition for "style" I propose the following: "distributions of linguistic behavioral elements such that particular sets of those elements occur predominantly within particular sets of corresponding speech events." Thus those elements of variation in language that can be thought of as "stylistic" are those that can be seen to be context-sensitive.

In Persian, as pointed out in the last chapter, there are many forms of variation that are context-sensitive. In this chapter I am dealing specifically with sound variation in Persian. Some sound variation that might be considered more "morphophonemic" is dealt with in the chapter that follows. Some aspects of Persian morphology bear directly on sound variation, however.

There is a great variation in Persian in the use of words of Arabic origin across different social and cognitive contexts. A high incidence

TABLE 2

Persian Allophones

Phonemes	Allophonic Variants
Consonants	
/p,t/	Aspirated before vowels; released in syllable final position.
/k,g/	Aspirated before back vowels /a o u/; palatalized before front vowels /i e æ/ and in syllable final position.
/q/	Phoneme /q/ is described by Vogelin and Vogelin (1965: 211) as follows: "a back voiced velar stop [ġ] initially, back voiced velar fricative intervocalically [γ]; [ġ] occurs in /Cq/ and /qC/ clusters and medially as /qq/, and in final position; otherwise [γ]." [γ] is transcribed as [gh] in this study.
/r/	Voiceless initially and when the second element in final consonant cluster [R]; voiced elsewhere.
/m,n/	In combination with preceding vowel and following consonant (V/ⁿ/C), mark nasalization of preceding vowel and assimilate to the position of the following consonant. Otherwise /n/ is a dental and /m/ a labial nasal. Voiceless as second element in final consonant clusters [M N].
/l/	Voiceless as second element in final consonant cluster [L].
/'/	Anlaut before a vowel initially and in C'V environments, and a glide intervocalically. A distinction is made in this study between " ' " and " ' " in transliteration passages to reflect an orthographic difference between Arabic 'æyn (ع) and hæmzeh (ء). Phonetically there is no distinction between " ' " and " ' ". Phonetic observations about /'/ apply to both realizations. Initial " ' " is not transliterated, but initial " ' " is preserved.
Vowels	
/a/	Short [a] before /'/, final /h/, and final /n/; long [a:] in other environments.
/i/	Short before /'/, final /h/, and final /n/, before [a:] realized as [iy]; long [i:] in other environments.
/u/	Short [u] before /'/, final /h/, and final /n/, before [a:] realized as [uw]; long [u:] in other environments.
/æ/	Long [æ:] in environment /æ/ CC#; otherwise short [æ].
/e/	Long [e:] in environment /e/CC#; otherwise short [e].
/o/	Long [o:] in environment /o/CC#; otherwise short [o].

of use of technical words of Arabic origin is likely to be accompanied by attempts to produce characteristically Arabic sounds. In sermons and orations delivered by the religious clergy and certain educators, the pronunciation of /q/ tends particularly toward being a true unvoiced back velar stop. Similarly in such situations /'/, tends toward being a full glottal stop or at least heavy glottal structure. In oratorical speech, /a/ becomes lengthened in certain environments to an extreme and is lowered and rounded to become almost [ɔ:]. An off-glide [ʷ] is also added so that the general effect becomes [ɔ::ʷ]. This pronunciation of /a/ has no counterpart in Arabic. Super-segmental features, such as pitch and accent, tend to be greatly exaggerated in oratory as well. Note also the word /četor/ "how." Written with an orthographic /u/, the word is pronounced [četo:ʷr], not [četu:r], in most oratorical styles.

The most common context-sensitive sound shifts occurring in Persian are reduction and deletion of sounds in some instances and their retention in others. It is this type of variation that I will consider below. The general pronunciation quality that one finds in speech ranges from preciseness and exaggeration of contours (as that associated with Arabic forms) to slurring and elimination of entire final syllables. Within the vowel system, there is a tendency to centralize all vowels in some contexts. Vowel length varies from full retention in some contexts to virtual elimination in others. In general, then, the quality of the dimensions of sound variation in the language range from overdetermination—great care in pronunciation and maintenance of high contrast within the system, to underdetermination—slurring and elimination of contrasts throughout the system.

In the discussion that follows, I have attempted to move away from the tendency to describe stylistic variation in terms of discrete "levels," and toward description in terms of scaled polar opposite tendencies. Sound features described in the previous section of this chapter as characteristic of Standard Persian form one extreme on the polar scale, and the most extreme variants of these individual features, the other extreme. This method of description is adopted, and will be seen to facilitate a demonstration below of the correlation between variation in the second system and variation in perception of the nature of context on the part of interaction participants.

In addition to my own field investigations, I have drawn in this discussion on numerous insights from others. I have already mentioned the important studies in the field of Persian speech style by Hodge (1957) and Jazayery (1970). Significant and enlightening statements on style in Persian have also been made by Archer and Archer (1972), Boyle (1952), Hillman (1972, 1981), Modaressi-Tehrani (1978), Newton (n.d.), Shaki (1957), Vahidian (1343/1963), and Windfuhr (1979).

Stylistic Variation—The Consonantal System

The following principal variations are actively recognizable in the consonantal system of Persian.

1. Reduction of /'/ varies from realization as glottal stricture ['], with accompanying lengthening of a preceding short vowel, to deletion except following juncture. Arabic 'æyn (ع) and hæmzeh (ء) are both realized as /'/ in phonetic analysis, Elsewhere they are transliterated as " ' " and " ' " respectively.

/da'i/	"maternal uncle"	[da'i]	→	[dai]
/mo'omen/	"pious"	[mo':men]	→	[momen]
/mo'æssese/	"institute"	[mo'æssese]	→	[moæssese]
/ræ'd/	"thunder"	[ræ'd]	→	[ræd]

Note, however, the following form, which will be dealt with below:

/bæ'd/	"after"	[bæ:'d]	→	[bæ:d]
/bæd/	"bad"	[bæd]	→	[bæd]

As has been pointed out above, short vowels in formal Persian are normally lengthened preceding final consonant clusters. Therefore the lengthening of the /æ/ in /bæd/ can be viewed as the normal phonetic lengthening of /æ/ before the final consonant cluster /'d/. As in the case of /ræ'd/, the elimination of the final consonant cluster through the deletion of /'/ causes the vowel to remain short. In the case of /bæ'd/, however, there is danger of confusion at one stylistic extreme with /bæd/ (bad). The vowel in /bæ'd/ thus retains its length. Thus it can be established that vowel length for /æ/ and /e/ is phonemic in contexts where /'/ is deleted, whereas it is an allophonic feature for the vowel where /'/ is retained.

2. Reduction of /h/. /h/ is contextually deleted at morpheme boundaries and finally. Internally, slight glottal stricture is maintained intervocalically.

/sægha/	"dogs"	[sægha:]	→	[sæga:]
/mahi/	"fish"	[ma:hi:]	→	[ma:i]
/sobh/	"morning"	[sobh]	→	[sob]

The reduction of /h/, then, parallels structurally the structural changes observed in the reduction of /'/.

3. Reduction of /r/. /r/ tends to be entirely deleted as the second element of any consonant cluster in its variation across contexts. This deletion may extend across morpheme boundaries as well. Thus the objectifying suffix /-ra/ becomes /-o/ following consonants and /-ro/ following vowels.

/sægra didæm/	"I saw the dog."	[sæ:gra: di:dæm]	→	[sægo didæm]
/gobera didæm/	"I saw the cat."	[gobera: didæm]	→	[gorbero didæm]
/sæbr/	"patience"	[sæ:bR]	→	[sæb]
/æsr/	"evening"	['æ:sR]	→	['æs]

/r/ is additionally reduced in final position following short vowels:

/digær/	"other, more"	[digær]	→	[dige]
/næxeir/	"no" (emph.)	[næxeir]	→	[næxe]
/četor/	"how"	[četor]	→	[četo]

In other final positions, /r/ is devoiced:

| /pæresta:r/ | "nurse" | [pæresta:r] | → | [pærestaR] |

4. Reduction of /l, m, n/. Reduction of /l, m, n/ in final consonant clusters along with the reduction of /r/ in the same position reduces final syllables of the structure CVCC containing these consonants to CVC.

/jæšn/	"celebration"	[jæ:šN]	→	[jæš]
/sætl/	"pail"	[sæ:tL]	→	[sæt]
/esm/	"name"	[e:sM]	→	[es]

It should be noted in the reduction of /r, l, m, and n/ that when suffixed, these phonemes are retained. Thus, strictly speaking, their deletion is a neutralization in word final position. Thus:

/æbr/	"cloud"	[æ:bR]	→	[æb]
/æbre kuček/	"small cloud"	[æ:bre kuček]	→	[æbre kuček]
/sætl/	"pail"	[sæ:L]	→	[sæt]
/sætlha/	"pails"	[sæ:tLha:]	→	[sætla]

5. Representation of /q/. /q/ is represented before consonants as [x] in informal style, contrasting with its representation as [ġ] in formal style.[3] Thus:

/væqf/   "religious bequest"   [væ:ġf]   →   [væ:xf]

6. Assimilation of stops and nasals following fricatives. Stops and nasals following fricatives are usually assimilated to those fricatives. This includes stops following /q/, reduced to [x] in informal style, as above:

/sæxt/	"difficult"	[sæ:xt]	→	[sæx]		
/væqt/	"time"	[væ:ġt]	→	([væxt])	→	[væx]
/češmha/	"eyes"	[če:šmha:]	→	[češša]		

7. Reduction of stops following nasals and liquids. This reduction does not apply for all combinations. However, /d/ is assimilated to a preceding /n/, /b/ to a preceding /m/, and /g/ to a preceding /n/ when both elements in each pair constitute a final consonant cluster:

/čænd/	"how much"	[čæ:nd]	→	[cæn]
/jæng/	"war"	[jæ:ng]	→	[jæŋ]
/tomb/	(an island in the Persian Gulf)	[to:mb]	→	[tom]

8. Conversion of affricate to corresponding stop in final consonant cluster. There is a tendency for the initial fricative in a cluster of two fricatives in word final position to be replaced by a weakly pronounced stop in the same position.

/bæxš/	"luck"	[bæ:xš]	→	[bæ:(q)š]
/kæfš/	"shoe"	[kæ:fš]	→	[kæ:(ṗ)š][4]
/ræxs/	"dance"	[ræ:xs]	→	[ræ:(q)s]

9. Elimination of juncture. Elimination of phrase internal juncture results in phrase contractions in many instances.

/mohæmmed'æli/	[mohæmmed 'æli:]	→	[mændæli]
(proper name)			
/mæšhædi hæssæn/	[mæšhædi: hæssæn]	→	[mæšihæssæn]
(proper name)			
/šah 'æbdol 'æzim/	[ša:h 'æbdol 'æzi:m]	→	[šæbdolæzim]
(shrine near Tehran)			

Let us summarize the variation of consonantal phoneme quality and distribution between contextually determined styles.

a. In general, the principal axis of variation consists of reduction of consonantal elements.

b. Reduction of consonantal elements tends toward elimination of word final consonant clusters.

c. Syllable count for both words and phrases is also reduced.

d. In some cases where consonants are deleted, two vowels co-occur, an impossibility in Standard Persian.

Implicational Scaling in Stylistic Variation

In all cases of consonantal sound deletion, it is possible to set up implicational scales to characterize the variabilities in deletion that are based solely on the phonetic environments where deletion occurs. For example, it is possible to establish an implicational scale for /h/ deletion as follows:

/h/ is deleted in an unstressed syllable

1. in word final position $\quad /h/ \rightarrow \emptyset \; / \; \dfrac{\#\;(\#)}{[-\text{stress}]}$

2. prevocalically $\quad /h/ \rightarrow \emptyset \; / \; \dfrac{X \quad V}{[-\text{stress}]}$

3. preconsonantally $\quad /h/ \rightarrow \emptyset \; / \; \dfrac{X \quad C}{[-\text{stress}]}$

The three deletion rules form an implicational scale where rule 3 implies the other two. Thus, intervocalic deletion of /h/ implies that word final /h/ will also be deleted. Preconsonantal deletion of /h/ implies that all three delegations will occur. The following examples attest to this:

1. a. nega kon be in ha
        "Look at these!"
    b. *negah kon be in a
2. a. Radar æm nægof ke to nabudi
        "Rahdar (also) didn't say that you weren't there."
    b. *Radar hæm nægof ke to nabudi
3. a. Mæmud, man æm mixam inaro nega konam
        "Mahmud, I too want to look at these."
    b. Mæmud, man hæm mixam inaro nega konam
    c. *Mæmud, man hæm mixam inhara negah konam

Example 1 shows deletion of word final /h/ with no deletion of prevocalic /h/ in the phrase internal plural marker *ha*. The reverse pattern of deletion is stylistically unacceptable. Similarly in example 2 the preconsonantal /h/ in the proper name Rahdar is deleted along with prevocalic /h/ in the phrase internal construction with *hæm* (too, also). Deletion of preconsonantal /h/ without corresponding prevocalic deletion is unacceptable. Finally, preconsonantal /h/ in the proper name Mahmud can be deleted, but only when other /h/ deletions are also performed,[5] as shown in examples 3a, b, and c.

The two other implicational scales that will prove relevant for the discussion to follow involve the deletion of /r/ and the reduction of final consonant clusters. /r/ is deleted initially following internal morpheme boundaries as well as word finally following both consonants and vowels. Written as deletion rules, the three tendencies take this form:

$$
\begin{aligned}
1. \quad /r/ &\rightarrow \ \emptyset \ / \ C\underline{\hspace{2cm}}\#\# \\
2. \quad /r/ &\rightarrow \ \emptyset \ / \ X \ \#\underline{\hspace{2cm}}Y \\
3. \quad /r/ &\rightarrow \ \emptyset \ / \ V\underline{\hspace{2cm}}\#\#
\end{aligned}
$$

Thus the following:

4. a. četor šod, in ketabro næyaværdid
        "How is it that you didn't bring this book?"
    b. četo šod, i ketabo næyaværdi
    c. četour šod, in ketabo næyaværdin
    d. *četo šod, in ketabo næyaværdid
5. a. čeghadr xub šod, in ketabro aværdid
        "How good that you brought this book."
    b. čeghad xub šod, i ketabo aværdi

    c. čeghad xub šod, in ketabra aværdin

    d. *čeghadr xub šod, in ketabo aværdid

6. a. četor šod, an ghædr bi-ædæb šodi*

       "How is it that you've become so impolite?"

    b. četo šod, un ghæd bi-ædæb šodi

    c. četor šod, un ghæd bi-ædæb šodi

    d. *četo šod, an ghædr bi-ædæb šodi

The examples above demonstrate the interdependency of the three rules in the three words *četor* (/r/ is deleted as per rule 3), *ketabra* (/r/ is deleted in the objective particle /-ra/ as per rule 2), and *ghædr* (/r/ is deleted as per rule 1). In Examples 4a–d, it is seen that rules 2 and 3 may be applied together, and rule 2 may be applied without rule 3, but if rule 3 is applied, rule 2 *must* apply.

Examples 5a–d and 6a–d set up similar relationships for rules 1 and 2 and rules 1 and 3. Thus the rules are properly scaled in their present order.

As has been mentioned above, there is a general tendency in Persian to reduce word final consonant clusters to a single consonant. However, this reduction does not proceed according to a simple rule. At times the second element in the consonant cluster is deleted, and at other times it is not. The following examples illustrate. Examples 6a and 6f show the deletion of the second element in the cluster. Examples 7a, b, and c show the retention of both elements.

7.	a.	/æbr/	"cloud"	[æ:br]	→	[æb]
	b.	/sætl/	"pail"	[sæ:tl]	→	[sæt]
	c.	/sæxt/	"difficult"	[sæ:xt]	→	[sæx]
	d.	/dust/	"friend"	[dust]	→	[dus]
	e.	/čæšm/	"eye"	[čæ:šm]	→	[čæš]
	f.	/jæmb/	"next to"	[jæ:mb]	→	[jæm]
8.	a.	/zærd/	"yellow"	[zæ:rd]	→	[zærd]
	b.	/væqf/	"religious bequest"	[væ:ġf]	→	[væxf]
	c.	/šæms/	"sun"	[šæ:ms]	→	[šæms]

If we examine the sounds that are preserved in final consonant clusters versus the sounds there is a tendency to reduce in varying speech styles of Persian, we see that affricates (/f,v,s,z,š,ž,č,j,h/) have the greatest tendency to be retained as the second elements in a consonant cluster. Stops are retained in about half of all possible combinations, and liquids and nasals (/r,l,m,n/) are nearly always deleted when they occur in second position in a consonant cluster. This can be seen when observing the changes that occur for all possible final consonant clusters, as shown in table 3.

If we look at the phonological environment in which deletions most often occur, we see that the second element in a final consonant cluster has the greatest possibility of being deleted when the first consonant in the cluster is a fricative and the greatest possibility of being retained when the first consonant is a liquid. The two tendencies of consonant classes, both to be deleted and to condition deletion, are summarized in table 4.

Sound Variation in Social Context

In the last section of this discussion I identified the dimensions of contextualization of interaction in Iran as embodying three principal components: perceptions of a social ethic, perceptions of an individual ethic, and perceptions of a specific arena of activity. In order to make the present argument slightly more cogent, I will review the specifications of these perceptual dimensions briefly here.

As dealt with extensively above, in Iran considerations of perceptual relationships to others in terms of hierarchies of unequal relationships and complexes of equality relationships are highly active in governing individual interaction behavior. Furthermore, correct marking of these differences or similarities in human interaction is an activity that consumes immense amounts of time and energy in any social situation in Iran. The system of *tæ'arof* in Iranian interaction, which one might gloss in English as "ritual courtesy," provides a tool for the constant assessment of the qualitative nature of the social differences that exist between members of any particular constellation of individuals who find themselves in a particular arena of interaction at any one time (cf. Loeb 1969; Beeman 1976a). Because inequality is relative to shifting constellations of individuals, hierarchical relationships require constant testing and thus an over-determined communicational system for that testing. Equality relationships have, on the other hand, no need of being tested; they embody an ethic of absolute sacrifice and absolute understanding between individuals involved in them.

These two dimensions, which I characterized with Douglas's terms "grid" and "group," constitute a social ethic when they are projected onto particular situations of interaction. The interactions one antici-

TABLE 3

Stylistic Reductions in Persian
Final Consonant Clusters

Consonant Cluster		Applicable Rule
First element	Second element	
+ strident	+ plosive	[+ plosive] → ∅ / [+ strident] _____
+ strident	+ sonorant	[+ sonorant] → ∅ / [+ strident] _____
+ strident	+ strident	$\begin{bmatrix} + \text{strident} \\ a \text{ grave} \\ b \text{ diffuse} \end{bmatrix} \rightarrow \begin{bmatrix} + \text{stop} \\ a \text{ grave} \\ b \text{ diffuse} \end{bmatrix} / \underline{\hspace{1cm}} [+ \text{strident}]$
+ strident	+ plosive	$[+ \text{plosive}] \rightarrow ∅ / \begin{bmatrix} + \text{sonorant} \\ a \text{ grave} \\ b \text{ diffuse} \end{bmatrix} / \begin{bmatrix} a \text{ grave} \\ b \text{ diffuse} \end{bmatrix}$
+ sonorant	+ sonorant	No change
+ sonorant	+ strident	No change
+ plosive	+ plosive	No change
+ plosive	+ sonorant	[+ sonorant] → ∅ / [+ plosive] _____
+ plosive	+ strident	No change

TABLE 4

**Deletion Tendencies for Consonant Types
in Persian Final Consonant Clusters**

	Tendency to be deleted as second element in consonant cluster	Tendency to be associated with deletion of second element when serving as first element in consonant cluster
Highest	Liquids/Nasals (+ sonorant)	Fricatives (+ strident)
Second	Stops (+ plosive)	Stops (+ plosive)
Lowest	Fricative (+ strident)	Liquids/Nasals (+ sonorant)

pates in some specifiable future context cause one to consider how to identify that context and what to do about outward appearance (and mode of communication) to meet the principles of interaction and environment operative in that context.

In the Iranian situation, then, the perception of symmetry and asymmetry between oneself and other actors constitutes the basic core of the *social ethic* underlying immediate interaction situations. The pragmatic communicative reflex of that social ethic is overdetermined communication for situations that one perceives as embodying asymmetrical relations within which one must find one's own place and underdetermined communication for situations that one perceives as embodying symmetrical relationships that demand openness, sacrifice, and absolute understanding.

The individual *expressional ethic* concerns a person's feeling about his *ability* to operate within different contexts—the degree of "freedom" he feels in personal expression in interaction. Being able to deal freely with people and say whatever one wishes is expected of situations involving symmetrical relationships. This same behavior in situations involving asymmetry in social relations has already been identified earlier in this discussion and glossed as *por-ru'i* [lit. full-face (brashness, audacity)]. As has been mentioned, in asymmetrical situations one is expected to be cognizant of the status of perceptual superiors and restrict one's behavior, exhibiting humility, reticence, and bashfulness. However, as has also been mentioned, if one is humble, reticent, and bashful in situations where it is not expected, one may be labeled with equal pejorativeness as *kæm ru* (lit. little-face).

Restricted expression in asymmetrical relational situations means, paradoxically, that the codes of expression must be highly overdetermined and redundant in order for understanding to take place at all. In the Iranian royal court on state occasions, very little went on other than exact formulaic ritual greeting reinforced by body gestures that replicated the elaborated language. In private, with an old schoolmate, body postures are totally relaxed, almost amorphous, as individuals sprawl on a carpeted floor and speak with expressions that may be incomprehensible to anyone but the two individuals involved because of the extreme communality of understanding that both share.

The immediate situation impinges on behavior as it is defined as *birun* (outer) or *ændærun* (inner). These two concepts are extremely meaningful and potent in Persian, corresponding as they do to the Sufistic concepts of *zaher* and *baten* (cf. Beeman 1980; Bateson, Catherine et al. 1977), the external and internal aspects of one's individual psyche. Traditionally the inner *ændæruni* was the most private secluded area of a man's residence—the women's quarters. The *biruni* was the place of public reception. These are not just physical locations, but states of mind as well.

Whether a situation is defined as more *birun* or *ændærun* affects the social relations between individuals. Two brothers sprawled on the floor when alone in a room will pull themselves to a cross-legged sitting position when their father or an uncle enters the room. A son addresses his mother more respectfully in public and in the presence of her brothers than in private. Two intimate friends defer to each other politely when with others in a public restaurant over, say, a place to sit, but feel free to seat themselves anywhere when alone together. This is due in part to the ethic governing symmetrical interpersonal relationships mentioned above, where individuals are expected to protect the interests of their friends and intimates. The proverbial Persian admonition *zaher-ra hefz kon* [protect the external (appearances)] extends to one's symmetrically related intimates. Thus one demonstrates to others that one's brother, cousin, companion, or crony is a person worthy of respect.

One also must protect one's own external appearances. Ostentation, fine dressing, and fine manners are the hallmark of Iranian social relations. One never understates one's own social position in situations defined as *birun*. Thus behavior in general in *birun* situations, as opposed to *ændærun* ones, is overly determined, overstated, and highly redundant.

The three dimensions thus combine not only to contextualize behavior, but also to form interlinked semantic dimensions along which various kinds of behavior can be understood as appropriate or not. To restate this basic pattern, then, we may see it as consisting of a correspondence among the three dimensions I have mentioned above: (1) the controlling social ethic—asymmetrical versus symmetrical social relational prescriptions; (2) the controlling individual ethic of behavior—restricted versus free expression in social interaction; and (3) the controlling arena of activity—*birun* or outside situations versus *ændærun* or inside situations. Arranged schematically the three dimensions appear as shown in table 5.

I now wish to suggest that there is a direct correspondence between the dimensions that I have identified as determining contextualization in Iranian interaction and the dimensions of stylistic variation within the sound system of the language. I have chosen a number of examples from my own recordings and field notes drawn from various contexts, and I will attempt to show that the speakers' perceptions of sociocultural context correspond to their actualization of the sound system in language.

1. Deletion/retention of /h/
   Case a.
   i. sohbæt æz in bud ke ba hæm šærik bešim
       "The talk was about this, that we become partners."

   ii. ma sælamætíet sobæt midarim, xoda enšalla hefzet kone
       "We speak of your (2 sg.) health, God (we hope), protect you."

TABLE 5

**Factors Controlling the Contextualization
of Iranian Interaction**

	Pole A Situations	Pole B Situations
Social ethic	Asymmetrical ("grid")	Symmetrical ("group")
Individual	Restricted expression (*Kæm ru'i*)	Free expression (*por ru'i*)
Arena of activity	Outside (*birun*)	Inside (*ændærun*)

The two passages above were recorded for the same person on two different occasions in Gavaki. The speaker is a semi-blind middle-aged man who makes his living partly by trading and partly by performing religious recitations of the martyrdom of Imam Hosein (*ro*ʷ*zeh*) in people's homes in the village. The contrasting word in the two passages is the word *sohbæt* (speaking, conversation), where /h/ is deleted in the second realization, but not in the first. The first passage was recorded when this informant was speaking to another faculty member from Pahlavi University and me about his background and occupational history. This was in a public area of the village outside the man's own home where other persons in the village were listening to the conversation, and during the first three months of my stay in the village. The second passage was recorded approximately six months later, after I had gotten to know this man fairly well. We were joking around with my tape recorder, I urged him to say something, and this passage was spoken half in jest. The informal, intimate nature of the passage is marked by the use of the second person singular pronoun as well.

Case b.
i. væ xeili hæm, færzetan, mæmnun mišim
    "And we will, for instance, be very grateful also."

ii. i čiz æm dros kon
    "Fix this thing too."

Both passages are again spoken by the same speaker, as in case a. The first passage is not, strictly speaking, a natural production. I was asking the informant to produce speech that would be used by someone towards someone else from whom he wanted to extract a favor. The word *hæm* (too, also), which is used in collaboration with *xeili* (very) to form a unitary phrase, has the full retention of /h/ in this case. In the second case, which occurred during the same conversation, an order was being given to the man's same aged male cousin to fix the charcoal in the brazier on the floor. Both conversations took place in the man's home with only me and the cousin present. As one would expect in the relaxed, intimate situation, /h/ in *hæm* was deleted.

Case c.
i. væ un negah kærd væ did ke un dare tæjavoz mikone be
    zamineš

"And that one looked and saw that the other was
encroaching on his land."

ii. æli, særet, særet, nega kon be xoda
     "Ali, your (2 sing.) head, your head, look for God's sake."

The speaker in both of these cases was a farmer in the village. The
first interview was taken by one of my field assistants who was questioning the man on recent disputes in the village over land and water
rights, usually a fairly sensitive issue. The /h/ in the word *negah* (looking, observing) is retained here, even though some other common
colloquialisms are found in the passage [*un* for *an* (that), *dare* for *daræd*
(he has—used in constructing the progressive tense of the verb *tæjavoz
kærdæn* [to encroach, violate])]. The term *tæjavoz* is not often used in
common parlance and gives additional confirmation that the speech
is being carried on at a rather restricted, nonintimate level. In the
second example, the imperative warning issued in the second person
singular was directed toward this man's brother-in-law, who was also
his partner in farming in a work situation where I was a passive
observer. The element of free expression combined with the social
intimacy of the two partners correlates with the deletion of /h/ in the
word *negah*.

    2. Deletion and retention of /'/
        Case a.
        i. hič vaxt næræfte'íd aqa-ye bimæn?
           "Haven't you ever gone, Mr. Beeman?"

        ii. æmma ræfti unja, didi
           "But you've been there, you've seen."

        iii. čun næræftí hič væxt, nemidunesti
           "Since you have never been, you didn't know."

The examples above were provided by a military officer with whom
I was acquainted in Tehran. The first sentence was uttered on our
first meeting together in his home in his formal sitting room, the
second several months later at a family supper, and the third to his
wife at that same supper, contrasting the retention of /'/ in stronger,
more formal situations with its deletion in a slightly more relaxed,
intimate setting.

Assessing the stylistic distribution of /'/ is problematic for a number of reasons. The presence of /'/ in perfect verb forms corresponds with the use of the second plural ending /-id/, although not always so. Technically, the second person singular form *ræfte'i* should be possible, but it remains from my and my informants' experience only a textbook example. In example iii, the final syllable in the verb form *næræfti* (you hadn't gone) is stressed rather than the first syllable *næ-*, to distinguish the perfect tense from the simple past. (The normal negative past is shown in *nemidunesti*.) This feature of stylistic variation within the morphemic system of the language will be examined further.

Case b.
i.   æz moghe-ye šoru'e jælæse xaheš mikonæm æz aghayan
     hærf næfærma'id
     "From the moment of the beginning of the meeting, I
     request of the gentlemen not to speak."

ii. filmeš ke šoru šod didæm mænsur nisseš
     "When the film began I saw that Mansur wasn't (there)."

The two utterances were given by the *kædkhoda* of Gavaki on different occasions. The first occasion was at a meeting to determine the monies and goods to be exchanged between two families preceding a pending wedding. The setting was partially informal, and this sentence was used partly in jest by the *kædkhoda* to set off the formal business from the social preliminaries of the meeting. The second occasion was an amusing narrative to his friends about a trip to Shiraz where he lost track of his son. The retention and deletion of /'/ in these occasions correspond to these changed circumstances. The formality of the first situation is marked as well by the pronunciation of the term *aghayan* rather than *aghayun* and the more elevated verb form *hærf færmudæn* (lit. to command speech). The relaxed quality of the second situation is marked additionally by the deletion of /t/ in the word *nist* (he isn't) and the enclitic -*eš* (he, him).

Case c.
i.   čænd dæf'at dide'æm šæxæn. . . .
     "Several times, I have seen personally. . . ."

ii. čæn dæfe raftæm Širaz didæm. . . .
     "Several times.I went to Shiraz, I saw. . . ."

Both of these sentences were produced by a student at the University of Tehran with whom I was acquainted. The first sentence occurred when he was speaking to one of the faculty at the university about a subject related to his field (architecture). The second sentence comes from a conversation with me about Shiraz in his apartment. The contrasting form is the word *dæf'e,* which he pluralizes in the first sentence to *dæf'at* with full retention of /'/ and uses in the singular without /'/ in the second instance.

3. Reduction of /r/
    Case a.
    i. xu hala četo šod če ghæd šod
        "Okay, now, how is it, how much is it?"

    ii. un qædr 'ælaghmænd hastim ke hær færmayeš. . . .
        "We are so affectionately disposed (toward you) that any request. . . ."

    iii. četor mitonim šomara bištær bebinim
         "How can we (arrange to) see more of you?"

All three of the sentences above were spoken by the head of the village association in Gavaki. The first sentence came in a long interchange with five of the man's neighbors while they were weighing wheat that they had cultivated partially in common during the previous growing season. The interchange was jocular and occurred during the work situation. The weighing was taking place in the courtyard of one of the man's neighbors. The reduction of /r/ in the two words *qædr* (amount), realized as [ghæ:dR], and *četor* (how) corresponds with the informal, internal character of the event. The other two sentences were spoken in leave-taking toward the brother of one of my field assistants—a respected elementary school teacher who had been resident in Gavaki some years before and had used the occasion of my field research to return to the village. The head of the village association was speaking to him in the public area in front of the village walls as he was about to get on a bus to return to Shiraz. The public, hierarchical situation demanded formulaic speech to a degree. In the two sentences, the retention of /r/ is *qædr* and *četor* corresponded stylistically to the tone of both the conversation and the context.

Case b.
i. bayæd begi "xeili ozr mixam, xeili mæzræt mixam"
   væ æz in hærfa
   "You have to say, 'Pardon me, I'm sorry,' and
   words like that."

ii. næ baba, be tor-e koli oz xastæn inja nemikonæn
    "No, people don't ask (each other's) pardon here
    in general."

These two sentences came from different villagers in Gavaki with whom I was talking about the ways poorer villagers can deal with higher-status persons in making requests. The person in sentence i was giving several hypothetical forms for use with the one or two wealthy farmers in the village. The two phrases '*ozr mix^vam* and *mæ'zeræt mix^vam*[6] could be used to get the person's attention in beginning the request. In these hypothetical cases, *ozr* is retained in final post-consonantal position. My informant's friend remonstrated with him about his use of the phrase '*ozr x^vastæn*. This time, however, he was not speaking hypothetically to a higher-status individual but to an intimate equal. Moreover, he was not speaking in order to make a request, but to chide, an act he would perform only with an inferior or an equal, and never in public. All of these bespeak a nonhierarchical, intimate, private situation. In this case, the deletion of /r/ correlates with the circumstances.

Case c.
i. væ un næsihætra dad be mæn ke
   "... and he gave this advice to me, that ..."

ii. hič væx næsiyæto ghabul nemikonæn
    "They never accept advice."

The two instances were taken from the same person, in this case a clergyman in Shiraz. The first sentence was from a sermon of his, delivered during the month of Ramazan in the mosque. The second was from a private conversation he had about Islam in contemporary society and, in particular, among his own congregation. The contrast between sermon style and casual conversational style in the man's private quarters is marked twice in the word *næsihætra* (advice; obj.), in both the reduction of /h/ to an intervocalic glide and the elimination

of /r/ in the objectifying particle /-ra/. The use of the third person
plural form /-n/ rather than /-nd/ in sentence ii is a consonant cluster
deletion consistent with the reduction of /r/.

4. Consonant cluster reductions
   Case a.
   i. A: bioʷ hær če migoftæm
      B: bogu če ghæde
      A: nemæxad, bioʷ beriz bioʷ bolæn kon hærf-emæn
         dorosse
      A: "Come on, whatever I say (is right)."
      B: "Tell me how much."
      A: "Forget it, come on, pour, come on, lift it up,
         what I've said is right."

   ii. kamelæn dorost, hič vaxt næyamæd piš-e ma.
       "Absolutely right, he never came to see us."

   iii. un yeki doroste, ma æhle in kar nistim
        "That one is correct; we aren't the kind to do that
        sort of thing."

The three sentences were spoken by the head of the village association of Gavaki. The first interchange occurred during a work
situation where the weighing was taking place. The consonant cluster /st/ in the word *dorost* (correct) is reduced both in word final position and in conjunction with the enclitic /e/ (is). Additionally, the
cluster /nd/ is seen to be reduced to /n/ in the verb *bolænd kærdæn*
(lift up). Sentences ii and iii come from an interview that the head
of the village association was having with the head of the local government health and family planning office about difficulties the village was having with the former local doctor. This was in conjunction with a visit the official was paying to the village to show some
guests the medical facilities that had been established there. The official was putting the head of the village association on the spot here
by interviewing him in front of his guests on a sensitive issue. The
retention of the cluster /st/ both in final position and before the enclitic in these two sentences correlates with the hierarchical, formal,
public quality of the interchange.

Case b.
i. . . . ruzi ke 'ælahæzeræt ræftænd. . .
". . . the day on which his majesty left. . . "

ii. . . . momkene nækonæn a
"It may be that they won't do it, you know!"

Both of these sentences come from a meeting between a provincial official and a body of planners and university personnel. The first sentence was part of a statement made to the entire group. In this, the final cluster /nd/ in *ræftænd* [he (third person plural used honorifically) left] maintains its full value. The second sentence was issued as an aside to a high university official seated to the right of the provincial official after the official had made an exhortation to the group. The reduction of /nd/ to [n] and the use of the expletive *n* mark this sentence as a private comment to an intimate in the midst of the public meeting. It is slightly paradoxical that the reduction of the third person plural verb ending could occur in all referential contexts save where it is used honorifically to refer to a single person. The use of this form will be taken up in the next chapter.

In all of the examples above, I have attempted to demonstrate that the movement from one stylistic extreme to another in the pronunciation of particular speech elements tends to be correlated with particular social and cognitive contexts. In general, the tendency for /h/ and /'/ to be deleted, the tendency for /r/ to be deleted, and the tendency for final consonant clusters to be reduced all increase as (1) the *social ethic* being invoked tends toward that of symmetrical social relationships, (2) the individual engages in free as opposed to restricted expression, and (3) the arena of activity is perceived as more "inside" than "outside."

Thus far I have provided an account of stylistic sound variation and its context of occurrence, but my purpose in this discussion, as stated previously, is to go beyond this simple description and attempt an explanation of the reasons why *these* particular variations occur and why they occur in the *way* they do. In order to attempt an explanation of the reasons why particular sounds are deleted in some social contexts, it is necessary to have a little more information about the sounds in question and their role within the Persian language. Any explanation of these phenomena at this point is bound to be speculative to a degree. My attempt to explain the variation discussed so far centers on formulating an account of how sounds in language are conceived and perceived by speakers and dealt with in the pragmatics of conversational interaction.

Redundancy and Sound Reduction in Persian

An important and interesting study of sound distribution in Persian was completed by Jiři Krámský over thirty years ago (1948). In this study, Krámský, in an extensive computational survey, investigated the frequency of participation of classes of sounds in various positions in Persian monosyllabic words. Krámský begins by listing the structures of possible monosyllabic words in Persian. These structures correspond to Persian syllable types as well:

V	CV
VC	CVC
VVC	CVCC

By considering diphthongs as VV, Krámský adds the following two classes:

CVV
CVVC

Matthews (1956) concurs with Krámský except for the final two "diphthong types." Nye (1955) adds the combination VCCC, which is limited to the French loan words *tæmbr, septambr, novambr,* and *desambr.* Scott (1964) reduces the six primary types cited above to four by extending the distribution of /'/ to initial position. Thus, for Scott, "the canonical shape of the syllable in Persian can be represented as CV (C) (C) (C)" (Scott 1964: 27). Scott's argument for establishment of /'/ initially is based on the recognition of phrase internal open juncture as an "emic" unit in Persian (Scott 1964: 29), a position also supported by Hodge (1957).

Krámský in his 1948 study establishes a broad set of distributional data for the consonants and vowels of Persian. Basing his survey on E. H. Palmer's *A Concise Dictionary of the Persian Language* (1924), he separates words of Persian origin from those of Arabic origin. For the purposes of this discussion, Krámský's type of monosyllables have been collapsed to conform to Scott's typology (thus Krámský's VC is subsumed under CVC, etc.). Diphthongs are treated as single vowels.

Krámský does not include *tæmbr* in his inventory, so the CVCCC form is eliminated from this study as well.

Adapting Krámský's data in this way, the following distribution for monosyllabic forms is obtained:

Syllabic Form	Persian Origin	Arabic Origin
CV	47	14
CVC	416	214
CVCC	184	575
Total	647	803

Thus it can be seen that for monosyllabic words, the form CVC as we have defined it is the most common among words of Persian origin and the form CVCC is the most common among words of Arabic origin. Additionally, it is found that for all forms all consonants may appear initially. In the form CVC all consonants may appear finally as well. Vowels may appear in combination with any initial or final consonant in the form CV of CVC.

What will prove to be of particular interest in this discussion is the construction of final consonant groups in the combination CVCC. There are fifty possible consonant clusters occurring at the end of monosyllables of Persian origin. There are, however, 178 possible terminal consonant clusters for words of Arabic origin. Groupings of membership in clusters are shown in table 6. Percentages represent the proportion of all existing positions as elements in consonant clusters filled by each consonant class. Thus 125 of all first elements in final consonant clusters in words of Persian origin are plosives. Col-

TABLE 6

**Distribution of Persian Phonemes
In Final Consonant Clusters (Monosyllabic Forms CVCC)**

	Persian		Arabic	
	1st element	2nd element	1st element	2nd element
+ Plosive	6 (12.0%)	22 (44.0%)	53 (29.8%)	48 (27.0%)
Average	1.0/member	3.66/member	10.6/member	9.6/member
+ Strident	20 (40.0%)	17 (34.0%)	76 (42.7%)	76 (42.7%)
Average	1.81/member	1.54/member	9.5/member	9.5/member
+ Sonorant	24 (48.0%)	11 (22.0%)	49 (27.5%)	54 (30.3%)
Average	4.8/member	2.2/member	12.5/member	10.8/member

umns of percentages all add to 100. Averages show the distribution of consonant cluster positions among all members of consonant classes (total number of existing elements in each position divided by total number of members in each consonant class). This provides a rough index of the participation of each consonant class in the elements of final consonant clusters. Compare this data with consonant distribution for final consonants of monosyllables of the form CVC in table 7. Combining the Persian and Arabic origin forms from table 6, the data for table 8 are obtained.

As can be seen, the fricatives dominate as final consonants in the final consonant clusters of Arabic origin but do not dominate in the final consonant clusters of Persian origin. On the other hand, fricatives do dominate as the final consonants in the form CVC for words of Persian origin and for all CVC monosyllables in the language, whereas they do not dominate in words of Arabic origin.

TABLE 7

Distribution of Persian Final Consonants
(Monosyllabic Forms CVC)

	Persian	Arabic	All
+ Plosive	82 (20.7%)	38 (32.7%)	120 (22.5%)
Average	13.6/member	7.6/member	20.0/member
+ Strident	165 (41.2%)	29 (24.1%)	214 (40.2%)
Average	15.8/member	3.62/member	19.4/member
+ Sonorant	149 (37.6%)	49 (42.2%)	198 (37.2%)
Average	29.8/member	9.8/member	39.6/member

TABLE 8

Distribution of Persian Consonantal Phonemes
In Final Consonant Clusters (Monosyllabic Forms CVCC)

	1st Member	2nd Member
+ Plosive	59 (21.5%)	70 (30.7%)
Average	9.83/member	11.83/member
+ Strident	96 (42.1%)	93 (40.8%)
Average	8.72/member	8.82/member
+ Sonorant	73 (32.5%)	65 (28.5%)
Average	14.6/member	13.0/member

However, fricatives considered individually are the *least productive* group in terms of occurrence per member in final consonant clusters. Because the occurrence of fricatives in final consonant clusters is less frequent than that of plosives or liquids/nasals, individual fricatives must carry out a greater function of differentiation for Persian speakers and thus carry a greater information load. Thus, it would be reasonable to assume that for a speaker of Persian, a consonant cluster would be more readily identifiable by its fricative component than by its liquid or plosive component.

Liquids, by having the widest distribution, are also the most expendable class of sounds in terms of the information they carry. This is to say that a word of the form CVCC that was only partially understood would have a greater chance of being comprehended if the liquid/nasal component of the cluster were incomprehensible than if the plosive or fricative element were reduced. As will be seen in the following section, in the comparison of stylistic extremes in Persian there is a tendency to reduce all syllables to the form CV or CVC. It will be hypothesized that the reduction of consonants in final consonant clusters in one stylistic dimension bears a direct relationship to the frequency of distribution of those reduced consonants in another stylistic dimension.

No careful statistical count has been made of phoneme distribution for multisyllabic words in Persian. However, a short examination of Persian vocabulary will show that CVCC sequences can occur only preceding morpheme boundaries or juncture. Consider the following example:

> gorgha mærdra gaz gereftænd
> "The wolves bit the man."

Dividing this sentence into syllables (/) (cf. Scott 1964) and indicating morpheme boundaries (-), the results are as follows (# indicates word boundaries):

> #gorg⁄ ha # mærd ⁄ ra # gaz # ge⁄ref / t-ænd #[7]

I can find no consonant cluster in Persian that does not occur preceding a morpheme boundary, with the possible exception of several proper names that in fact combine morphemes in their construction:

Shahrbanu   Sabz'æli
Mehrbanu   Gorg'æli

which are often transcribed

Shahr-banu   Sabz-'æli
Mehr-banu   Gorg-'æli

Even words based on Arabic participles and verb forms beginning with /'est-/ or /most'/, when followed by a triliteral root beginning with /'ein/ or /'alef/ (anlaut is realized as a *hæmzeh*), vocalize preceding the /'/ of the root. Thus we see [#este'emar] (colonization, imperialism) and not *[#est'emar]. Similarly, and not surprisingly, since initial consonant clusters do not occur, foreign words such as "spaghetti" and "steak" are transposed into ['espageti] and ['este:k].

We can see then that the structure of individual syllables in standard Persian parallels that of monosyllabic words. All consonantal phonemes may occur in all positions. Consonant clusters occur only at morpheme boundaries or preceding internal phrase junctures. However, consonant clusters followed by a suffixed vowel are "split." Thus the syllable CVCC, which can only appear in terminal position, when followed by a suffix, particle, or enclitic of the form V, VC, or VCC becomes CVC + CV, CVC + CVC, or CVC + CVCC, accordingly. As will be seen, the proclivity for breaking up internal consonant clusters is such that even in styles where the highest retention of consonant clusters occur, there is a tendency for initial consonants in CV or CVC suffixes to be deleted and for the final consonantal element of a preceding consonant cluster to be attached to the vowel. The following examples serve to illustrate:

/mærd væ zæn/ becomes /mærd o zæn/
with the syllable structures mær/d-o # zæn

/mærdan/ (men) has the syllable structure mær/d-an

My argument proceeds through a consideration of consonants in two ways—as unified classes and as individual units within classes. I must here regretfully abandon my resolve not to label either of the stylistic extremes I have referred to throughout the discussion. The stylistic pole where, hypothetically, all consonant clusters are retained will be labeled as Style A, and the hypothetical stylistic pole where maximum cluster reduction occurs, Style B. These may be thought of in conjunction and correspondence with Pole A and Pole B as described in Chapter 4 of this discussion. There are probably an infinite number of stylistic variants that fall *between* Syle A and Style B on an implicational scale. It should be understood that in saying Style A or Style B, I am indicating a *directionality* on an implicational scale rather than an actual concretized style. Occasionally when a concrete noun is needed for purposes of English syntax I may refer to Style A or Style B as "stylistic extremes." This does not change my insistence that they are *tendencies,* not things.

As a class, fricatives have the highest participation as terminal consonants in monosyllabic Style A words, for both the form CVC and the form CVCC. In terms of the degree of participation per member of each consonant class, liquid/nasal consonants are much higher for CVC words and for CVCC words.

If we further consider only the second element in consonant clusters of Style A monosyllables, we see that in terms of class participation, fricatives occur most often as final elements in clusters, then plosives, and then liquids/nasals. In terms of individual item participation, however, the situation is exactly reversed; liquid/nasal consonants have the highest average participation in Style A final consonant clusters as the second element, followed by plosives and then fricatives.

Taking account now of the retention in Style B of consonants represented in Style A final consonant clusters, we see that the order of retention parallels the order of average participation as second consonant in terminal clusters. Table 9 summarizes this conclusion.

It should be noted that in a comparison of the consonant clusters at the two poles of stylistic variation, two intertwined phenomena are at work. One is retention and the other is deletion. We can only speculate as to the actual relationship between participation of a consonant in one style and its deletion or retention in another. The above correlation is both broad and tentative, and it needs further investigation. Krámský's original categories of consonants are very broad indeed, but they have been retained throughout the discussion so that his very interesting data could be examined to the fullest extent possible. Despite these fairly serious drawbacks, however, a regular pattern does seem to emerge here, one that has correlates in other aspects of stylistic variation in Persian.

Returning to Krámský's study, we see that in Style A, /r/ is the consonant that has the most frequent participation in final position for all words in Krámský's sample. Indeed, /r/ has the greatest par-

TABLE 9

**Preservation of Style A Consonant Clusters
In Style B Linguistic Contexts**

	Highest	Second	Lowest
Participation by sound class as second element in final consonant cluster-Style A	fricatives (+ strident)	plosives (+ plosive)	liquids/nasals (+ sonorant)
Participation by average class member as second element in final consonant cluster-Style A	liquids/nasals	plosives	fricatives
Style B retention of sound in corresponding Style A final consonant clusters	fricatives	plosives	liquids/nasals
Deletion of sounds from consonant clusters in Style B	liquids/nasals	plosives	fricatives

ticipation of all consonants in all positions. Returning to our earlier account of stylistic variation between stylistic extremes as presented in the preceding section, we see that /r/ is the only consonant that is reduced not only in consonant clusters but in CVC forms and as an initial consonant following internal phrase juncture, with the exception of /h/ and /'/, which I will treat as a special class below.

As I stated at the beginning of this section, I am attempting here to account for the regular variation exhibited in Persian style by formulating an account of how sounds in language are conceived and perceived by speakers. In strictly linguistic terms, a dichotomy is seen between whole classes of sounds perceived individually as members of classes and sounds perceived as totally separate without regard to class. This assumption forms the skeleton for the working discussion that follows.

Taking the problem of consonant deletion in Style B as an example, in Style A it can be said that as the final element in consonant clusters, fricatives dominate in frequency of participation as a *class* over other consonant classes. However, it can also be said that collectively, as a class, fricatives dominate in terms of the information content that they carry, since individual members of the class have the lowest degree of participation in consonant clusters. Liquids and nasals exhibit opposite characteristics, having a low frequency of participation as a class in consonant clusters but also having low information content as a class, due to a high individual member participation in consonant clusters.

Based on this reasoning, it is possible to make the following sketch of predictive hypotheses for Persian:

1. Deletion of consonants is a qualitative variational feature by which styles in Persian contrast with each other.
2. If a consonant in a cluster is to be deleted, it will be the final consonant.
3. The probability of a final consonant being deleted increases as a function of the information carried by the class of sounds participating in the cluster (as shown in table 10.)

The pattern that we set up for consonant deletion in consonant clusters works very well for the case of /r/, which, as mentioned above, has the highest participation of any sound element in Persian, according to Krámský. According to the schema in table 10, one would predict its deletion in a wider variety of situations because of its low information content, which is in fact the case.

TABLE 10

**Probability of Deletion of Second Element
In Final Consonant Cluster**

		Information Carried by Second Element		
		+ Strident high	+ Plosive medium	+ Sonorant low
	high + strident	low	high	high
Information Carried by First Element	medium + plosive	medium	medium	high
	low + sonorant	low	medium	low

/h/ presents a much more interesting case. Krámský lists /h/ as a fricative. However, /h/ does not behave like other fricatives in its deletion pattern. In point of fact, its deletion pattern resembles that of /'/ much more than that of /f, v, s, z, etc./. Both /h/ and /'/ are associated with vowel length and accent in their usage, which is retained when the sounds are deleted. Thus:

9. a.	/šoja'/	"courageous"	[šoja']	→	[šoja:]
b.	/bæd/	"bad"	[bæd]	→	[bæd]
c.	/bæ'd/	"afterwards"	[bæ:'d]	→	[bæ:d]
d.	/ræfte'id/	"you (pl.) have gone"	[ræfte:'id]	→	[ræfte:id]
10. a.	/mah/	"moon"	[mah]	→	[ma:]
b.	/ruh/	"face"	[ruh]	→	[ru:]
c.	/sægha/	"dogs"	[sægha]	→	[sæga]

Vowel length shifts in Persian stylistic variation will be discussed at length below. Here let it suffice to state that the range of extremes in unmodified stylistic variation in vowel length in Persian can be seen as follows:

/a:	i:	u:	/a	i	u
		→			
æ	e	o/	æ	e	o/

The presence of either /h/ or /'/ in either stylistic pole creates a special situation. The vowel preceding these sounds becomes *marked* in terms of the vowel system for each stylistic pole. After /h/ or /'/ normally long vowels a:, i:, and u: are shortened at one pole; short vowels æ, e, and o are lengthened. At the other stylistic pole both sets of vowels are lengthened, thus causing them to be likewise marked at the other end of the opposite stylistic pole where vowel length does not occur as a regular feature. For examples of this, see items 9a, 9b, and 9c, and 10a and 10b.

Examples 9d and 10c give situations where /h/ and /'/ are associated with the only suffixes in Persian with initial consonants, which are accented. The accents are retained at both stylistic poles as the characteristic of the particles in question, even as /h/ and /'/ are deleted.

In the first instance, then, /h/ and /'/ are redundant particles with respect to the marked nature of vowel length and accentuation that accompany them. The contrastive vowel length is retained at both ends of the stylistic pole, and the redundant /h/ and /'/ are dropped. In the second instance, the accents characteristic of the two suffixes are retained as the distinguishing characteristic of those particles, and the redundant /h/ and /'/ are again deleted.

The approach taken here can also lead to better structural information about a given language when used as an explanatory device. For example, let us return to the point, made above, that /h/ does not behave like the other fricatives, that its deletion pattern in Style B resembles that of /'/ more than that of /f, x, z, etc./. In Style B, both are deleted in roughly the same pattern. If the two are set up as a class and compared with the other three classes given here, we find that information content for the class is high, but that frequency is extremely low. The combined factors do not give the class very much strength in final consonant cluster position, and the members of the class are in fact deleted, contrary to what would be expected of /h/ if it were considered to be a fricative.

The discussion above has presented only one kind of suggestion about how one kind of structure in language can be seen to prefigure regular variation in correlate. In viewing the changes that take place in the vowel system of Persian between stylistic extremes, the element of redundancy within the system is discussed. It should be noted, though, that redundancy is another way of expressing the concept "low information content."

Redundancy in Interaction and Sound Reduction

What I now mean to suggest is that there is a definite relationship between the pragmatic nature of the contexts in which sound deletions occur in Persian and (1) the types of sounds that are deleted and (2) the pattern of their deletion. In general, in contexts where individuals assume the social ethic associated with asymmetrical social relationships, where they feel the imperative for restricted expression, and where they feel that they are in a context that is defined as "outside" rather than "inside," their behavior is *in general* more overdetermined, more redundant, and more overstated. This is one of the ways that individuals have of signaling to others what kind of situation they feel themselves to be in and what kind of behavior they will be engaging in during that situation. Situations where symmetrical relations determine the social ethic, where personal expression is free, and where the situation is felt to be more "inside" than "outside" demand behavior that is *in general* less determined, less redundant, and more understated. This is not to be thought of as an absence of the behavioral elaboration occurring at the other situational pole, but rather is a positive set of actions that individuals use to demonstrate that they are in a symmetrical, freely expressive, or "internal" situation to other persons who participate in that situation.

Linguistic behavior in such situations should follow the general pragmatic principles that obtain for all behavior. This is, it should be more redundant and overdetermined at one pole and less redundant and less determined at the other pole. In fact, I have given some indications that this is the case. In the same instance of sound deletions, it is the most redundant elements with the least information content that have the greater probability of being deleted in contexts where a general reduction in redundancy is required as a concomitant of the action that can be carried out in those contexts.

Stylistic Variation—The Vowel System

So much confusion has existed in the past among scholars engaged in the study of classical Persian about the status of the vowel that it is doubtful that it will ever be known what the exact status of vowel quality and vowel length were in Persian before the twentieth century. Classicists were in the habit of interpreting the vowel system as consisting of three long vowels and three short vowels that corresponded directly to them in terms of sound quality:

| long | ā | ī | ū |
| short | a | i | u |

It is not possible to tell now whether these reflected actual sounds or were the result of romanization of Persian orthography, for which no clear indication of the short vowels was ever made. In exact transcription, the Arabic diacritics *fæthe, kesre,* and *zomme*[8] were used, which in classical Arabic were given the values /a i u/ as above. Further confusion results when it is realized that in classical Arabic the qualitative correspondence between long and short forms was fairly close.

Shaki's article of 1957 attempts to correct the above situation by pointing out that in fact the short vowels are qualitatively different from the long vowels, as well as differing in length. His proposition is the one that has been accepted throughout this discussion:

long	ā:	ī:	ū:
short	æ	e	o

In addition, as has been shown, allophonic variations in standard Persian produce lengthened short vowels and shortened long vowels. The allophonic length feature is of little importance in standard Persian, since long and short vowels are in complementary distribution allophonically. At the extreme ranges of stylistic variation, complementary distribution is retained. The patterns of complementary distribution differ between the two stylistic extremes, however, and it is the contrast in distributive patterns that can be said to characterize the variational difference between the two systems of vowel length. The two systems can be roughly compared, along with classic Arabic, as shown in table 11.

Speculatively, an account for loss of vowel length in Style B might be sought in a comparison of Persian and Arabic elements in the language. In classical Arabic, vowel length is indeed phonemic, where in Persian it is redundant, since vowels differ in quality as well as in length. Arabic forms entering Persian adapt to Persian vowel quality, and thus length for them becomes redundant.

The following additional changes occur at two extreme stylistic poles:

$$1. \quad /a/ \;\rightarrow\; [u] \; / \left\{ \begin{matrix} m \\ n \end{matrix} \right\}$$

TABLE 11

**Pole A and Pole B Vowel Systems
Compared with Arabic**

	Pole A	Pole B
Predominant	a: i: u:	a i u
	æ e o	æ e o
Allophonic	a i u	a: i: u:
	æ: e: o:	æ: e: o: (ə, ɨ)

Arabic

æ:	i:	u:
æ	i	u

Thus:

/tehran/	"Tehran"	[tehran]	$\rightarrow$	[teːrun]
/rehan/	"basil"	[reyhan]	$\rightarrow$	[reyhun]
/nan/	"bread"	[nan]	$\rightarrow$	[nun]

This particular feature is characteristic of Tehran and is represented in other areas of the country insofar as Tehran dialect has been adopted as a standard. However, this pronunciation feature is not present in some important areas of Iran, such as Kermanshah and Gorgan.

$$2. \; /æ/ \rightarrow [ə] \; / \; \underset{[-\text{stress}]}{\rule{2cm}{0.4pt}} CaX$$

Note: this does not apply across morpheme boundaries. Thus:

/ænar/ "pomegranate" [ænar] $\rightarrow$ [ənar]

$$3. \; /e/ \rightarrow [ɨ] \; / \; \underset{[-\text{stress}]}{\rule{2cm}{0.4pt}} \begin{array}{l} C \, (C) \, V \\ + \text{ high} \\ + \text{ front} \end{array}$$

$$4. \; /o/ \rightarrow [ə] \; / \; \underset{[-\text{stress}]}{\rule{2cm}{0.4pt}} X$$

$$5. \; /o/ \rightarrow [o^w] \; / \; \#\#$$

The tendency for the midvowels /æ e o/ to become centralized where they appear in unaccented syllables at one end of the stylistic pole is at first difficult to account for. However, it could be maintained that their centralization leads to symmetry within the vowel system. Thus the total vowel system could be represented in its two stylistic extremes for unaccented syllables as follows:

iː		uː	i	u
e		o	$\rightarrow$	ɨ
æ				ə
	aː			a

In general, then, the following remarks can be made concerning stylistic variation within the vowel system of the language:

1. Length of vowels is an important stylistic dimension. At both stylistic extremes the *contrastive patterns* of long and short vowels, rather than simple length, characterize the style.

2. In general, the stylistic variation in the vowel system involves the retention or deletion of systematically redundant features.

3. There is some indication of a tendency toward symmetry within the vowel system at one pole, with lower contrast, and asymmetry with higher contrast at the other.

It has already been suggested that modification in Style B would be in the direction of elimination of elements carrying low information content within the contrastive system of consonants. Redundant features carry little or no information; thus the elimination of vowel length in informal style fulfills the general pattern derived for the system of consonants discussed in the previous section.

Arabic versus Persian

I have tried thus far to confine my discussion of stylistic variation in Persian to the sound system of the language itself. At several points I have made references to the dichotomy that exists between Persian and Arabic vocabulary in Persian, but did not pursue a close comparison of the two systems. I now wish to suggest that the few general points that have been raised with regard to the kinds of differences that exist between stylistic extremes in Persian also conform to a pattern in which less redundant styles in Persian (styles tending toward Style B) seem to represent patterns that are more characteristic of the "Persian" element in Persian than do more redundant styles (ones tending toward Style A). Stated in other terms, certain structural features in Style A are more "Arabic." In situations that embody a highly familiar context, these elements tend to be replaced by features that are more distinctly "Persian."

The first of these is the reduction of "Arabic" sounds in general. Chief among these is /'/, which does not occur as a phoneme in any word of Persian origin, but only as an *anlaut*. I have suggested that /h/ and /'/ might be considered to form a consonant class. Considering that the back velar stop /q/ is realized as [x] or its voiced counterpart [ɣ] in many contexts (occurring in many words of Persian origin), this leads one to suspect that all glottal stricture is functionally something "non-Persian" in two ways. First of all, consonant clusters themselves are far more frequent in Arabic than in Persian. Thus their elimination constitutes itself a kind of Persianization. Secondly, elimination of final consonant clusters reduces syllable structure to the CVC or CV form in most cases, which is more characteristic of Persian than Arabic, where, at least for monosyllables, CVCC forms seem to be more prevalent.[9]

Third and finally, the length distribution in the vowel system of Style B more correctly reflects the functional contrasts that exist between Persian vowels, eliminating elements that are contrastive in Arabic but noncontrastive in Persian. This conclusion is particularly tentative, since nearly all other Iranian languages do have contrastive length in their vowel systems (Vogelin and Vogelin 1965), making it difficult to tell exactly what elimination of length in Style B could signify.

It should be reiterated, finally, with regard to the above line of argument, that the proportion of Arabic-origin words increases dramatically in formal speech situations and oratory,[10] lending some additional support to the proposition that movement from more to less determined style (Style A to Style B) may proceed on a continuum: greater to less Arabicization in all linguistic features.[11]

Systemic Processes and Stylistic Variation—A Summary

I have tried to accomplish two things in this discussion. The first has been to sketch a preliminary model for the investigation of stylistic variation in language. The second has been to attempt an analysis of one aspect of stylistic variation in Persian, that variation relating to the sound system of the language.

Restricting myself to a bipolar comparison of stylistic data characterizing tendencies in the variation found in different styles, I have tried to demonstrate how regular stylistic variation can be understood as proceeding from structures characterized by the system of sound pattern and sound distribution within the language. Two types of variation were seen to operate between stylistic extremes: deletion and sound replacement. Criteria for either deletion or replacement were hypothesized to proceed systematically from (1) configuration of frequency of participation of classes of consonants in specific combinatory structures, leading those classes which combined lower information content per class member with lower frequency of occurrence to be deleted or replaced, (2) tendency toward elimination of contrastive redundancy, and (3) tendency toward symmetry.

I have tried to demonstrate that the particular stylistic variations that occur in the Persian sound system are neither random nor accidental, but are directly correlated with the cultural nature of the perceptual contexts of their occurrence in actual social usage. Thus, a particular set of forms can be seen as functioning to increase or decrease redundancy in a particular linguistic interaction because the sociocultural context in which the utterance containing those forms occurs requires a greater or lesser degree of definition and determination in order for the information to proceed appropriately. An individual's own realization of speech forms is, of course, dependent on one's own perception of the situation one finds oneself in and the ability to negotiate the nature of that situation with coparticipants in interaction. Thus, it is never possible to predict with absolute accuracy which forms will occur in which abstract context.

Finally, it was suggested that the use of forms that tend to decrease redundancy in speech also tends to create speech structures that are more Persian than Arabic. Speech forms that are closer in structure to the root stock of a language seem almost universally to have a more intimate, less formal quality. This factor will play an important role in the argument of Chapter 6 in discussing stylistic variation in Persian morphology.

VI

PERSIAN SOCIO-
MORPHOLOGY

Morphological Variation

Stylistic variation in the morphological system of Persian occurs primarily in two distinct areas: the verbal system of the language and the pronominal system. The material I wish to treat in this section consists primarily of those morphological items that are directly substitutable for other items in sentence constructions. Chapter 7 is a discussion of the construction and use of varieties of phrases, idioms, and locutions.

As with stylistic variation in the sound system of Persian, as seen in the previous chapter, variation in style within the morphological system is subject not to criteria of grammaticality, but rather criteria of appropriateness. Thus the use of one pronominal form in place of another does not constitute a grammatical difference, but rather a difference in the fit between the form of the utterance and the nature of the context within which the persons involved in the production and interpretation of that utterance see it as occurring.

Still, stylistic variation in Persian morphology is not without structure. Within the lexical system, the variation that occurs is limited to substitution in a rather small class of verbs, and a number of pronouns and pronoun substitutes. Within the structure of the verb, variation occurs primarily in the pronominal endings. From this small repertoire[1] of building blocks, Iranians are able to construct a system of verbal style that is enormously rich and flexible, one that proves to be highly versatile in the social situations it is able to handle. I will demonstrate in Chapter 7 that Persian morphological variation is "shaped" to conform to the needs of those social situations. More precisely, the pattern of choice in lexical items available to a Persian speaker can be seen to map directly onto the system of social differentiation in interaction outlined in Chapter 4 of this discussion.

The Elements of the Persian Verb: A Conventional Description

Grammars of Persian generally state that the Persian verb has two stems to which various prefixes and suffixes may be attached to obtain the full range of forms for the verb. Stem I is generally called the "present stem" in standard grammars, and Stem II, the "past stem." Stem II invariably terminates in one of the allomorphs /-d -t -id/, hereby noted as {-D}. Because the infinitive of the verb is created through suffixation of Stem II with /-æn/, this stem is often treated as primary in Persian teaching grammars. Indeed, it does seem that derivation of Stem I proceeds regularly from deletion of the final morphemes of Stem II occurring in reverse order from the infinitive, as shown:

Infinitive	Stem II	Stem I	
xabidæn	xabid	xab	"to sleep"
xordæn	xord	xor	"to eat"
baftæn	baft	baf	"to weave"

The picture becomes slightly more complex for verbs that exhibit vowel and/or consonant shifts:

Infinitive	Stem II	Stem I	
taftæn	taft	tab	"to twist"
duxtæn	duxt	duz	"to say"
dadæn	dad	deh	"to give"
neveštæn	nevešt	nevis	"to write"
æfzudæn	æfzud	æfza	"to increase"

If the forms of Stem I are inspected, the distribution of the allophones of {-D} can be clearly seen, as well as the changes necessary in Stem I to obtain Stem II. Stem II is thus formed according to the following formulae:

    1. Stem I + /-id/

    2. Stem I with internal consonant or vowel shift +
        a. /-d/ if /r/, /n/, or a vowel is final in Stem I
        b. /-t/ if /s/, /f/, /š/, or /z/ is final in Stem I

The first of these formulae is by far the most productive in forming Stem II of a verb. In fact, many verbs that form Stem II according

to the second formula above have parallel forms derived according
to the first formula. These secondary forms have at times taken on a
slightly variant meaning or a more colloquial feeling [e.g., inf. *reštæn*,
II *rešt*, I *ris* (to spin) as opposed to inf. *risidæn*, II *risid*, I *ris* (to spin)].
Jazayery (1969) cites sixty-six such forms that are derived not only
from Stem I of the verb but also from other parts of speech [e.g., *bus*
(kiss), *busidæn* (to kiss); *ræxs* (dance), *ræxsidæn* (to dance)].

Stem I may not appear in verbs without being prefixed by either
the particle /mi-/ or the particle /be-~bo-/. Stem II remains unprefixed
or is prefixed with /mi-/ in some forms. The prefix /næ-/ is also used
with both stems.

The number of simple verbs used in modern Persian is very small,
and for this reason a great number of compound verbs or "verbal
expressions," in John Andrew Boyle's parlance (Boyle 1952), are formed
using adverbs and prepositions, nouns, adjectives, or verbal particles
in conjunction with one of about twenty simple verbs. Examples of
these verbs follow:

1. adverbs, prepositions + verb
dær amædæn	"to come out"
dær gozæštæn	"to die, pass over, forgive"
piš bordæn	"to win, gain the upper hand"
bær daštæn	"to lift up"
pæs dadæn	"to give back"

2. prepositional phrases + verb
be ja aværdæn	"to perform, accomplish"
be kar bordæn	"to use, make use of"

3. noun + verb
hærf zædæn	"to speak"
guš kærdæn	"to listen"
dæst dadæn	"to shake hands"
čane zædæn	"to bargain"
væ'de dadæn	"to promise"
yad daštæn	"to remember"

4. adjective + verb
bolænd kærdæn	"to raise"
baz kærdæn	"to open"
peida kærdæn	"to find"
gom kærdæn	"to lose"

5. parts of other verbs + verb

gir kærdæn	"to get stuck"
gir aværdæn	"to get, obtain"
ræft o amæd daštæn	"to exchange visits with"

6. derivatives of other verbs + verb

kušeš kærdæn	"to try" (kušidæn)
porseš kærdæn	"to ask" (porsidæn)
gerye kærdæn	"to cry" (geristæn)
setayeš kærdæn	"to praise" (sotudæn)

The "compound" verb in Persian, as illustrated above, is extremely important in the construction of the language. As Mohammad Ali Jazayery has pointed out, "there is scarcely a simple infinitive for which there is no synonym in a compound infinitive: often there are several. There are, however, not a few compound verbs which are without simple-verb synonyms. Such is the case in /tærjome kærdæn/ (to translate); /rahnema'i kærdæn/ (to guide); /be kar bordæn/ (to use); /sæbr kærdæn/ (to wait); etc. (Jazayery 1969).

In the use of the compound verb, only the verbal element is inflected, the initial element remaining unchanged. As a rule, however, the elements are not separated syntactically in actual utterances, the exception being the optional attachment of a pronominal object to the initial element in the compound verb. Thus we see *pas dadæm* (I gave back), *pæseš dadæm* (I gave it back). Compare the simple verb *zædæm* (I hit), *zædæmeš* (I hit him, her, it).[2]

Verbs are suffixed with the following personal endings for all forms:

Person	Singular	Plural
first	/-æm/	/-im/
second	/-i/	/-id/
third	/-ø, -ad, -ast/	/-ænd/

Both the personal verb endings and the enclitic pronominal object will be treated in greater detail in the following section.

It should be noted here that the third person singular ending has three forms used with different verb stems. /-æd/ is used with Stem I, /-ø/ with Stem II, and /-æst/ with the "participle," which is Stem II suffixed with /-e/, which then takes the primary stress for the word [-e] unless followed with a personal ending.

True compounds are formed through the combination of suffixed forms of Stem II [with /-e/, thus inf. *xordæn* (to eat), II *xord*, part. *xordé*], followed by auxiliaries, which are in fact fully conjugated forms of the verbs *budæn* (to be) or *šodæn* (to become). The result is inf. *zædæn* (to hit, strike), part. *zædé* (hit, struck), *zæde'æm* (I have hit), *zædé budæm* (I had hit) [with Stem II form of *budæm* (to be)], *zæde bašæm* (that I have hit) (with Stem I form of *budæm*), *zæde mišævæm* (I am being hit, will be hit) [with Stem I form of *šodæn* (to become)], *zædé šodæm* (I was hit) (with Stem II form of *šodæn*).

Stem I forms of verbs and Stem II forms prefixed with /mi-/ are characterized in standard Persian grammars as progressive tenses,[3] although their actual usage admits a wider range of usage. Stem I forms prefixed with /mi-/ regularly have a simple present time designation, can indicate future time, or can indicate continuous, progressive, or habitual action. Stem II forms prefixed by /mi-/, regularly past tense, indicate conditional and subjunctive moods as well as past conditional progressive or habitual action.

"True" progressive forms, as indicated by the use of the verb *daštæn* (to have), as a kind of auxiliary verb preceding the Stem I or Stem II forms of the principal verb: thus *daræm mizænæm* (I am hitting), *daštæm mizædæm* (I was hitting). This construction constitutes something between a true verbal construction and an idiomatic expression, because it is defective in forms other than those analogous to the two above,[4] whereas true compound constructions are conjugated through all forms of the verb.

A form designating the future is found in Persian, but its use is somewhat limited. It consists of the unprefixed Stem I form of the verb *xᵛastæn* (to want) with personal endings, followed by Stem II: thus *xᵛahæm zæd* (I will hit). This formal future form does not contrast easily with any other grammatical form. It is in fact a future formed on a stem used for past tense formation in compound with what was formerly (now obsolete) an aorist.

Negatives are formed in all instances by the prefixation of /næ- ~ ne-/ (hereafter næ-). In forms prefixed with /be-/ , /næ-/ replaces the /be-/. In forms prefixed with /mi-/, the /næ-/ is placed before the /mi-/. In compound forms the /næ-/ is prefixed to the Stem II form; likewise for the future. The true progressive tenses have no negative. Thus the particle /næ-/ is prefixed to /mi-/ and to Stem II, and replaces /be-/. Another negative verb prefix, /mæ-/, is obsolete and is encountered today primarily in poetry. Its distribution is the same as that of /næ-/.

The Pronoun System

Pronominal reference in Persian is accomplished in several different ways: through personal verb endings, as mentioned above; through separable pronominal forms; and through enclitic pronominal forms. It is useful to consider pronominal forms formally as consisting of two types: separable and affixed. I will consider suffixed pronominal forms briefly first, since the bulk of formal stylistic variation occurs within the separable pronominal system.

Suffixed pronominal forms can be considered formally as a single system, where the combination of the pronominal form with verb stems, adjectives, nouns, and other pronominal affixes results in differential interpretation of the pronominal form. The basic system is set forth in table 12.

Verbal suffixes are actually enclitic verb endings. They can be suffixed to either verb stems or adjectives to provide a nominative reference:

| ræft | "went" | ræfti | "you (sg.) went" |
| zešt | "ugly" | zeštænd | "they are ugly" |

Nonverbal suffixes can be appended to nouns or verbal affixes, providing a genitive or objective reference, respectively:

TABLE 12

Pronominal Suffixes in Persian

Person	Nonverbal Affixes		Verbal and Nonverbal	Verbal Affixes	
	Plural		Singular	Plural	
1	-eman		-æm		-im
2	-etan	-et**		-i	-id
3	-ešan	-eš	(-eš) see below	-æd*	-ænd
				-ø	
				-æst	

*as mentioned above
-æd   with present tense verb stems
-ø   with past tense verb stems
-æst   with participial stems in periphrastic verb forms
          and adjectives.
  **There is some difference among commentators about the vowel quality of this suffix. Some would write it /-æt/. I preserve the /-e/ throughout.

| ketab | "book" | ketabeš | "his book" |
| zædæm | "I hit" | zædæmet | "I hit you" |

A ø third person verbal suffix is sometimes replaced colloquially[5] with the third person nonverbal affix:

| ræft | "he went" | ræfteš | "he went" |
| bud | "he was there/here" | budeš | "he was there/here" |

This is observed primarily with intransitive verbs, as the /-eš/ suffix with transitive verbs can be interpreted as an object:

$$\text{zædeš} = \text{zæd} + ø + \text{eš} \qquad \text{"he hit} \begin{cases} \text{him} \\ \text{her"} \\ \text{it} \end{cases}$$

Nonetheless, it is sometimes the case that the nonverbal affix is omitted with transitive verbs when the object is unspecific or unimportant. In these cases, reference to the action of a third person on an object creates an ambiguity where it is not clear whether the /-eš/ suffix refers to the actor or the subject:

zædæmeš $\text{"I hit} \begin{cases} \text{her} \\ \text{him"} \\ \text{it} \end{cases}$

zædæm	"I hit (something unspecified)"
zædi	"you hit (something unspecified)"
zæd	"he hit (something unspecified)"

zædeš $\text{"he hit (something} \begin{cases} \text{her} \\ \text{him"} \\ \text{it} \end{cases}$

Separable pronouns are represented in the following paradigms:

Person	Singular	Plural
first	mæn	ma
second	to	šoma
third	u	išan

The reflexive pronouns are formed through the combination of the term *xod* (self) with the nonverbal affixes mentioned above:

xodæm	xodeman
xodet	xodetan
xodeš	xodešan

Another set of reflexive pronouns is formed through a combination of *xod* with the separable pronouns:

xod-mæn	xod-e ma
xod-e to	xod-e šoma
xod-e u (rare)	xod-e išan

A set of demonstrative pronouns also is used in pronominal reference:

in "this one"	inha these ones
an "that one"	anha[6] those ones

Inha and *anha* are used in alternation with *išan*.

Stylistic Requirements within the Morphological System

The above sketch outlines the basic structure of the verb and pronominal system of Persian. However, this system can be extended and transformed stylistically in any number of ways. Given my statements on the nature of stylistic variation thus far, extensions and transformations of the basic morphological system of Persian should reflect the social needs of individuals situated in contexts of interaction. The range of stylistic choice available to speakers of the language should facilitate carrying out behavior that is both appropriate and strategically viable.

Social appropriateness and strategic viability are judgments that analysts can make about behavioral routines of various sorts that can be observed in the regular actions of others. In ethnographic analysis, one is able to discover general behavioral routines that are characteristic of the society under question, primarily because of the need of individuals to present uniform accounts of their actions to others in social encounter, even though motivations in all social action may

differ greatly from person to person. Some of these routines for
Iranians have been dealt with above.

Now, just as I have tried to demonstrate that certain phonological
stylistic variables in Persian relate to perceptions of the nature of the
contextualization of behavioral routines in social interaction, in the
account to follow I will show how morphological variables in the verbal
and pronominal systems facilitate the behavioral routines included
under the rubrics of *tæ'arof, partibazi,* and the exercise of *zerængi* as
outlined above.

Tæ'arof and *partibazi,* as I have mentioned, are terms that gloss
behavioral routines activated when persons are constrained to deal
with differential perceptual status. *Zerængi* involves behavioral routines that frustrate other persons' ability to interpret one's own actions.

The linguistic needs for *tæ'arof* routines consist of a set of devices
that allow for the implementation of the social goals embodied in
tæ'arof. As mentioned earlier, one important strategy people use in
dealing with others is to indicate elevation of the status of the other
person in interaction, placing a positive value on the action of those
others and to indicate depreciation and lowering of one's own status
while placing a negative value on one's own action. Furthermore, all
parties in interaction must be able to perform *tæ'arof* routines toward
each other.

The stylistic variational code used in the language of *tæ'arof* must
then contain at least three elements: (1) "other-raising" elements, (2)
"self-lowering" elements, and (3) a variational structure that allows
both sets of elements to be used simultaneously by all parties without
logical contradiction.

Partibazi is a system that emphasizes *sæmimiæt* (ties of intimacy). For
partibazi to be operative, *sæmimiæt* must be contained between individuals. Social routines that maintain *sæmimiæt* must contain language
forms that serve to reinforce equality and solidarity among participants. As has been stated above, reinforcement of solidarity consists
of two dimensions—the first, lack of either status elevation of the
other individual or lowering of self in private, restricted, group-
dominated (Pole A) situations and mutual reinforcement of status
elevation in public, free, grid-dominated (Pole B) situations.

In practicing *zerængi* to frustrate the interpretation of one's true
intentions, one might (among other things) use *tæ'arof* or *sæmimiæt*
reinforcing linguistic routines in an insincere manner in order to
enforce the ethics implied in either equal or unequal status situations
on others. One might also imply those same ethics as a correct interpretation of one's own actions. Thus conventions for the use of verbal

stylistic variation in Persian must include this possible usage for the language of *tæ'arof* and *sæmimiæt*.

In establishing the requirements placed on linguistic stylistic variation by the needs of Persian social interaction, it should be noted that three different elements of variation are taken into consideration: (1) that certain linguistic forms must vary; (2) that they must vary in a particular way, i.e., the variation itself must have a particular "shape"; and (3) that there must be conventions for the exploitation of both the variant elements and the shape of the variation.

All three of these elements bear a direct relation to appropriateness of behavior and effectiveness of behavioral strategy. Thus, if one does not use a linguistic form with a person of higher status that is a proper indicator of that person's status, one risks having one's linguistic behavior judged inappropriate. If one uses one verbal form correctly, but does not adjust other language elements to conform to the variation "shape" established by the use of the first term, the linguistic behavior might likewise be inappropriate.

Choosing the correct variant is also vital for social communicative strategies. In elevating a person in status linguistically in order to compel him or her to *behave* like an elevated individual, one must choose the proper degree of elevation or else risk having the stratagem fail through "overplaying one's hand." Likewise, one must choose the proper variational shape to make the stratagem work and so constrain the social structures that allow for the interpretation of variational elements that the stratagem is not detected. For example, as will be seen below, an important stratagem consists of elevating through language a person with whom one is very intimate in order to create an impression. In doing this, one must not also use linguistic forms that demonstrate that one *is* intimate with the person being elevated, thus demonstrating that one is "in cahoots" with that person at the same time.

In the discussion to follow, I will explore the linguistic devices that are used for all three complexes of linguistic routines—*tæ'arof*, *sæmimiæt*, and *zeræengi*—in order to demonstrate, as in the last chapter, not only that stylistic variation exists in the morphological system of Persian, but also why those particular elements vary, and why they vary in the way that they do.

The Language of *Tæ'arof*

As I have mentioned, within social situations in Iran, status relationships are dependent on the configuration of individuals present at any one time. Thus, it becomes vital for individuals engaged in interaction to be able to place themselves and others within some status hierarchy that obtains for any one particular interaction: that is, to be able to define and redefine themselves and others as the situation shifts. A great deal of individual variability in skill comes into play here, since one may be adroit or clumsy in estimating one's own position in the social constellation of the moment.

The more adroit operators in interaction will not be limited to reacting passively to a social hierarchical situation they see as "given." Playing on the ambiguity that exists in all such social encounters, they will be able to seize the opportunity to define status for other participants. By using linguistic and behavioral forms appropriate to a given status, they are able to make incumbent on others not only a relative hierarchical rank, but also the social ethic associated with that rank. To this end, stylistic variation in Persian morphology becomes an extremely important social tool. Two principal stylistic devices form the core of *tæ'arof* language: (1) alternative self-lowering and other-raising forms and (2) singular versus plural forms used in reference to individuals.

As mentioned above, linguistic variation that facilitates *tæ'arof* routines and incorporates both self-lowering and other-raising dimensions is reflected through lexical substitution in both the verbal and the pronominal system. Within the verbal system, the bulk of this substitution is accomplished through the use of varying compound verbs or "verbal expressions" as outlined above. Typically, the structural scheme for substitution consists of a simple verb of Persian origin alternating with a compound verb, consisting itself of an element often of Arabic origin plus a simple auxiliary verb of Persian origin. The configuration can be represented as in figure 2.

It should be pointed out that though these alternative stylistic forms differ in social intent and in the consequences that follow from them in the course of an interaction, their "action reference" is the same. Thus, in translating a Persian text, one should ideally consider these forms as correlates to only one English verb. To illustrate, let us take the verb *dadæn* (to give).

Dadæn is the most neutral form for "to give" and is a verb of Persian origin. It would be used mutually by status equals or in contexts where perceptions of relative status are irrelevant or difficult to fix. Also meaning literally "to give" is the form *tæqdim kærdæn*, but with reference to one's own lower status vis-à-vis the person one is addressing.

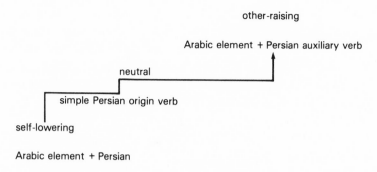

Fig. 2. Self-Lowering and Other-Raising in Persian Lexical Substitution.

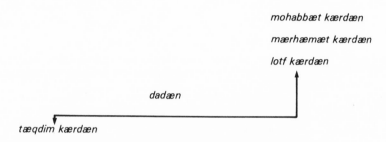

Fig. 3. Lexical Substitution for *Dadæn*.

For references to others (either present or absent) one uses *lotf kærdæn,* *mærhamæt kærdæn,* or *mohabbæt kærdæn* in order to indicate an address-ee's higher status vis-à-vis the speaker. These forms also mean literally "to give." The status-differentiated connotations are reflected in the etymology of the forms, however. An examination of the literal mean-ing of the Arabic roots gives little reason to suppose that they have been selected arbitrarily. Translated literally, *tæqdim* in Arabic means "offering." *Lotf* means "favor"; *mærhamæt,* "indulgence"; and *mohæbbæt* "kindness." These are represented in figure 3.

To take another example, the complex of forms indicating "to say" differs from the pattern established above in having a Persian simple verb in its other-raising component. The neutral form *goftæn* alter-nates with the self-lowering *ærz kærdæn* (lit. to petition) and other-raising *færmudæn* (lit. to order, to command) as in figure 4.

Here again, the action referred to is the same for all variant forms. The referential equivalence of these forms is demonstrated well in such interchanges as this:

Fig. 4. Lexical Substitution for *Goftæn*.

A: (makes statement)
B: *če færmudid?*
    "What did you say?"
C: *'ærz kærdæm ke* . . . (repeats statement)
    "I said that . . ."

The verbs in both cases must be translated as "said" in English.[7]

The verb *færmudæn* serves a double role, both as a stylistic variant of *goftæn*, as cited above, and as a productive auxiliary verb in forming other-raising variants of other simple verbs. Examples include *'enayæt færmudæn* (to see) for *didæn, mærqum færmudæn* for *neveštæn* (to write), and *meyl færmudæn* for *xordæn* (to eat). The productivity of this particular form is limited to verbs that require voluntary action. Thus any verb denoting voluntary action of an agent that forms with the auxiliary *kærdæn* can be made other-raising by the substitution of *færmudæn* for *kærdæn;* thus in the case of *dadæn* (to give) above, even greater status distance can be shown by the substitution of *lotf færmudæn* for *lotf kærdæn,* and so forth. Of course, *færmudæn* cannot be used in self-lowering forms. The imperative use of *færmudæn* is a very special verbal interaction in Iran and will be dealt with at much greater length below.

The restriction of *færmudæn* to verbs of voluntary action does not make it directly substitutable for *kærdæn* in all instances, as *kærdæn* is occasionally found in verbs that denote involuntary action. The tension between the general but incomplete substitutability of the two terms and the range of usage of *kærdæn* can occasionally be exploited in humor. For example, the verb *mordæn* (to die) has as an other-raising referential variant, *fowt kærdæn,* or possibly *fowt šodæn* [*fowt* Ar. (death, dying), *šodæn* (to become)]. In one episode of a popular television show, a villager wanting to be respectful and polite to an urban widow asked her how many years ago her husband *"fowt færmud,"* a very humorous instance of this potential misusage.

Three verbs of movement—*ræftæn* (to go), *amædæn* (to come), and *budæn* (to be)—are of particular interest in that they not only reflect other-raising and self-lowering functions, but they also indicate both restriction of movement and separation implied in the difference between high and low social status in social life. Indeed, the forms used at stylistic extremes for these verbs completely collapse all indication of movement in forms that reflect only stasis and relative status. For the three verbs, reference to higher-status persons proceeds on at least three levels of differentiation (see figure 5). On the first level, *ræftæn* is replaced by *tæšrif bordæn* (lit. to take one's presence), *amædæn* by *tešrif avardæn* (lit. to bring one's presence), and *budæn* by *tæšrif daštæn* (lit. to have one's presence). At the next level, all three are replaced by the forms *hozur yaftæn* or *hozur ræsandæn* (to find one's presence, to be conveyed) or *tæšrif færma šodæn* (approx. to confer or

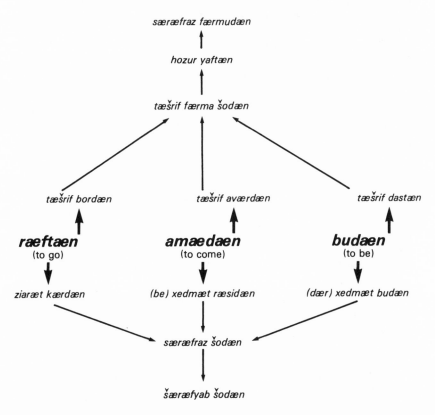

Fig. 5. Verbs of Movement—"To Go," "To Come," and "To Be." Lexical Substitution for /ræftæn/, /amædæn/, and /budæn/.

command one's own presence). Finally, the form *særæfraz færmudæn* is used, meaning literally "to command (another's) head to be raised"— thus, etymologically, to command honor for those to whom one goes and comes or with whom one stays. In context, however, as I have pointed out above, even such an elevated expression as *tæšrif færma šodæn* must be understood denotatively as "to go," "to come," or "to be."

A similar collapsing of forms occurs in self-lowering expressions. Both *amædæn* and *ræftæn* are replaced by either *ziaræt kærdæn* or *(be) xedmæt ræsidæn* (lit. to make a pilgrimage, to arrive in service). *Budæn* is replaced by *(dar) xedmæt budæn* (lit. to be at or in the service of). To indicate a greater status difference, all reference to personal action is obliterated in the forms *særæfraz šodæn* (lit. to have one's head raised— thus to be honored) and *šæræfyab šodæn* (lit. to become a recipient of honor).

Other verbs of movement that make action more explicit also fall into the above paradigm. Thus such verbs as *dær ræftæn* (to go out) and *xarej šodæn* (to exit), are replaced by *tæšrif bordæn* and other high-status stylistic equivalents; *ræsidæn* (to arrive), *tu amadæn* (to come in), *vared šodæn*, and *vorud kærdæn* (to enter, arrive) by *tæšrif aværdæn;* and *mandæn* (to remain), *sæbr kærdæn* (to wait—in the sense of "wait here"), and other verbs and phrases indicating nonmovement, such as *nešæstæn* (to sit—when used to mean "remain sitting"), *nærou* (don't go), etc., by *tašrif daštæn*.

Similar stylistic variation is observed within the pronominal system of Persian. Separable pronouns offer the possibility of using either singular or plural forms in first, second, and third person. This singular/plural alternation will be dealt with below. Lexical substitution conforming to the same pattern as seen in the verbal system is also found within the pronominal system.

In examining figure 6, note that self-reference varies from the neutral *mæn* to forms such as *bændeh, čaker,* or *nokær* (lit. servant, slave) or even *jan-nesar* (lit. soul-sacrificer) and reference to another who is present from the normal second person pronoun *šoma* to *jenab-e 'ali* or *hæzræt-e 'ali* (lit. highness, excellency). Other forms are *sær kar* (approx. head of affairs, primarily used for women and policemen) and *æ'lahæzræt* along with *olyahæzræt* (most high presence) for the shah and the shahbanu respectively.

A few special forms used to be utilized for various members of the royal family, such as *wala hæzræt* for the sons and brothers of the Shah and *sær kar'olieh* for the mother of the former Shahbanou. Terms used

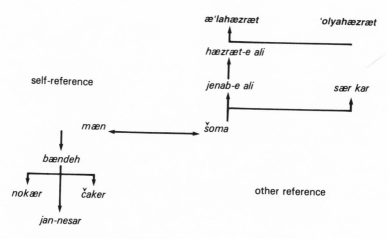

Fig. 6. Alternative Forms of Pronominal Reference.

pronominally for the royal family were also used in reference to them in preference to the third person pronoun. Thus one both addressed and referred to the shah as *æ'lahæzræt*.

The Singular/Plural Distinction as an Indicator of Status

Both singular and plural pronominal forms are used in first, second, and third person address and to refer to *single* individuals. The conventions for usage of each form differ, however. Alternative form distinction in single second person reference is found in many of the world's languages and in virtually all Indo-European languages. In Persian usage, the singular/plural distinction is used to indicate many different aspects of interpersonal relationships depending largely on pattern of usage and context. The second person plural, *šoma*, is, as mentioned above, thought of as a kind of "base" reference. I mean by this that *šoma* is appropriate in situations where personal knowledge about other people is minimal. It is of course the appropriate usage in other situations as well, but it is definitely appropriate where other information is lacking, as in a phone conversation with a stranger.

As in most European languages that incorporate differentiated second person address terms, the simple use of *one* term or another in Persian is not in and of itself enough to establish a status differential for interaction participants. It is the asymmetrical pattern of usage involving at least two participants that characterizes difference in status. Thus use of the second person singular form *to* does not in and of itself indicate that the person using the form feels that the person being addressed is of lower status. That person's lower status is only established and affirmed when the form *šoma* is returned by the addressee, establishing the asymmetrical pattern. As will be seen below, reciprocal *to* is used to indicate *sæmimiæt*.

The second person singular/plural distinction is also reflected in verbal endings, as in the paradigm:

> to rafti   "you (sg.) went"
> šoma raftid   "you (pl.) went"

This reflects alternative usages when addressing an individual.

An "intermediate" form has developed in Persian that allows for the use of *šoma* as a pronominal form but with a slightly less formal flavor. This is the verb ending *-in*, as in *šoma raftin* (you went).[8] This form does not indicate *sæmimiæt*, but it does not indicate formal distance either. It is a comfortable form for friendly face-to-face interaction in relaxed settings. It is, furthermore, most often a reciprocal form, rather than an asymmetrical one.

I have no data that shows asymmetrical -in/-id in interaction; however, there are a few cases of asymmetrical -i/-in in data collected from Gavaki, where the use of *-id* was not common except with persons from outside the village. In this case, persons were addressed with *-in* in verb endings by and reciprocated with *-i* to persons who perceived them as having a higher status within the village social hierarchy. Thus, the several *kædkhodas*, the head of the village association, a few of the merchants, and several large land owners regularly received *-in* and gave *-i* to landless workers and smaller landowners.

As a final note, in addition to the forms used above, there has begun to develop a true second person plural form that indicates more than one addressee. This form, *šomaha*, consists of the normal second person plural form with the pluralizer *-ha* attached. It is also possible to construct a more precise second person plural reference periphrastically, as in the phrases *šoma do ta* (you two), *šoma do næfær* (you two persons), *šoma se ta* (you three), and so forth.

The singular/plural distinction in the use of the third person is also used as a denotator of relative status in reference. The singular referent *u* (he, she, it) is replaced[9] when referring to a third person for whom one wishes to indicate respect or regard with the plural *išan*.

This plural form has come to be used almost exclusively to indicate relative status in verbal interaction, the true third person plural being indicated by *anha* (lit. those).

The greatest respect in reference is shown by not using a pronoun at all but referring to a person by title and name. Thus a hierarchy of reference is established that can be shown for the simple phrase "he went" (see figure 7).

An additional factor that affects third person reference concerns the perceived status of the person to whom information is being imparted relative to both the speaker and the person being referred to. Since status perceptions are relative in Iranian interaction, as I have stated several times thus far, it is possible to represent the various alternative situations three persons could find themselves involved in in terms of a matrix centering on the individual providing the reference to a third person in speaking with a second person. Thus, either the person addressed or the person referred to could be felt by the addresser as equal in status of himself ($=$), higher in status ($+$), or lower in status ($-$). The eventual reference form used, either *u* or *išan,* would be a function of the total configuration of the social perceptions of those present. If both addressee and referee are seen as higher or lower in status than the addresser, a further distinction is made as to whether one is higher ($++$) or lower ($--$) than the other.

In general, as can be seen in Table 13, reference is predicated on the perspective of the person having the highest status of the three persons involved. Thus, if the person being referred to is seen as being lower in status than the person being addressed, the form that is utilized is *u.* In cases where both referee and addressee are seen by the addresser as having higher status than himself but there is no further status distinction made between them, the form used in reference is *išan.*

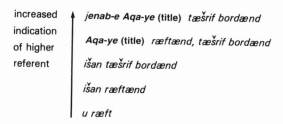

increased indication of higher referent ↑

jenab-e Aqa-ye (title) *tæšrif bordænd*

Aqa-ye (title) *ræftænd, tæšrif bordænd*

išan tæšrif bordænd

išan ræftænd

u ræft

Fig. 7. Status Differentiation in Third Person Reference for "He Went."

TABLE 13

**Differentiation in Third-Person
Pronominal Reference**

	Addressee	Referee	Form Used
a)	=	=	*u, išan*
b)	−	=	*u, išan*
c)	+	=	*u, išan*
d)	=	−	*u*
e)	=	+	*u, išan*
f)	+	+	*išan*
g)	+	+ +	*išan*
h)	+ +	+	*u*
i)	−	−	*u*
j)	−	− −	*u*
k)	− −	−	*išan*
l)	−	+	*išan*
m)	+	−	*u*

Several social relationships in interactions involving reference can be seen to be ambiguous, given the limited parameters used in this chart. When either the referee or the addressee is seen by the addresser as being his status equal, the further criteria of *sæmimiæt* must be applied in order to determine whether the reference will be *u* or *išan*. It is only in the case where addresser and addressee are seen as equal in status and reference is being made to a person seen as lower in status that the reference is clearly *u*.

Just as with second person address, the singular/plural distinction in referring to a single third person is maintained in verbal forms. Thus, corresponding to the *u/išan* pronominal distinction is the third person singular/plural verbal form, which I abbreviate here as the *-d/-ænd* distinction. Thus *u xord* (he ate) alternates with the higher-status *išan xordænd* (he ate).

The plural pronoun *ma* is used in preference to the singular *mæn* as an *alternative* to self-lowering pronoun substitutes to achieve about the same effect: a status elevation of the other person as either referent or addressee. The plural form has been suggested by Susan Bean (Bean 1970) to serve as a formalizing mechanism by making two-party encounters symbolically into multiparty encounters. The explanation given by one of my informants for the use of the first person plural form when referring to oneself in address and reference would seem to support Bean's observation: "In speaking favorably about another person one doesn't want to be so presumptuous as to greet him or praise him oneself. By using *ma* it is as if I am speaking for many in their praise or greeting. If I flatter a man *personally* he will assume I want a favor."

The statement above may be a little overdrawn, but the use of the first person plural is very widespread, especially among the middle and upper classes. Even in Gavaki and other villages, statements that reflect the opinion of perhaps only one person will be phrased in collective terms. Thus, instead of saying, "I hold a good opinion of you" in public to someone, it would be more common to say, "We all hold a good opinion of you" or, "All the people hold a good opinion of you."

Because the first person plural distinction extends to verbal endings as well as pronouns, the first person plural ending is commonly found with self-lowering stylistic forms, as in the following examples:

1. ræfti piš-e aqa-ye Doktor
    "Did you see (Mr.) Doctor?"
2. xedmæt-e išun ræsidim
    "I went to see him." (lit. we arrived at his service)
3. bebæxšid aqa-ye Mænučehri, mozahem šodim
    "Excuse me, Mr. Manucehri; I (lit. we) have disturbed."
    Næxeir aqa-ye Viliam, ma bændegan-e šoma hæstim
    "No, Mr. William, you're welcome." (lit. we are your slaves)

It should be clearly noted that use of the first person plural pronoun does not achieve self-lowering in and of itself—it is a way of showing respect through the diffusion of self rather than the humbling of self. It is perhaps for this reason that it is used so widely by the educated classes among themselves, in preference to such forms as *bændeh* (slave) as a substitute for *mæn* (I).

The singular/plural distinction in usage extends to possessive and enclitic object pronominal forms as well as separable pronouns and personal verb endings. Thus, one speaks to a person seen as higher in status about his book as *ketab-etan* [book-your (pl.)] rather than *ketab-et* [book-your (sg.)]. Having seen such a person, one says to others, *didæmešan* [I saw him (pl.)] rather than *didæmeš* [I saw him (sg.)].

Meaning and the Language of *Tæ'arof*

As mentioned in Chapter 4, the most common strategic principle in Iranian interpersonal interaction involves opting to indicate a lower status position for oneself while indicating elevated status for a person being addressed. Stylistic variation in the language of *tæ'arof* allows *both* parties in an interaction to indicate a lower status for themselves while elevating the status of the person they are addressing by maintaining two dimensions of lexical substitution, one for self-reference and one for reference to others. This stylistic device allows each party in interaction to "get the lower hand" by allowing *each* to practice nonreciprocal address and lexical usage. In this way, even nonintimate individuals who view each other as equal in status can move to an unequal status situation and, in their *mutual* use of nonreciprocal stylistic forms, maintain their equality.

In examining the verbs that are most affected by stylistic variation, we see that there are in point of fact very few that are subject to lexical substitution in situations involving status differentiation. What becomes more important in understanding the language of *tæ'arof* than a "glossary" of directly substitutable forms is an understanding of the *process* whereby whole areas of general semantic reference, such as "movement," become subject to lexical substitution and are collapsed into a few expressions that embody not so much the action performed as the cultural ethic implied in the action.

It is primarily verbs that express action and interaction that are most subject to lexical substitution identifiable as *tæ'arof*. "Going," "coming," and "remaining" are three actions that, for descriptive ethology or for a police report, may require strict distinction from each other. In Iranian social interaction, where one needs to find expressions for perceptions of relative status in all social interactions, whatever need there may be to express the precise nature of the action is "overwhelmed," as it were, by the need to express and emphasize the importance of the person doing the action. The presence of an important person at an event is secondary to the means he used to get to the event or his manner of arriving. In a cultural sense, the shah didn't really "go" anywhere, but he did often "honor people with his presence."

Thus, descriptions of the actions and movement of others must always embody a personal view. Another person moves relative to me if I am doing the speaking. If I then wish to comment on that movement to another person, or to the moving person, I must include in my description all the culturally relevant information necessary for it to be adequate and appropriate.[10]

Interactive domains indicated by such verbs as "saying" and "giving" involve transfers of goods and of words. As pointed out in an earlier part of this study, these domains of action are central to Iranian social relations in general. It is thus not surprising that they should be two areas of expression in which it is particularly important to be able to underscore and reiterate one's perceptions of the status of other individuals. Indeed, as has been shown, the etymologies for all verbal forms undergoing lexical substitution derive from words that embody the cultural ethics associated with social status differences in the Iranian "great tradition." Thus, for the verb *goftæn* (to say), the self-lowering stylistic variant really does derive from a form that emphasizes the notion of petitioning, and the other-raising form, the notion of ordering, as seen below in figure 8.

Thus, in Iran, individuals finding themselves in interaction situations where they feel it necessary to indicate the relatively more elevated status they perceive for another person can direct any of their references to action into one of the standard channels for lexical substitution and thereby underscore the status dimension. It is this feature of flexibility that makes the development of an exact glossary of *tæ'arof* difficult, if not impossible. The relatively free substitutability of *færmudæn* for *kærdæn* and other central forms in the many verbal expressions of the language is a productive feature that enlarges the potential breadth of status-marked usages considerably.

An understanding of the language used in *tæ'arof* then demands abandoning the notion that the meaning of the terms used resides in the verbal forms. What is meaningful for participants in interaction about verbal expressions that mark status is that a process of stylistic substitution is being employed, using terms that are culturally effective in emphasizing to all concerned: (1) *that* status differences of a particular equality are being indicated and (2) *what* the status differences themselves imply in Iranian cultural terms for the participants' future

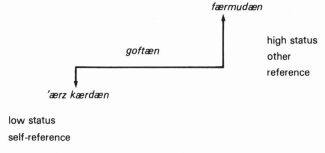

Fig. 8. Differential Status Dimensions for Stylistic Variants of "To Say."

actions. Any behavioral expression that is able to do these things—
verbal or otherwise—"counts" as *tæ'arof*.

If the above is understood, then the logic of variation found in
other areas of Persian morphology can be explained as well, even
though paradigms as clear as those for verbal and pronominal systems,
ones that contrast forms with each other in an exact formal way, cannot
be set up. Take, for example, the Persian prepositional system.

Direction toward a person or object can be indicated by numerous
prepositions in Persian: *be* (to, towards), *be su-ye* (in the direction of),
dær (to, into), *jæmb* (beside, toward the side of), *piš* (to, near to)—used
particularly for persons. In indicating elevated status for another party,
these are largely replaced with "fictive prepositions" that include some
etymological reference to the presence of the person in question, such
as *xedmæt-e* (lit. service of). These help to indicate elevated status of
another party, even in ellipsis. Thus the unmarked reference:

> Koja budi
> "Where were you?"

> piš-e Aqa-ye Mænučehri
> "with Mr. Manucehri"

contrasts with the following form, which indicates Mr. Manucehri's
higher status:

> Koja budi
> "Where were you?"

> xedmæt-e Aqa-ye Mænučehri
> "with (lit. service of) Mr. Manucehri"

The phrase *dær hozur* (lit. in the presence of) is used in a similar
manner. The use of these prepositional phrases allows one to indicate
elevated status for another, especially in reference, without having to
indicate a lower status for oneself. This is particularly useful when
rendering an account of one's actions to an individual to whom one
does not want to appear as a status inferior. Thus one may say, *ejazeh
bedid inra tæqdim konæm xedmæt-e jenab-e 'ali* [lit. give permission that I
offer this (to the) service of your excellency] but provide an account
of the same occurrence to another as *uno dadæm xedmæt-e jenab-e modir*

[lit. I gave that (to the) service of the excellency director], using the common verb *dadæm* rather than the self-lowering *tæqdim kærdæm*, as one might wish to do in the actual presence of the director. Similar distributions are made for prepositional phrases indicating direction away from an individual. The principal preposition here is *æz* (from), which becomes extended to *æz xedmæt-e*, *æz hozur-e*.

Although the appropriation of the singular/plural distinction (or in some cases the second person/third person distinction) to indicate perceptions of the relative social status of individuals is widespread in Indo-European languages, the meaning of this distinction must nonetheless be ascertained for each language and each culture area individually. The meaning of variation in this area for users of Persian cannot be established without taking into account the totality of situations for its usage. If, as in the example of lexical substitution above, we allow the basis for our conclusions about the meaning of this variation to rest on contrasts inherent in the pattern of usage for alternative forms rather than in formal contrasts inherent in the forms themselves, we will come closer to understanding how individuals use this type of variation to create meaning in interaction to make themselves both understood and accountable.

The singular/plural distinction differs markedly from the lexical substitution paradigm treated above in that it has no pattern of usage that serves the function of self-lowering. It does have a pattern that serves to demonstrate the perception that another has a lower status than oneself: the pattern of asymmetrical usage. To achieve self-lowering in this case, one must use one of the first person pronoun substitutes, such as *bændeh* or *čaker*. If we then combine the patterns of lexical substitution and pronominal usage, we see that a tool is created for social interaction that allows for the clear ascertaining of an actual hierarchy of status perceptions obtaining for any given situation. As an example of the sort of calculus that can obtain in the interplay of the two variational schemas, note table 14.

This table derives from the fact that the self-lowering/other-raising distinction in lexical substitution functions both independently from *and* in conjunction with the singular/plural distinction. Thus the permutations and combinations of the different applications of the two stylistic distinctions are understood in highly different ways. Instance a. on the chart, representing mutual high regard or flattery, has already been discussed. Instance k., however, represents a more complicated situation. One party is practicing self-lowering and receiving

TABLE 14

Interaction of Persian
Sociolinguistic Processes

| Instance | Stylistic Process | | | | Interpretation |
	Self-Lowering	Other-Raising	Gives Plural	Receives Plural	of Status Perception
a.	+	+	+	+	Mutual high regard or mutual flattery
b.	+	+	+	−	Individual is really lower in other's estimation
c.	+	+	−	+	Impossible or deliberately humorous
d.	+	−	+	+	Individual allows other person to take the lower hand
e.	−	+	+	+	Mutual respect
f.	+	+	−	+	Impossible or deliberately humorous
g.	+	−	−	+	Very strange; perhaps self-lowering is done for benefit of third person not being addressed
h.	−	−	+	+	Mutual respect
i.	−	+	+	−	Individual is unwillingly put in lower position by another person
j.	−	+	−	+	Impossible or deliberately humorous
k.	+	−	+	−	Individual perceives self as inferior but does not want to give other persons their due

TABLE 14 (*Continued*)

Instance	Stylistic Process				Interpretation of Status Perception
	Self-Lowering	Other-Raising	Gives Plural	Receives Plural	
l.	+	−	−	−	Strange; individual seems to want sympathy from an intimate, perhaps wishes to ask favor
m.	−	−	−	+	Individual perceives self as superior to other person
n.	−	−	+	−	Individual put in inferior position by either person; a jockeying situation
o.	−	+	−	−	Impossible or deliberately humorous
p.	−	−	−	−	Mutual intimacy (*sæmimiæt*)

singular second person pronouns, but although he addresses the other person with the second person plural pronoun, he will not give him his full due by using elevated address or verb forms.

Table 14 is not designed to represent either complete or definitive explanations of the social language patterns found in interaction but rather to give a picture of the variety of social interpretations that participants in interaction are able to place on the configuration of the speech of others through just the application of four stylistic variables. Several of the instances in the table have been marked "impossible." This is because other-raising verbal forms must be accompanied by at least the second person verb ending *-in*, or *-id;* if a pronoun is used, it must be *šoma* and not *to*. The verb ending *-i* is inappropriate. Nevertheless, among students I have observed other-raising forms used with singular pronoun forms to achieve an ironic or humorous effect, in such forms as *'ærz kærdæm xedmætet* [I told (lit. petitioned) you (sg.) or *jenab-e to* (approx. your [sig.]) excellency]. As will be pointed out in the next section, one of the characteristics of the language of *sæmimiæt* is a denial of status differences, with a tendency to declare sincere devotion or praise for the other person. This to some degree fits those situations labeled as impossible in table 8, but without use of *tæ'arof* forms.

The language of *sæmimiæt,* as will be seen, involves lexical substitution patterns that vary according to perceptions of the context of interaction, as outlined in the previous chapter. Perceptions of contexts also affect the language of *tæ'arof,* especially in third person reference.

In the last chapter, the deletion of final consonant clusters was mentioned as a regular stylistic variational feature in Iranian verbal interaction, corresponding to individuals' perceptions of the contexts in which that verbal interaction occurred. The third person plural verbal ending is no less subject to this stylistic variation, even in respectful reference to a higher-status person.

It will be remembered that consonant cluster deletion was seen to occur more often in situations where social status is perceived as more symmetrical to embody free expression and to be seen in a more "inside" *ændærun* setting. These I labeled as Pole B situations: interactions in which a third person is referred to by others. These can clearly occur within a wide range of settings. The perception of the two parties engaging in interaction about the contextual setting of *their* encounter and their perceptions of the status of the third person they are referring to, relative to themselves, are clearly separate. Thus, in Pole B situations it should be possible to have *both* the use of lexical forms that indicate higher status for a person being referred to *and* phonetic shifts that indicate that the individuals engaged in the interaction perceive themselves to be in a Pole B situation.

Similarly, colloquial pronunciations that indicate regional dialect differences should also affect forms which indicate perception of higher status, such as the common tendency in many areas of Iran to pronounce /a/ before nasal consonants as [u].[11]

Considering together both stylistic variations that reflect perceptions of relative status and stylistic variations that reflect perceptions of contextual setting, we can obtain table 15's characterization of a portion of the variation seen for the phrase "he went."

Third person reference proves to exhibit an extremely interesting sociolinguistic stylistic variation, as shown in this example. The number of possibilities for variation is larger than in second person address

TABLE 15

**The Interaction of Perceptions of Status and Setting
in Determining The Form of "He Went"**

| | | Perceptions of Setting | |
		Pole A	Pole B
Perceptions of Status	Higher than addresser	*išan tæšrif bordænd* *išan ræftænd*	*išun tæšrif bordæn* *išun ræftæn*
	Lower than addresser	*u ræft*	*u ræf*

precisely because perceptions of a person's status relative to the speaker can be shown in situations that do not involve that person as a participant. Thus, respect for an absent individual can be shown in interaction, while at the same time, the verbal style used in conveying the message that the absent person is respected demonstrates that the situation is a relaxed one.

Consider the following example: Seated in the office of a government official who was conferring with a friend of his, both of whom were among those who participated in high government functions on a regular basis, I heard the sentence presented in the analysis below. Significant points of stylistic variation are underlined. (Translation: When his majesty arrived, he said that we should finish this business as soon as possible, and I said. . . .)

vaxt-i	ælæzræt	tæšfærma	šodæn	færmudæn
1	2a, b	3a, b	4a, b	5a, b, c

ke	zudtær	inkaro	doros	konim
		6 7	8	9

væ	mænæm	bišun	'ærz	kærdæm
	10 11	12 13a, b		14

Description and Interpretation

Points of Variation		
1.	x used instead of q in word *vaqt*	Pole B situation
2.	a. use of *æ'lahæzræt* in reference to shah	Relative status indicator
	b. deletion of both /h/ and /'/, elimination of juncture	Pole B situation
3.	a. use of *tašrif færma šodæn* in place of *amadan* or *ræsidæn*, (to come, to arrive)	Relative status indicator
	b. elimination of juncture deletion of /r/	Pole B situation
4.	a. use of third person plural to refer to actions of shah	Relative status indicator
	b. deletion of /d/ in final consonant cluster	Pole B situation
5.	a. use of *færmudæn* for *goftæn* (to say) in referring to shah	Relative status indicator
	b. use of third person plural ending to refer to shah	Relative status indicator
	c. deletion of final /d/ in consonant cluster	Pole B situation
6.	Elimination of juncture, assimilation of nasal /n/ to following /k/ as n	Pole B situation
7.	Use of object particle /ro/ instead of the more "Pole A" /ra/	Pole B situation

8.	Elimination of /t/ in final consonant cluster in *dorost*	Pole B situation
9.	Unclear whether speaker means that the Shah directly told *them* or that he told the speaker, who then is using the first person plural form to indicate status at the time of interaction with the shah	Relative status indicator
10.	Use of *mæn* rather than self-lowering pronoun	Indicator of relative status of two persons speaking
11.	The /h/ in the word *hæm* (also) is deleted, as well as the word juncture between *mæn* and *hæm*	Pole B situation
12.	Word juncture between *be* (to) and *išan* (him) is eliminated	Pole B situation
13.	a. *išan*, the plural form, is used instead of *-eš*	Relative status indicator
	b. *-išan* pronounced [-išun]	Pole B situation
14.	*'ærz kærdæm* used in place of *goftæm* (to say)	Relative status indicator

The rough analysis above obliterates the essential quality provided by the narrative of the fusion of status perceptions and contextual perceptions. The impression the hearer gets on hearing this sort of speech is not that one is deferring to the shah in an informal situation, but that the speaker is the kind of person who has occasion to report on his dealing with a higher superior in an informal setting. The reporting is both informal and respectful. Thus the conversation is comfortable, not pompous, and properly deferential to the third party not present. In addition to the actual event reported, then, the speaker has *created a means for his reporting of that event to be interpreted by a listener through his use of stylistic variants*. Such an ability is essential in handling the language of *sæmimiæt* and in being *zeræng*, as will be seen in the rest of this chapter.

A Note on Superior-Inferior Address

As pointed out above in the use of pronouns, the superior-inferior relationship can be designated through the use of the nonreciprocal singular pronoun. Other verb forms can be used nonreciprocally in order to underscore the superior-inferior relationship as well, although their number is smaller than the stylistic variations found in the language of *tæ'arof*.

The direct imperative of the verb is used in superior-to-inferior requests without even the use of such qualifiers as *bi zæhmæt* (without trouble) as prefixes. Some particularly strong demands use verbal forms that underscore the duty of inferiors to superiors. Thus, the imperative of *dadæn* might be *ræd kon!* (lit. to return, relinquish). Even more to the point is the order *betæmærgh* for *bešin* (sit!). The etymology of the former form is lost to most Iranians, but it derives from the Arabic and literally constitutes a command for the person ordered to roll and wallow in the dust.

The Language of *Sæmimiæt*

The indication of *sæmimiæt* in speech cannot be accomplished through use of language in a single speech event. The pattern of *sæmimiæt* consists of a pattern of usage that demands that stylistic choice involving lexical substitution vary from Pole A contexts to Pole B contexts. In general, *sæmimiæt* involves the *reciprocal* use of forms we have characterized as used in *tæ'arof* situations, in Pole A situations, and the *reciprocal* use of forms characterized as indicating superior-inferior relationships in Pole B situations. It is only when the full range of Pole A to Pole B situations is observed for two individuals that the *sæmimiæt* pattern emerges.

As I mentioned earlier in this discussion, *sæmimiæt* underlies the operation of *pærtibazi* in Iranian society and consists of ties of intimacy, equality, and friendship. It is antithetical to *tæ'arof*, in that it embodies a denial of status differences. The ethics implied in *sæmimiæt* are those of loyalty; communality; and absolute, unquestioning reciprocity.

The arena of institutionalized *sæmimiæt* is, as stated earlier, the intimate gathering—either formalized, as in the *dowreh*, or nonformalized, as in the gathering of village men outside of a shop during leisure time or the regular but unannounced visiting taking place between close urban friends at any time. However, ties of *sæmimiæt* are active in other kinds of situations as well, as intimates are expected to defend and support each other against the social dangers of an unscrupulous world.

Sæmimiæt in a very real sense is perceivable primarily only for individuals that are *sæmimi* with each other. They are, after all, the only two persons who always see both parties in all contexts. Thus their own perceptions of the language each uses toward the other is one of the foundations on which the relationship is perceived to exist. Individuals can have a falling-out with each other if the pattern of correspondence between language forms and contexts of occurrence is ruptured without a reasonable explanation apparent.

Given, then, that the language pattern involved in *sæmimiæt* serves not only to indicate but to support the constitution of the social relationship between individuals, it is not surprising that the linguistic forms used in the overall pattern serve to reinforce the ethics inherent in *sæmimiæt*. One set of forms, those that are realized in Pole B situations, serve as a constant indicator to intimates that they are equal and that their relationships are reciprocal. The other set of forms demonstrates the loyalty and support that intimate equals expect each other to demonstrate in Pole A situations, by identifying and presenting each other in the most favorable light.

The first set of forms, or Pole B forms, consists of reciprocal nonuse of status differentiating verbal and pronominal forms. In general, as stated above, there is reciprocal usage of forms that indicate superior-inferior relationships. Thus, direct commands are made instead of requests, and second person singular pronouns and verb endings, rather than second person plural forms, are used in address.

Sæmimiæt can be extended so far as to involve terms of insult in place of other address forms. Young men in particular will use terms such as *kos-keš* (pimp), *madær-qæbeh* (son of a whore, lit. shameful mother), *pedær-sæg* (son of a dog, lit. father-dog), and such terms.

Direct sexual reference is generally avoided in this kind of intimate banter. When I asked young male informants whether a term such as *kun-deh* (passive homosexual, lit. anus giver) or similar insults can be used to indicate *sæmimiæt*, most imagined that such terms might be used endearingly by very coarse people, but no one could imagine using such language himself in this way, unless as a joke.

The few verb forms used in superior-inferior demands can be used reciprocally in *sæmimiæt* relationships. In this case, the use of *ræd kon!* for *bedeh* (give) implies that the person who is being asked for something is obliged to give whatever is being asked, just as in the superior-inferior relationship. However, the basis for that obligation is different. Individuals should ideally have no personal right to keep for themselves anything that is needed by an intimate equal. Giving on request is not rendering the other person his due, as one would to a superior, but fulfilling the personal obligation implied in the *sæmimiæt* relationship. Similarly, visiting for intimate equals is not the *ziaræt* (pilgrimage) of *tæ'arof*, but rather *sær zædæn* [to hit (one's) head], roughly equivalent to "dropping in," as one does not need to pay a formal visit when one wants to see intimates.

Interjections increase in Pole B *sæmimiæt* language, as do remonstrances and chiding, such as *borou, dige* (approx. aaah, go on!), *ey baba* (lit. oh dad!), used as an expression of surprise, and other such statements. Utterances such as these help to structure the entire interaction and will be covered in greater detail in the chapter dealing with discourse structures, to follow.

The Pole A pattern of the language of *sæmimiæt* is in many ways indistinguishable from reciprocal *tæ'arof*, except that lapses into Pole B *sæmimiæt* form as asides between intimate participants in a setting involving general people are always imminent for the duration of the Pole A speech event.

A little thought will reveal that usage of forms identical to those used in reciprocal *tæ'arof* can be exchanged appropriately between two persons alone. The reduction of participants to two or more intimates, whether through making an aside or through the departure of others, precipitates the return to Pole B forms, whereas true *tæ'arof* continues as long as the speech event is identified as continuing in its original state.

Examples of the switching of forms between intimates are numerous. The following example will serve to illustrate. At a meeting of a committee of the local office of the Iranian Plan Organization, the provincial governor and the chancellor of the university were both in attendance. The two men sat next to each other. The provincial governor addressed the group thus:

> Ba komæk-e jenab Aqa-ye Doktor Sæfa'i mitævanim
> "With the help of his excellency Dr. Safa'i we can"

> in kara zud tæmam konim.
> "this work soon finish."

> Aqa-ye doktor momken æst
> "Honorable doctor, is it possible"

> dæstur befærma'id
> "for you to order"

> ta pæsfærda
> "by the day after tomorrow"

> in gozareša beferestænd
> "that they send this report"

> xedmæt-e aqayan?
> "to the service of these gentlemen?"

> (Aside)
> Ino dari, hazer e, mæge næ?
> "You have it; it's ready, isn't it?"

And the chancellor answered:

> "Færda be-et telefon mikonæm"
> "Tomorrow I'll telephone you."

In the case above, the governor refers to the chancellor using status-raising forms and *færmudæn* in place of *kærdæn* for the verb "to order." In asking him to do something, he prefixes the substance of the request with the phrase *momken æst* and turns it into a question for his assent rather than an order. He additionally does not ask the chancellor to send the report himself, but to have "them" send it. Second person plural verb endings are used to refer to the chancellor, and the preposition *be* (to) is replaced by *xedmat*.

In the exchange with the chancellor, both parties use second person singular forms and drop into regular Pole B sound deletions. The phrase *mæge næ?* turns the statement into a foregone conclusion, giving the governor no way to answer "no" directly. The report was indeed not ready, so the chancellor postponed his explanations to the governor, one assumes, until the next day.

In summary, the language of *sæmimiæt*, like the language of *tæ'arof*, is not recognizable through specific identification of particular terms. It is only recognizable as a pattern that integrates and correlates the use of terms with their stylistic variational equivalents across particular speech-event contexts. In using this pattern of stylistic variation, one reinforces and underscores the *sæmimiæt* relationship that gives rise to it, making incumbent on partners in that relationship the ethics of reciprocity, communality, and loyalty implied in it. This in turn serves as the basis for such social institutions as the *dowreh* and *pærtibazi*.

The Language of *Zerængi*

There is no specific set of lexical forms that one can associate with the successful practice of *zerængi* as it has been treated throughout this discussion. On the contrary, all lexical and morphological variation structures thus far discussed facilitate "the clever dissimulator" in interpersonal interaction.

The language of *tæ'arof*, as I have described it above, provides the means for marking and indicating the status of other persons as one intends. Persian does not contain the rigid references for categories of individuals that are found in some Oriental languages. Further, because perception of one's own status and those of others is variable according to the social constellation one finds oneself in, the degree of ambiguity inherent in any encounter can be seized by a person who is *zeræng* and defined as he sees fit by the use of *tæ'arof*, which is appropriate not, perhaps, to the actual social situation, but rather to the social situation that the *zeræng* individual *desires to be in force*.

The system of lexical variation is further arranged so that more than one person can use *tæ'arof* expressions simultaneously. The feature of the variational system that allows this is its simultaneous self-lowering, other-raising capacity. Through this, all individuals involved in interaction can control the attribution of status they wish to place on others and obscure their own status. "Taking the lower hand" has been dealt with at length above as the most effective social strategy in interaction. The system of lexical variation described here allows everyone to employ this strategic device to his best advantage. The total result is a degree of obscurity about rights and obligations that can be employed to the advantage of any person clever enough to seize the opportunity.

Still, being *zeræng* with one's language means using it in creative ways. At one point in Tehran, I wanted some information from an official but was doubtful about my ability to obtain it. A friend of mine, who would be regarded by most persons as a much higher-status individual than I, decided to help me. Preceding me into the official's office, he announced my arrival to him. Once I was in the office, my friend represented me to the official using elaborate other-raising verbal forms. He used other-raising forms toward the official as well, but it was clear that his verbal language to me and in reference to me was much *more* other-raising than the language he used toward the official. This, combined with effusive self-lowering phrases, helped my friend create the impression of a status hierarchy, for the duration of the interaction, that had no reality at all. I was on the top of the hierarchy, the official in the middle, and my friend on the bottom. In fact, my friend and the official were in some absolute sense about equal in status, and I was considerably lower. This bit of *zerængi* worked perfectly, and I received the information I wanted without delay.

The supportive language used between persons who share a relationship of *sæmimiæt* in Pole B situations also is a form of *zerængi*, albeit a collective practice. Using higher status-marked language toward intimates for the benefit of others obscures the *sæmimi* relationship for those others and benefits the person being addressed in his dealings. He is still free to practice self-lowering as a strategy and so loses nothing and gains a good deal in this interchange. This situation reflects directly Loeb's study of the Shiraz *knisa,* cited above, where the honor of leading prayer could be obtained only by having it pressed on one by a close equal.

Pronominal usage between intimates often constitutes obscured information for others who have no knowledge of the relationship. In particular, normal patterns of pronoun usage seem to vary in different relationships. In a survey of students at Pahlavi University I was surprised to find that there was no entirely predictable pattern of pronoun usage between students and their parents. A clear pattern might have emerged had the survey been more fine-grained, taking economic, religious, and educational background into consideration, as well as the age difference between parent and child.

The group of students surveyed was about equally divided in using the second person singular pronoun or the second person plural pronoun with the mother. Nevertheless, it was universally the case that students reported that they practiced pronoun switching in order to indicate their emotional attitude toward their parents. Displeasure would be indicated by a reduction of a normal second person plural usage for an individual to a second person singular, or the raising of a normal second person singular usage to a second person plural to achieve sarcasm. Addressing parents in the presence of others, particularly older relatives, would always involve the use of the second person plural pronoun or a phrase such as *jenab-e 'ali* or *sær kar* for a woman. A person who used the second person plural pronoun with his or her relative in private, however, could demonstrate displeasure by continuing to use that form rather than moving to a more honorific one.

Addressing servants falls into this pattern as well. It was reported by the students surveyed that servants were normally addressed with the second person singular pronoun; only on special occasions (such as a visit from one of the servants' own older relatives) or as an indication of approbation would they be addressed with the second person plural pronoun. The same second person plural form could be used sarcastically to indicate displeasure in private, however, and an honorific phrase used with a servant would definitely indicate a cold anger.

Unless an outsider knew the family rather well, it would be impossible to tell for sure what was being indicated by a particular pronoun usage. The interpretation of this kind of message remains private, within the closed circle of the family, though there are definite principles of communication that seem from my brief survey to operate on a fairly general level in Iranian society.

The pattern of pronoun usage within the family leads to yet another area of language usage that tends to obscure the true motives and feelings of the speaker: the general area of flattery and displeasure. Flattery is achieved through a complex of linguistic and nonlinguistic message management, which will be dealt with extensively in the next chapter. Displeasure and anger are difficult to deal with in public, Pole A situations in Iran. As pointed out above, the great pressure for individuals to protect outside appearances has important religious and philosophical roots. Thus a growing displeasure in a social encounter is often handled by the displeased party by a gradual increase in polite language—a growing cold reserve not unlike flattery in its outward form. If we can speak generally of a pattern of indicating displeasure in Iran through running counter to an expected communication pattern, other-raising forms could be effective only as a communication of displeasure for someone who would not be expected to receive this behavior from the other party. Since, as I have cited several times, most interactions embody a degree of ambiguity that is hard to overcome except by seizing control of the situation oneself, when another person is practicing other-raising it is not always clear whether he is pleased or displeased. One thing is clear: he certainly cannot be accused of insult.

One pattern of displeasure indication is unambiguous. This is the total denial of interaction with an intimate with whom one is displeased. In Persian this is known as *qæhr budæn*. The phenomenon is well described by Bateson et al. (1977), who point out that withdrawing communication from an intimate places pressure on the entire social network in which both are involved to force the parties who are at odds with each other to reconcile their differences. This is an excellent solution to a problematic "falling out," where either party would lose face if forced to be the initiator of a reconciliation. The most interesting aspect of *qæhr* from the standpoint of this discussion is that when two people decide not to speak to each other, the actual issue over which they had a disagreement becomes more or less lost in the social pressure for reconciliation. It is in effect a way of removing an issue from consideration. Oftentimes, the parties forcing an end to the *qæhr* will not even listen to the two sides' arguments. Indeed, becoming *qæhr* with another intimate may be one of the most effective obscurist tactics one can use with those individuals with whom one is *sæmimi*.

Conclusion

This chapter has dealt with varieties of morphological variation and its use in social interaction. I have tried to demonstrate that the repertoire of variation that is available to individuals is the repertoire that facilitates basic social patterns of interaction outlined in Chapter 4. Further, morphological variation considered in this way corresponds with and incorporates patterns of phonological stylistic variation treated in the previous chapter.

In Chapter 7, I attempt to demonstrate how these patterns of stylistic variation are incorporated into interactional routines in such a way that social meaning is communicated between interaction participants.

VII

THE SOCIO-SYNTAX OF IRANIAN INTERACTION

Purposive Use of Stylistic Variation

One purpose of this study has been to underscore that an adequate description of style in language must go beyond a mere listing of variant forms that may be in some way or another equivalent. It must also demonstrate how the use of these variant forms facilitates purposive language use in such activities as humor, sarcasm, and social manipulation. In Persian, as has been described in the preceding chapters, a great deal of this verbal activity is accomplished through lexical substitution.

I have consistently posed an alternative to the view that language usage is *merely* reflective of the circumstances of interaction. Of course, language usage does reflect reality; to maintain that it does not would be foolish. But it also can be used strategically to shape the nature and definition of that reality. Indeed, language can in fact be seen *always* to affect the definition of the context in which it occurs, even if it is used only to maintain that context in its existing state. In this way, the forms of words issuing from a speaker's mouth cannot bear a totally arbitrary relationship to the context in which they occur— they both define and are defined by it in a dynamic, interactive manner (cf. Friedrich 1979).

In Chapter 1 of this book, I spoke of *appropriateness* and *effectiveness* as important speaker skills—the former consisting of the ability to use language in accord with social expectations, the latter, to veer from social expectations strategically in order to change the definition of elements in the communication context. The skillful speaker must be able to exercise both abilities. In order to do this one must take into account a number of factors, among them (1) one's own intentions (e.g., "I want to make a good impression," "I want to convince them to leave soon," "I want to be totally unobtrusive," etc.); (2) components that will be prominent factors in the context in which one's language will be interpreted (e.g., "If the room is too hot, they won't pay attention," "I wonder if I'm dressed too informally," "If her wig slips one more inch, I'll burst out laughing and ruin everything," etc.); (3) the way the speech event will be interpreted ("Will they think this is a request?" "Will they realize I'm angry?" "If I speak softly, will they think I'm well-mannered, or just timid?" "My God, how could I say such a stupid thing! They'll think I'm an idiot!" etc.).

Having taken account of these factors, the skillful speaker will know what language to use and how to use it, in order to steer the situation in a way that will best suit his or her aims. Few speakers are so skilled that they are always able to achieve exactly what they set out to do in interaction. Most are satisfied with anything short of disaster. Moreover, few can be entirely certain whether their efforts were successful or not ("I hope that went all right," "I think he was convinced, but I'm not sure," "I got the impression that she liked me," etc.).

I do not wish to convey the impression that language skills are used solely for self-serving manipulation in interaction. Most interaction seems to be largely aimed at secure, uncomplicated maintenance of predictable interaction and unchanged social relationships. Thus, interaction has a strong bias toward appropriateness skills. Nevertheless, the maintenance of a steady state in interaction requires skill—it requires as much skill, indeed perhaps more, not to offend as to offend; not to argue as to argue; not to appear ridiculous as to appear ridiculous purposely.

The observer of language use can understand how speech is used in these instances only through a careful view of the total system of language use in all contexts. The purposive use of language then appears as a function of the configuration of the whole system.

Chapters 5 and 6 have concerned themselves with what I have termed the socio-phonology and the socio-morphology of Persian, respectively. The use of variation in speech events to achieve social ends, as I have characterized it above, can be thought of as the basis for a kind of "socio-syntax" in Persian.

It would have been possible in this study to restrict discussion of syntax and stylistic variation to sentence-level ordering of linguistic elements, but this would be misleading. The sentence is not a natural unit in social interaction. In order to understand principles of structure above the morphological level in speech, one must deal with the sequencing and structure of far more than single subject-predicate units of the spoken word. This is particularly true if one also wants

to explore, as I have attempted to do in this study, how these elements
are understood to have the meanings they do in interaction.

There are two broad areas that I wish to cover in describing the
socio-syntax of Iranian communication. The first has to do with *operational functions* in the construction of conversational structures. These
operational functions have to do with the business of moving an interaction from start to finish through all of the potential operations
and suboperations that may be involved.

This area of communication is rarely dealt with in sociolinguistic
theory. It is absent, for example, from the inventories of Jakobson
(1960; see Chapter 2), Hymes (1972, 1974), Geertz (1960), Brown
and Gillman (1960), Brown and Ford (1961), Bernstein (1972), and
Labov (1972). Still, it is a terribly important function of speech—a
logistic component, if one will. Operational functions involve more
than merely proper sequencing of elements in the linguistic code.
They also involve the cultural definition of stages and events. An
interaction opening, for example, is a culturally defined social event
as well as a linguistic event—the two cannot, in fact, be conveniently
separated, but must be considered simultaneously.

In Iranian interaction, we are especially constrained to understand
these operational functions in their full cultural context. Like other
language areas dealt with in this study, these operational functions
involve stylistic variation. The use of one form in preference to another in the construction of any given interaction sequence, as well
as the choice made to use one of several possible sequences, are both
subject to interpretation of the sort proposed in Chapters 5 and 6.

The second area of the socio-syntax of communication, *pattern configuration*, has been dealt with in general terms in Chapter 2 of this
study under the rubric of message management. At this point, I wish
to return to treat it in a more analytic manner. Pattern configuration
can be thought of as a congruent structuring of the elements of communication so that a desired form for the event as a whole emerges
for participants. The configuration thus created can be seen as a
systemic *gestalt* where the combination of all elements forms a framework governing the interpretation of individual elements occurring
within that framework. This concept is not unlike Gregory Bateson's
notion of "play" (1956a, 1956b) or Goffman's "keyings" (1974).

A gestalt construction model of message management differs significantly from most approaches to communicative events, such as
those of Jakobson, Hymes, and others mentioned above. These traditional approaches in sociolinguistics emphasize the dissection of the

communicative event into its subcomponents; the gestalt approach emphasizes understanding of the nature of the total interaction event through the understanding of the *nature of the interconnectedness* of the communicative functions embodied in the entire configuration. This approach makes it possible to deal with materials that have been difficult for linguists and anthropologists to analyze in the past, such as embarrassing situations (why are they embarrassing?), humorous encounters (why are they funny?), insults (why does someone feel offended?), misunderstandings (what is the basis for the misunderstanding?), and interpersonal attraction (why do those people feel attracted under just these circumstances?).

The communicational structuring of humor provides an easy example of how this approach can operate. No individual element of speech or behavior is intrinsically humorous. To understand why some things can be made to be funny or are interpreted as being funny, one must understand the systemic nature, the gestalt, of the event in which those elements are embedded. In humor, the total configuration of circumstances reaches the point where tensions generated between new elements and existing elements within the interactional structure are identified as "humor-producing." For American humor, these tensions might qualitatively be interpreted as contradiction, redefinition, anticipation and fulfillment, and so forth.[1] Successful comedians are able to get people in the mood to laugh by constructing just those configurations in their performances that will render their statements and actions humorous.

Just as humor and the construction of the gestalts in which humor can be generated are culturally variable (do Americans really understand British humor?), so are all other configurations in message management. Though one may be able to go so far as to describe the principles for construction of communication events in another cultural system, in this study I have determined to go further. In keeping with the aims of my first chapters, I have tried throughout to explain why certain configurations of elements are found and are used actively in purposive communication for Iranians.

This answers many of the questions raised in Chapter 2, in which I suggested that many of the themes that non-Iranians detect in the warp and weft of Iranian daily life consist of generalized principles of communication necessary for the conduct of social interaction. Linguistic forms in interaction and their construction in communicative gestalts should conform to these generalized communication practices.

In Iranian interactional pattern configuration, as has been shown, processes of sound variation and lexical substitution play an integral role. These processes take on the dynamic aspect of connecting the immediate communication event with broader cultural patterns governing perceptions of context and social differentiation of individuals as seen in Chapters 3 and 4.

Operational function and pattern configuration thus are both ordering principles in governing the shape of interaction. Operational function governs patterns of sequencing—syntagmatic structuring in Saussurian terms. Pattern configuration insures congruence of elements—paradigmatic structuring, if one will. Both are necessary in shaping the logic of ongoing communication. In terms of speaker abilities as well, each provides important points for orientation as interaction proceeds.

One can monitor operational function, checking to make sure that an interaction is still "on track." One monitors pattern configuration to insure that all elements mesh properly. When either principle is awry, interaction also reels out of control. Here one can come into accord with traditional investigators of syntax in language, for speakers will easily detect when one or another principle is out of kilter.

Both principles likewise allow for creativity, even change. Just as a musician can modulate from key to key, so can adept communicators begin with one operational function, transit in midinteraction, and end up in another. Thus a casual greeting sequence can lead into a serious discussion pattern; what begins as an angry attack can segue into a humorous interchange. In pattern configuration, that which had the gestalt of an informal chat can end up as a sales pitch. What one thought was a violent outburst is discovered to be a plea for attention. The principal problem for speakers is keeping their bearings as they weave their way through the flow of ongoing communication.

A Problem in Operational Function:
The Use of the Imperative of *Færmudæn*

To illustrate the approach set out above for the description of purposive language, I wish to consider the case of the imperative of the verb *færmudæn* (to command), which has already been encountered in its use as a stylistic alternate auxiliary form for several other verbs. The imperative of *færmudæn* is often translated as "please." In point of fact, it is an operational form that can be used or interpreted correctly only through careful attention to its congruence to other elements present in the communication event where it is used.

In general functional terms, one uses the imperative of *færmudæn* to elicit an action on the part of another. An appropriate response to this verbal form must always address itself to the implied action— either a compliance in performing the action or a declination. Thus an appropriate response to an imperative *færmudæn* might be seating oneself, taking a glass of tea, speaking, proceeding through a door, or declining to do any of these or any other implied action.

The imperative of *færmudæn* is subject to the same sorts of morphological variation cited in the previous chapter of this discussion. Thus, there are three forms for the expression commonly used:

> befærma'id
> befærma'in
> befærma

These forms correspond roughly to the use of the singular and plural second person pronouns (Chapter 6). Thus, in employing any form of *færmudæn*, social distinctions can be signaled through the choice of pronoun ending. In general, however, the principles operating for the use of singular versus plural second person pronominal endings are imperfectly realized for befærma(*'in/'id*). Their normal function is almost overridden by the function of the imperative of *færmudæn* in triggering interactional operations between individuals.

The first of these operations is that of immediate invitation. All forms of the imperative of *færmudæn* can be used to indicate invitation, but not by all persons. The *-id* form is proper for everyone, as in *befærma'id tu* (come in), *befærma'id ča'i* (have some tea), or *befærma'id* and a gesture toward a chair (sit down). Persons who see themselves as status equals will issue an invitation using the form *befærma*. In this instance, the use of the term is the same as *befærma'id*. In issuing invitations of this sort, the imperative of *færmudæn* is followed immediately by a phrase or a gesture that indicates the action that one is being invited to fulfill. The use of this phrase can be seen in operational terms as a means of effecting a change in the activity state of the individuals engaged in interaction, and doing so smoothly, by providing a means for making performance of a specific action incumbent on the other person.

Changing one's own activity state is done via the reciprocal of invitation: asking permission. Thus transitions in the activities of an interaction are framed verbally with these operational forms, as in the following example:

> (B enters Manucehri's store.)
> A: *sælam'æleikum* (stands)
>   Hello.
> B: *sælam aqa-ye Mænucehri, Hal-e šoma xub-e*
>   Hello, Mr. Manucehri; how are you?"
> A: *æz lotf-e tun* (moves something off of a chair)
>   "Well, through your kindness."
>   *befærma'id* (gestures to the chair)
>   "Please sit."
> B: *ba ejaze-ye tun*
>   "With your permission."
> (B sits.)

This sequence demarcates the first activity state involving the individuals in the interaction. *A* above moves to change the activity state of both individuals by inviting *B* to sit. *B* reciprocates by asking *A*'s permission to sit. If we consider that *A*'s invitation to sit is a literal command for *B* to take charge of the situation, *B*'s acknowledging *A*'s permission reciprocates in the same way, by throwing the option for change of activity state back to *A*. The sequence continues:

> A: *Yallæh!* (rises as B sits)
>   "Allah!"
> B: *Hal-e tun xub-e, en ša ællæh*
>   "Your health is good, by the will of God."
> A: *Æl-hæmdu lillæh*
>   "Praise God."
> B: *Hal-e owlad četour-e*
>   "How is the health of the children?"
> A: *Æz mærhæmæt-e tun, do'a-gu-ye šoma hæstæn*
>   "By your kindness, they pray for you."
>   *ča'i mixorid*
>   "Will you drink tea?"
> B: *Xaheš mikonæm vas-e mæn zæhmæt nækešid*
>   "Please, don't take trouble for me."

A: *Zæmæt nis. Æhmæd, ča'i bio, zud baš!*
"It's no trouble. Ahmad, bring tea; be quick."
(Conversation . . . Ahmad brings tea on a tray)

A: (Takes tray, offers tea to B by holding out tray to him.)
Befærma'id
"Have some."

B: *Ba ejaze*
"With permission."
(Takes tea and sugar, and drinks.)

In this sequence, the new activity state is again marked off by health inquiries at the beginning. If there is a break in the conversation and *B* still does not want to break things off, he can renew the current activity sequence by another round of health inquiries. *A* signals a new activity, tea drinking, by inviting *B* to take a glass of tea. *B* again reciprocates by acknowledging that he is doing so "with permission." In this sequence of events, anything else that could serve as a significant change in the positions of physical attitudes of participants would also be appropriately marked.

Interaction sequencing of this type occurs when one party in an interaction is clearly on home territory, or on territory that is more his than the other person's. In this regard, two persons in a public place may occasionally jockey for control of the "host" role in the interaction, each anticipating the needs and wants of the other, and prefacing his moves with *befærma('in/'id)*. This can be a way of seizing some control of the situation by regulating and marking off the actions of the other individual. As my informants are quick to point out, however, there is also an element of genuine concern involved, as well as a desire to minimize all possible discomfort for the other individual. I have no doubt, having traced the course of several friendships during the period of my research in Iran, that solicitous attention to one another in this way can be taken as a sign that both parties want to establish ties that are more *sæmimi*.

Even between individuals who are *sæmimi* with each other, actions are marked off in much the same way. The invitational offer may be advanced to the beginning of the interaction, and it takes the form *befærma*. My informants point out that one stereotypic pronunciation with elongation, high stress, and high pitch on the second syllable (*-fær-*) is characteristic of the *jaheli* or "tough" class of males found mostly in urban centers. An excellent discussion of this stereotypic character type is seen in Bateson et al. (1977). The *jahelis* and their cultural relatives, *lutis* and *pæhlevans*, are in many ways idealizations of the ethics of *sæmimiæt*, among other things. This class is traditionally depicted as hanging out in tea houses and other public locales. Thus their usage of *befærma* is contextualized in a setting where any person on the scene would be able to issue a real invitation to a person entering to sit, drink tea, eat, etc.

The second person singular verb ending can also be insulting to persons who feel that they should be addressed using the second person plural ending. The form *befærma* can constitute an obscene insult, equivalent to "get fucked," indicating that one should "ingest" something other than food. In Isfahan I witnessed a man, angry at another, point to his leg and say *"befærma, ino boxor!"* (Here, eat this). The formula was perfect for two lower-class intimates; however, the invitation was obscene in connotation. Further, if the two did not in fact see themselves as intimates, the insult would be compounded by the second person singular form.

Befærma'in is less widely encountered than its equivalent in other verbal forms. I have collected only a few instances of it. One class of instances was noted in Gavaki for persons for whom *-in* as a second person verb ending alternated exclusively with *-i*, with no clear *-id* ending present for verbs used with other villagers. In urban areas, the few cases of this form I have run across seem to be attempts to strike a medium in intimacy indication between *befærma* and *befærma'id*.

I have characterized one of the reciprocal forms that can be used to counter the imperative of *færmudæn*, namely the acknowledgment of or direct request for permission. Others include various phrases that throw the action back upon the person who issued the invitation, such as *xaheš mikonæm, ested'a mikonæm,* and *tæmænna mikonæm,* which might be rendered in English as "please, I beg, I insist," and the like. These are stock phrases one hears a great deal, but only the limits of imagination bound the phrases one might use to attempt to reverse the direction of invitation. Though the order in which a task is carried out by two or more persons is indicative of how they have eventually structured their relative statuses for that encounter (highest status being acquiesced to by lower status), the onset of jockeying over order in carrying out an activity also marks a real transitional point in the total interaction itself, as mentioned above.

Understanding the pattern set up by use of the imperative of *færmudæn* makes it possible now to see that other verbal phrases and nonverbal acts operate functionally in the same way to demarcate activity spheres in interaction. As we would expect, the variations correspond to both different perceptual status relationships and different perceptions of context for individuals.

In general, extreme deference is shown by removal of oneself from the activity in which both persons might participate. In the example above, where tea was being served, Ahmad (the son of *A*) brings tea, but then steps back out of the room to avoid even being considered in the action. A hostess passes a tray of sweets around the room, occupying her hands so that she cannot be subject to verbal jockeying over taking the sweets. A servant or low-grade office worker stays several paces behind a superior to avoid a mutual confrontation at a doorway, even though both might have just participated in an interchange of words. Total withdrawal cannot be dealt with easily. It is a "trump card" in activity change. To emphasize the deliberateness of the gesture one can fold one's hands and cast one's eyes to the floor. This act of abjection leaves the other party so helpless that it can on occasion even arouse a sort of frustrated anger on the part of the person who must give in and proceed first.

Direct imperatives as indicators of change of activity state in interaction are used both between close intimates and for interactions between clearly ranked superiors and inferiors. In the former case, the "inchoative" with the first person plural ending *-im* is often the form used, as in *berim* (let's go), *boxorim* [let's eat (or drink)], *bešinim* (let's sit), etc. Persons whose status vis-à-vis one another is clearly vastly different in their perceptions are unlikely to be involved in mutual activities where there would be any question of who would initiate a mutual action. Persons who know themselves to be the status inferior of others may, as stated above, refuse to become involved in situations where, for example, one would be forced to precede someone one considers a superior. This might also mean refusing to drink tea or refusing an invitation, even though one might prefer to accept.

We have then in the imperative of *færmudæn* an expression that facilitates an important operational function in interaction. It constitutes a verbal message that serves in changing the activity state in which two (or more) individuals are involved. This leads to the discovery of a range of similar operators that serve to mark these changes in activity as well. Thus the course of an interaction can be clearly delineated in its physical aspects by these active verbal clues. Each change operator further reflects the interactors' intents and overt assessment about the social climate in which the interaction is proceeding. In terms of mutual activity states, then, an interaction can be schematically represented as follows:

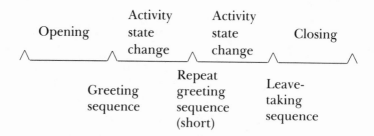

Before we can understand why the imperative of *færmudæn* is a particularly appropriate linguistic form to use for activity state changes between certain kinds of individuals in certain kinds of settings, we must understand how internal activity state changes in interaction relate to the two principal activity state changes—those that bound the interaction as a whole—the opening and closing.

Openings and closings must be dealt with on a more basic level of interaction than the use of specific words—namely, on the level of the role of ordering or participating in interaction, and its relationship to general socio-cultural parameters. The key to ordering lies, I believe, in the problem of "first greeting" in Iranian communication. This is summed up by the general principle that inferiors must acknowledge superiors first, but it is for the superior to initiate actual interaction beyond the exchange of greetings. This principle is illustrated nicely in telephone sequences. I cite first Ervin-Tripp's characterization of American telephone sequencing (1969:29, after Schegloff 1968) for comparison:

American

Summons Sequence:	Summons + Answer + Continuation + Response
Summons:	Courtesy Phrase (to stranger)
	Attention to call (to non-stranger)
	Telephone bell
Answer (phone):	Greeting 1 (+ identification [office])
Continuation:	Greeting 2 + (identification) + Message
Response:	(Deferral +) Reply to Message

Iranian

Summons:	Telephone bell
Answer:	Acknowledgment

Continuation: Request for Interaction (+ Message 1)
Response: Request for Identification
Continuation: Identification + Greeting 1
Response: Greeting 2 (only if party calling is known to speaker)
Continuation: Greeting 3 + Message

In Iranian telephone conversations, the interaction can only proceed after the calling party has identified himself or herself. The caller does so at the request of the person being called. Thus it is the called party's prerogative to continue the conversation by allowing the caller to introduce his or her presence into the situation by stating his or her name. For the caller to launch into the conversation without being acknowledged through a request for a name or recognition on the part of the called party would be an intrusion. Likewise, for the person being called to offer the first identification would display a slight lack of self-respect. For women this would definitely be the case. In Schegloff and Sacks's study of American telephone behavior, it is assumed that anyone calling is seen as having a "reason for calling." In Iran this is not the case. Persons being called have the option to commit themselves to interaction or not.

Face-to-face encounters operate on the same principle, but with a different set of parameters that deal not only with factors already mentioned, but also with setting. If one person comes to see another in a setting that is "home turf" for the person being visited, the visitor is put in the role of guest, and thus in an elevated status. The visitor can deny the right to guest status in any number of ways during the interaction, but if he or she chooses to press the prerogatives of the guest position, it is certainly possible to do so. The individual being visited can short-circuit the guest-host relationship in two ways: by refusing to see the person in question or by treating the visit as supplication. The former is a common tactic in Iranian bureaucracy and is highly effective for the most part. If individuals are is able to protect routes of access to themselves, they are also able to protect their prerogatives in decision-making and keep individuals from putting a social hammerlock on them by approaching as guests. The latter tactic is difficult to employ except toward those who are clear inferiors. In this way, haughty landlords, officials, and prominent persons one encounters in day-to-day interactions in Iran may attempt to protect their prerogatives as best they can in a world of potential clever favor-seekers. Nonetheless, the persons initiating a visit also put *themselves* in a subordinate role by having "made the first salaam"—by having greeted first. As guests they are then placed in a superior position. Thus the opening of the encounter is characterized by the marking of the visitor as both subordinate by virtue of his having come to see the other person, and as superior by virtue of his being a guest. The host is honored and placed in superior position by virtue of having received the greeting, and in a subordinate position by virtue of having taken the role of host.

The general set of interactional dynamics played out in this encounter is identical to those explored in the last chapter in explaining why the language of *tæ'arof*, when used in interpersonal situations, facilitates *zerængi*. A system of morphological stylistic variation, which facilitates simultaneous self-lowering and other-raising on the part of both parties, allows each person to "get the lower hand" voluntarily while elevating the person he or she is interacting with. One is elevated by the other person and has no control over the other person's self-lowering behavior. In the guest-host situation, each person voluntarily practices self-lowering, the guest by "taking the trouble" (*zæhmæt kešidæn*) to come and honor the host, and the host by accepting the person as a guest.

The imperative of *færmudæn* carries out the very same simultaneous action in one verbal gesture. The infinitive carries the dictionary meaning of "to order," "to command," and it is indeed used in this way in a legal sense. (A royal written order is a verbal noun derivative: *færman.*) However, it is the kind of word that can never be used in self-reference (the correct term for one's own commands is *dæstur*). Thus, the use of the imperative of *færmudæn* constitutes a literal command on the part of one person for another person "to command." This seems a paradox. Persons issuing orders place themselves in a subordinate position, and yet they are in a superordinate position through having given an imperative. Moreover, it is only the subordinate host who can issue this form to begin with. This situation is of course not really paradoxical: the person who is eliciting action is, through this lexical device, vitiating the force of the imperative statement. The person complying with this request is in the position of command in complying. We see here a recapitulation of the maneuvers involved in the self-lowering, other-raising strategies dealt with earlier. Using the imperative of *færmudæn* is a safe way to elicit action from another, no matter what his actual relative status vis-à-vis the speaker, since use of this form avoids having to issue an actual command to a higher-status person. Reciprocally, a higher-status person shows politesse and good taste in not imposing his status by eliciting action using this verbal form.

Most often, the action being elicited is to the benefit of, or for the comfort of, the person being addressed. An invitation to do something, such as sitting, or eating, is perhaps the commonest example. This is not always the case. However, this use of *færmudæn* also encompasses unequivocal commands. Thus, the imperative of *færmudæn* constitutes a generalized *stimulus to others to take action*.

The elicitation of goods or action from others is an act which is, as I have maintained above, central to Iranian interaction in general. Further, this action can have the connotation of either an *order* or a *petition* (cf. Chapter 4). The use of the imperative of *færmudæn* presents one way to elicit action without petitioning or ordering, by *shifting the focus of the request to the person who will be carrying out the action*.

Using the imperative of *færmudæn* is a particularly useful way to issue an invitation, since an invitation itself already constitutes a statement that the invitee is elevated above the inviter. To accept an invitation is to exercise rights gained through the acknowledgment of one's due as a higher-status individual. Hence a "command to command" is indeed the license of a guest. Invitations issued with *færmudæn* are of an "immediate" variety, however, and generally require acceptance through a response at the moment of the issuance. An invitation for a more distant time, say an invitation to dinner on a subsequent day, would be issued in more elaborate terms.

Thus, in the use of the imperative of *færmudæn* in situations where it is appropriate, we have an operational device that marks activity state transitions by continually recapitulating the social situation that characterizes the *entire* interaction. The use of the imperative of *færmudæn* constitutes that sort of message, characterized by Bateson and Goffman, that reminds participants in interaction that the interaction is of a particular sort, and that it is continuing to be that same sort and has not changed from its basic orientation, *despite the changes in activity states that have occurred during the course of the interaction.*

To sum up, the use of the imperative of *færmudæn* can be seen as an important behavioral device used to effect changes in activity states of participants in the course of interaction. Moreover, the use of the imperative of *færmudæn* to accomplish these activity state changes is interdependent with contextual and behavioral factors that establish guest-host relationships between and among participants. The imperative of *færmudæn* is appropriate in such situations insofar as it recapitulates operationally the sorts of perceptual status-balancing that occur in the guest-host situation, through both ordering the conventions governing greetings, cited above, and the other self-lowering, other-raising behavioral routines practiced in such situations.

Turning to other communicational devices that serve to facilitate change in activity states, we would expect to find that they too correlate with the participant's perceptions of the social context at the time of the interaction. I have mentioned two such devices: direct avoidance of interference with the activity of another on the part of a person who wishes to be seen as lower in status; and the use of direct imperatives by intimate equals and by persons who see themselves in higher status positions than those with whom they are interacting.

The former device recapitulates the ethic of stasis and separation treated in Chapter 3 of this discussion. It might be argued that in a real sense a person who avoids possible interference with another's activity is not interacting with him. In Iran, however, there is a good deal of studious avoidance of behavior that would interfere with the actions of persons seen as higher-status. The example of the tea server who has no hands free to serve himself has already been cited. Another way a tea server might deal with the same situation is to set the tea down and withdraw quickly before anything can be said, since even waiting to be thanked might be seen as a presumption on the relationship. Traditional women serving food or bringing anything to a male guest will often transfer the articles through their children (who, if small enough, are "socially neutral"), not only to maintain proper modesty, but also to avoid having to deal with the status relationship that must be marked in the transfer.

Parallels between this situation and Whorf's well-known observations about grammatical categorization should not be missed: just as a speaker must take into account such information about objects one wishes to talk about as shape, size, granularity, animateness, etc., in order to speak grammatically, one must likewise take social information into account in order to construct an ongoing string of appropriately meaningful behavior. The avoidance of interaction that might interfere with another's activity in Iran is tantamount to saying that there is no social time that I as an actor can share with that person so that a change in what he or she is doing (or what I am doing) needs to be marked for us. I wish to demonstrate that this person is of sufficient status to be totally free to do as he or she likes without being reminded by me of possible obligations with regard to me. The avoidance of behavioral interference also constitutes recognition that one *could* make behavioral obligations incumbent on the person being deferred to, if nothing more than an obligation to acknowledge the person practicing deference should he or she enter the room.

Direct imperatives have much the same force in activity state transition as second person singular pronominal forms and verb endings: they help to recapitulate the ethics of absolute communality between intimate status equals and serve to reinforce the ethic of duty when received from a person demonstrating status superiority. In the latter case, normal interchange would involve a direct imperative for action initiated by the superior individual and a petition of some sort or another issued by the status inferior.

To illustrate the latter example, in the office of the governor general of Fars Province, I was in attendance on a minor official. The tea server brought his regular round of tea, and there was one glass left over after all the seated individuals had been served. The official motioned the server toward a villager standing in a corner near the door, and the server gave him the last glass of tea. The man did not want to accept, and began a flattering protest to the official (who, after all, had been the one to offer the tea). The official became irritated and said:

mæge mixa'i tæ'arof koni vas-e ye ča'i! Mæge ki hæsti, to!
"Are you *tæ'arof*ing over a glass of tea! Who do you think you are!"

ča-i-ye to boxor dige![2]
"Drink your tea, you!"

The proper behavior in this case would have been for the villager to wave the tea server away, and look in the other direction without saying a word. The fact that the man had some business with the official made his clumsy protesting suspect (offering the tea gave him an opening to practice verbal other-raising with the official). Additionally, by interacting with the official over tea-drinking he was being extremely presumptuous—acting as if he were a guest when he was not of the category of person who could be a guest; indeed, his position, standing in the corner away from the other seated persons, demonstrated this.

Real invitations between status inferiors and superiors must be set up in advance and are issued as petitions. An employer will go to the wedding of a servant's son or daughter if told in advance that it is a wedding and if issued an invitation in proper form. But an offhand invitation will be interpreted as something else—most often a move to break the interaction event, or a proper closing. A common example of this occurs when one person accompanies or conveys another to his or her home. The invitation at the door to come inside for tea or for dinner is a sincere expression—of thanks or regard—but it is rarely a sincere invitation, even though issued as a petition, such as:

> *momken-e xedmæt-e šoma bašim beraye šam*
> Is it possible to be at your service for dinner?

> *Ejaze midid beraye šoma yek ča'i dæm konæm*
> Will you permit me to brew you some tea?

Such situations give the guest (he who was accompanied or conveyed) a final opportunity to turn the tables and place himself in a subordinate position. The conventional use of these petition-invitations is so widespread for purposes of closing off interactions that everyone (except foreigners) knows not to accept them. If an invitation is sincere, it will be repeated up to three times after the first denial. Even then it is rarely wise to accept unless one is willing and ready to begin the gradual move toward intimate equality.

As stated previously, intimate equals are free in each other's presence to make absolute demands on each other or to suggest any action on the part of each other. Mutual imperatives are issued freely as action state transition markers, both in the second person and the first person plural. The use of petitions, or *befærma'id*, between such persons would be construed as humorous or an indication of displeasure.

Taking an overall view of the language used in action state transitions in interaction, we see that participants regularly use communicative forms that indicate an orientation to a basic mode of Iranian interaction at each point where a shift in activity takes place. These communicative forms are not arbitrary, nor are they inexplicable. They are part of the general communicative strategies that individuals use with each other, in that they serve to establish and reinforce the social ethics that obtain for the interaction. They are, at the same time, accounting procedures that individuals use to inform each other of the nature of the imperative frame that they wish to obtain for the duration of the interaction.

Communicative operators for Iranian interaction are listed in table 16. Cultural principles that form the content of that which is being marked appear in the second column of the table, and the conse-

TABLE 16

**Operators in Action State Transition
in Iranian Interaction**

Communicative operator		Cultural principle	Consequence for interaction
1.	Noninterference	Raising and separation of high-status individual	Total freedom of action for one party
2.	Asymmetrical petition	Request for action stated as petition from lower to higher status	Invocation of noblesse oblige or duty ethic on party addressed
	Asymmetrical order	and as order from higher to lower status	
3.	Imperative of *færmudæn*	Both parties practicing self-lowering and other-raising	Balance between parties
4.	Use of simple imperative (go! take!)	Expression of equivalence between intimate equals	Freedom of action for both parties

quences for interaction produced by use of the operators in the third column.

The four operators presented in table 16 might be characterized as (1) asymmetrical symmetry, (2) asymmetrical asymmetry, (3) symmetrical asymmetry, and (4) symmetrical symmetry, where the first element of each term refers to the social relationship between the parties that is being expressed. The second element refers to the correspondence between the forms that are being given and those being received by each party. For operator 1, the parties are presented as unequal, and neither interacts with the other. For operator 2, parties are presented as unequal, and both give terms different from those they receive. For operator 3, parties are presented as equal, and both give terms different than those they receive. For operator 4, both parties are presented as equal and give the same terms they receive.

Thus, a complicated system of social ethics and behaviors, of linguistic coding and communication strategies can be reduced to a simple set of *differences*—in Bateson's words, "differences which make a difference" in important cultural terms. Cognitively, the task becomes one of establishing whether another person is to be designated in overt behavior as different from oneself and establishing how that difference is to be marked. Choosing whether forms used in interchange are to be symmetrical or asymmetrical is a negotiated problem for all parties in interaction.

Shifts from normal usage of these operators are often noted in Iranian interaction, particularly in humor and irony; however, understanding of humor and irony in the use of these forms for participants in interaction requires perception of a different order of difference than simple status distinction. In the United States, there are many behavioral devices that allow one to "break frame," i.e., to publicly renounce a schema of interpretation obtaining at a given moment. The mechanisms for doing this are detailed by Goffman in a good number of his writings. In his study, "Role Distance" (in *Encounters*, 1961), he suggests that devices such as humor and irony help individuals to de-identify themselves with the "activity system" in which they are engaged. Goffman maintains that this "role distancing" has social value in allowing superiors in an activity situation to relax the restrictions of the status quo. For subordinates to do this is likely to be seen as a refusal to keep their place, a rejection of authority, or indicative of low morale (Goffman 1961:128–129).

In Iran it is difficult to create humor, irony, or insult without a fairly full personal knowledge of individuals with whom one is involved. In the case that one knows and is known well by those with whom one is interacting, it becomes possible to see whether the language being used in interaction is in fact appropriate for the kind of interaction being carried out with that individual. If *not*, then it is likely that humor, irony, or displeasure is intended. Deliberate mistakes in the use of verbal forms may also be used with persons one knows well with the fair assurance that they will not be interpreted as grammatical mistakes, but as deliberate inconsistencies.[3]

In order to interpret deliberate inconsistencies in speech usage, one must first be able to recognize a usage as inconsistent. This requires personal knowledge of a speaker's conventional usage. Secondly, one must be able to understand, within the ongoing history of one's own social interaction with a particular individual, what the consequences of his usage are likely to be for the specific interaction event. Interpretation of this sort requires knowledge of a history of patterns of interaction that are highly personalized. That individuals can keep track of complexes of many such personal histories has been pointed out by Harvey Sacks (original punctuation preserved):

Lets say someone visits your house some non-first (N) time. And they walk through the house and say, "gee, that's new, isn't it?" And you say, "Yeah, I got it a couple of months after the last time you were here," or "I just got it," etc. Now, consider that as one of the ways in which, as between two parties, one goes about showing the other 'how much you're in my mind'; i.e. as between the times I visit you, I can, on many given occasions see, in looking through your place, the sort of changes that have been made, and show them to you. I can find things that have changed in 'our time'; i.e., time that is only marked by our relationship, and that you too, can see—even though maybe lots of people come over to your house—that this item was not purchased since February 1967, but that it was purchased after my last visit, whenever that was. So that you keep these kinds of calendars and objects in mind, and you have them in such a way that you know what's in this one's house; and in that way you keep an attention to them. (Sacks 1970:21–22)

In the same way that one can keep track of objects and time with persons with whom he interacts, so one can keep track of the history of interactions.

Linguistic operators in action state transition also vary in form according to the perceptual context of the interaction, as described in this study. Thus even the glottal stricture ['] of *befærma'id* may be highly pronounced or eliminated entirely, depending on a speaker's perception of the interaction event as a situation closer to Pole A or Pole B in nature.

In conclusion, I began this section with a discussion of one set of linguistic forms—variants of the imperative of the verb *færmudæn*—and tried to demonstrate how these forms function as operators in the ongoing stream of interaction, facilitating the transition from one point in the interaction to another. In doing this, I have tried to expose a whole class of linguistic operators to which the imperative of *færmudæn* belongs, which all serve the same motor function in the serial structure of interaction sequences in facilitating action state transition. These operators can be seen, however, to serve another function as well: that of reinforcing the interpretive frame within which the interaction as a whole occurs.

A schematic picture of these Iranian operators, then, would include a set of communicative form usages situated within three structures: (1) ongoing interaction as transition between action states; (2) perceptual context as a realization of a situation lying somewhere on a continuum between Pole A and Pole B situations; and (3) the totality of the ongoing history of personal interactions between the individual and other participants. The interpretation that is made of any one operator, then, depends on making a series of simple discriminations. The three discriminations cited above are repeated in table 17.

The general analysis I have provided here of a single set of terms has applicability for other communication operators, as will be shown in the section that follows.

Other Communicational Operators

The set of action state transition operators dealt with in the last section can be correlated with a set of operators that function in the linear ordering of discourse elements in Persian. These consist of

TABLE 17

**Discriminations and Consequences
in the Use of Communicative
Operators in Action State Transition**

Discrimination	Consequence
1. Is there a difference between the action state preceding and the action state to follow?	1. Establishes form as operator in action state transition (or not)
2. Is this more a Pole A or a Pole B situation?	2. Establishes phonological style
3. Is the person being interacted with significantly different socially than oneself?	3. Establishes base for expectations of communicative form
4. Are the language forms being used by the other person the same as the ones being used by oneself?	4. Establishes communicative operator
5. Are the language forms used by the other person different than the forms he uses in similar circumstances?	5. Establishes need for further interpretation

phrase introductions, interrupters, confirmers, and miscellaneous re-address forms. For the purpose of this discussion, I provide an analysis of the first of these below.

Phrase introducers are used by a speaker to preface a declarative remark. They cannot be used to preface a question or a direct command. Informants often describe a phrase introducer as a hesitation phrase; however, observation of actual use seems to indicate that it is also a means of taking the floor in discussion. The phrase introducer *can* be used repeatedly at any hiatus in a person's comments as hesitation or punctuation and as a means of keeping the floor. The formulae used in this operator fall into four broad categories:

1. an expansion of a formula based on the word *'ærz*
2. a formula based on *migæm*
3. ø
4. a direct order to listen

The *'ærz* formula can be expressed as follows:

$$
'\!ærz + \left\{ \begin{array}{l} \text{form of} \\ \text{\textit{kærdæn}} \\ \text{(to do)} \\ \text{form of} \\ \text{\textit{šodæn}} \\ \text{(to become)} \end{array} \right\} + \left\{ \begin{array}{l} \text{\textit{xedmæt}} \\ \\ \text{\textit{hozur}} \end{array} \right\} + \begin{array}{l} \text{second person} \\ \text{plural} \\ \text{pronominal} \\ \text{form or other-} \\ \text{raising} \\ \text{equivalent} \end{array} + \textit{(ke)}
$$

Thus is yielded a multitude of forms, a few examples of which follow:

    'ærz mikonæm   hozur-e   hæzræt-e'ali   ke
    'ærz mikonæm   xedmæt-e jenab-e'ali
    'ærz šavæd hozur-etan   ke
    'ærz mišævæd xedmæt-e   šoma
    'ærz konæm   ke
    'ærz šavad
    'ærz mikonæm
    'ærz beše

It is this form that is most often encountered as a phrase introducer. As one might by now suspect from following this entire discussion, this is the form used in status differentiated situations or in situations where both parties are practicing other-raising and self-lowering. The differential forms allow for the incorporation of different degrees of reference to other individuals present. As mentioned above, the verb form *'ærz kærdæn* is the self-lowering equivalent for "to say." Thus, in introducing a phrase, it is possible to recapitulate the self-lowering, other-raising operation before reaching the message one wishes to convey. This works retroactively in at least one case. If I, as a high-status person, greet another person first, I have exercised *tæ'arof* and have taken a lower-status position. His reply might not be "sælæm," but rather " *'ærz kærdæm* [past tense], sælæm," implying, at least, that he *did* (or meant to, or should) greet first.

The *migæm* formula for phrase introduction is much less extensive:

$$migæm + \begin{Bmatrix} ke \\ ha \end{Bmatrix}$$

Migæm is the Pole B form for *miguyæm* (I say) and is used to preface remarks between equals in situations that are closer to Pole B in nature. The relative clause introducer *ke* lends emphasis to the message to follow, while the particle *ha* emphasizes the fact that a remark is being made, and thus is a stronger bid for attention and the floor than unemphasized *migæm*.

An imperative command to listen can be given by a superior to an inferior, or by two intimates. The usual form is *guš bedeh*, the imperative of *guš dadæn* (to listen). The questions *mišenævi?* and *guš midi?* (are you hearing? are you listening?) are equivalents in this case.

The elements that make up the *'ærz* formula should be readily recognizable from the preceding chapter. They consist of materials that are used in the construction of the language of *tæ'arof* as already set out. The various expansions of the formula thus involve a range of indicators that vary from the greatest separation in status marking to the least. In order to test the range, I had printed out all the variants of the *'ærz* formula I had encountered in my fieldwork and presented them to twenty informants in Shiraz and in Gavaki, asking them to arrange them in order as they saw as appropriate, explaining the ordering to me. The task was difficult, but it yielded some interesting results. Shorter versions of the *'ærz* formula, such as *'ærz miše* and *'ærz beše*, were said to be *sæmimitær* (more sæmimi), but not really indicative of a close relationship. The shorter forms were also said to be less *ræsmi* (formal) than the longer. Those that involved the pseudo-prepositions *xedmæt* and *hozur* and other-raising pronoun substitutes, such as *jenab-e 'ali*, were both the least *sæmimi* and the most *ræsmi*.

As we look again at the function of the phrase introducer as an operator in interaction, the range of variation delineated by my informants can be explained in somewhat greater detail. The phrase introducer, as has been mentioned, can be used both in gaining the attention of others and in marking the beginning of one's turn at speaking. This occurs when one is expected to speak in discussion or when one is asked by another a direct question that requires an informational answer. Use of a phrase introducer to preface a response indicates that the responder sees himself as at least equal in status to the person asking the question. Because the *'ærz* formula in its more elaborate version involves other-raising pronominal substitutes and pseudo-prepositions, following the principle of taking the lower hand in social situations, the actual forms used in sentence prefacing could be the same in both social situations above. This makes the process of using phrase introducers different from the process of using action state transition operators, as shown in the last section, where status differences could be seen as far less ambiguous, as reflected in the linguistic operator.

The key to understanding phrase introduction lies in determining situations where turn-taking matters in interaction. All phrase introducers create a separation between the remarks of the previous speaker and the speaker using the phrase introducer. They also attract attention. These two functions can be considered as interacting with each other, creating a scale that encompasses both a marking of relative status and a marking of contextual perceptions.

Marking the juncture between speakers is an operation analogous to marking the change in activity states between individuals. Just as activity state changes must be marked by behavior that recapitulates and sums up the constellation of social reality at each moment, so must junctures in turn-taking mark the continuing state of the social order as each individual takes the floor. Further, in Pole A situations, as has been mentioned, the marking of the social order must be more highly determined than in situations defined as merely Pole B.

Of course, status marking in turn-taking does not matter for all situations. If everyone enjoys the right to speak freely and openly, as in Pole B situations, the relative status-marking function of the phrase introducer is eliminated and only the attention-getting function remains, as in the *migæm* formulae and the imperative *guš bedeh.*

A graphic representation can be constructed, then, that plots these two functions against each other and provides for a rough distribution of phrase-introduction forms (see figure 10).

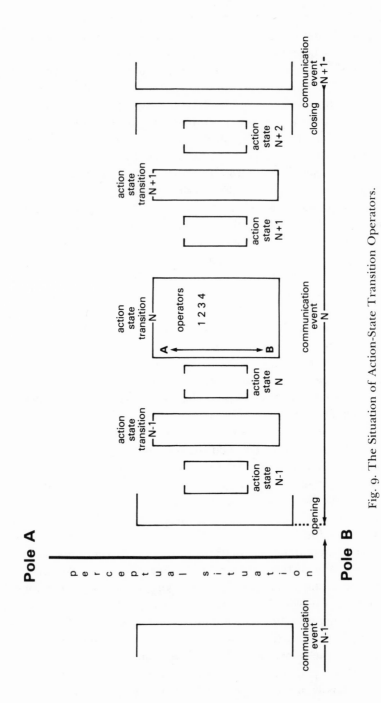

Fig. 9. The Situation of Action-State Transition Operators.

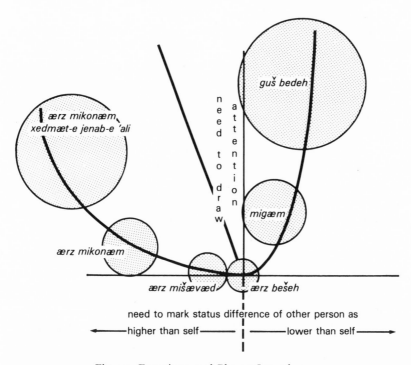

Fig. 10. Functions and Phrase Introducers.

Figure 10 shows a few representative phrase introducers set in spheres of applicability for the two functions mentioned above. Status marking is seen as the need to indicate that the person to whom one is speaking is higher or lower than oneself. The diagram is impressionistic, but it reveals an important tendency in interaction. Remarks that may be used to indicate the lower status of another person also are used with equals. The attention-getting functions of these remarks is thus primary, overriding the status-marking function. The overall curve of phrase introduction operator variants is represented, then, as a hyperbola. Note carefully that the axis of the hyperbola is skewed in the direction of the need to indicate that others have a higher status than oneself. This is a graphic representation of what I have referred to above as the principle of taking the lower hand.

The whole question of nonprefaced remarks and how to account for them raises a series of interesting general issues for this analysis. I have found, first of all, a good number of instances where persons interacting with others whom they know and feel to be of higher status than themselves do not preface their remarks at all, but make them both perfunctorily. A second set of occasions occurs where persons use these markers only irregularly throughout a conversation. Finally, there seems to be a third set of cases where nonprefacing is used strategically.

The second case above is partially explained in a consideration of other linguistic operators in interaction—in particular, address forms, which will be considered at length below. Address forms serve some of the same functions as phrase introducers and may be combined with them to form a long introduction to a remark. This combination will also be dealt with below. In any case, the need to mark status and the need to attract attention through phrase introduction can be reduced to zero through the use of other operators to fill these functions.

In order to account for the first set of cases of nonprefacing, it must be understood that there are some relationships in Iranian social life that simply do not admit full interaction between parties. One is the relationship between men viewed as having high status and those women who see themselves as lower in status. Freedom of interaction is frustrated and distorted by taboos against socializing between the sexes. Another of these sets of relationships involves older children and adults. Very young children are allowed a great deal of liberty in their interaction, but as they approach puberty, they are made aware that they must not intrude on higher-status persons by taking the initiative in conversation.

These sorts of prohibitions on interaction relate directly to the feature of social life mentioned in the previous section of this chapter: status marking and the principle of the first *sælæm*. It will be recalled that whereas the lower-status person must greet first, the higher-status person has the prerogative of continuing the interaction. Thus, beyond the *sælæm*, a lower-status person may not initiate substantive remarks without risk of being labeled perjoratively as *por-ru* (rude, brash). Going one step beyond this, initiation of greetings further implies that an individual actually is enough connected with the person he is greeting to have a genuine status relationship with him. Some persons are simply too low socially, too unknown, or too taboo to have *any sort* of relationship with a person they view as high in status, a stranger, or sexually taboo. To use *tæ'arof* expressions or enter into elaborate greeting sequences has possible social implications (as has been emphasized repeatedly throughout this discussion), even if the person is on the lower end of the hierarchical scale. If it would be presumptuous for an individual to claim any social relationship that would imply obligations of any sort, then that person is placed in a tremendous bind if forced to interact with the higher-status or taboo person. The reaction is often silence or terse and unceremonious remarks.

The visitor to an Iranian village may be surprised at the way he or she is treated on occasion. Something the visitor needs is hustled into the room by a woman, her chador pulled around her face, without comment. A direct question is answered by a perfunctory reply without any verbal ceremony whatsoever, actions that contrast sharply with those of the men of the same family or neighborhood. A telephone conversation with urban servants can also yield the same unceremonious behavior, especially if one is not known in the family.

In any case, the "need" to indicate perceptual status differences in this case is reduced to zero, since to call attention to that status relationship is itself undesirable. It is situations like this that lead many Iranians and Americans to say that the lower socio-economic classes in Iran, including villagers, do not know how to use *tæ'arof*, not taking into consideration that their own presence as observers may be affecting the language of the people they are observing.

If our functional variables are interdependent, then an inability to express status relationship also involves an inability to use a linguistic device to call attention to one's own remarks. This makes interaction between individuals who have no right to interact with each other terribly difficult, a kind of double bind. The individual wants something or has to say something (as in answering a direct question), but has no code for expression that does not betray him or her in some way. In this case, even the nonprefacing of declarative statements, which persons who have minimal interaction rights with others are forced to employ, is an expression of a particular status relationship. It is wrong to interpret this behavior as a kind of mini-speech pathology. Such individuals are not diffident, reticent, nor shy when status relationships become regularized.

Pattern Configuration

Pattern configuration is one of the chief techniques of message management described in Chapter 2. This means, basically, managing one's use of stylistic variables in such a way that they form a pattern that forces their interpretation along certain desired paths, presumably with particular results in mind. The patterns can be those that are totally expected, such as one uses in employing appropriateness, or they can lead to redefinition, as in the use of effectiveness skills.

I have talked throughout this discussion of the practice of *zerængi* in daily Iranian life as a process of thwarting interpretation of one's own actions while interpreting correctly and acting on the actions of others. *Zerængi* is associated with verbal skill more than any other quality, and it is in the area of verbal skill that the greatest potential for the practice of *zerængi* exists.

It is in the general interactional routines of message management that the strategic use of stylistic variation reaches its highest levels of skillful usage. Ideally, one should be able in interaction to lock individuals one is speaking with into a position of action and reaction from which there is little escape, through verbal and nonverbal behavioral routines. One is brought inexorably to a particular position that has been engineered by an interaction partner. This need not be thought of as manipulative or malevolent. Intimate friends establish and remind each other of their bonds of friendship through language and behavioral attitudes. Intimate friendship has definite consequences for interaction, even as it is invoked. As one uses the verbal forms associated with *sæmimiæt* in conjunction with settings appropriate to their usage, subsequent verbal and behavioral forms are expected to effect interactional routines associated with the *sæmimi* relationship. One expects on experiencing the language of *sæmimiæt* that an informal invitation will be issued or that a request for goods or services will be made, one that must be complied with. The consequence of all of these things—proper language, proper behavior, proper thoughts—is highly satisfying in Iran and indeed is invoked in the ancient aphorisms of Zoroastrianism: *pendar nik, goftar nik, kerdar nik* (good thoughts, good words, good behavior).

Proper congruence of thought, word, and deed in unequal status situations is also satisfying. Many of my Iranian friends, on listening to me speak about verbal manipulation, have rebuked me for ignoring that it is pleasant and even exhilarating to behave with proper respect toward a person one *really* respects. One researcher reports that in a word association test with Iranians the term with highest correlation with *ehteram gozardæn* (to give respect) was *dust dastæn* (to like, to love).[4] Nor is it only the prerogative of intimate equals to swear allegiance, loyalty, and devotion to each other. Many subordinates would indeed "sacrifice themselves" for an individual who is not only higher in status, but more esteemed.

Because the behavior associated with interpersonal relationships and the action prerogatives that individuals have in these relationships are so strongly connected, the possibilities for verbal strategy are great.

As might be expected, the principal axis for the practice of verbal manipulation consists of locking persons into positions where they are forced to see themselves as higher in status and thus subject to the ethics of noblesse oblige.

A person wishing to make this strategic move uses self-lowering, other-raising stylistic forms in speech and behavior. He or she greets first, inquires elaborately about the health of the individual and his or her family, and makes direct reference to the dependence relationship that exists between the greeter and the person being greeted, and that person's family. This process is known in Persian as *xær kærdæn* [to make a donkey (of someone)], particularly when it is done with a specific end in mind. What distinguishes this process as a verbal strategy from the routines an individual must observe in a normal request of a high status individual is that the phrases and behavior are seen as more than the person deserves, or rather, more than the relationship between the two individuals deserves. The important formal feature of the *xær kærdæn* routine that distinguishes it from simple verbal etiquette is its metalinguistic quality. The contents of the messages being presented are not only stylistically marked for self-lowering and other-raising but refer directly to the status inequality and its associated ethic. Thus, one informant in Gavaki relates, "If I want something special from Hajji Mohammed (a wealthy landowner) I go to him and say '*Sælæm*', and all of that routine (*tæšrifat*) and then I say, '*jenab-e Hajji, hæzræt-e 'ali* (are) greater than all of us, and we couldn't live without your existence (*vojud-etan*). If it is in your power, if it is no trouble for you, please do this thing for me and we will be grateful.' And if he has become a donkey (*ægær xær šod*) he'll do it."

A routine such as *xær kærdæn* constitutes a whole interaction event that has a unity of style and content from beginning to end. It is a piece of rhetoric, in effect, that draws on a unified set of stylistic devices and messages to persuade a person to do something according to a set of cultural expectations.

A second routine does not constitute an entire interaction event but is used as a corrective device for interactions that somehow get out of hand. As a defense against an individual who becomes threatening or angry, one may attempt to cut off anger through acquiescence. This involves casting oneself in a lower status position than one deserves, in terms of both linguistic style and action. Simply not answering someone's accusation effectively serves as a self-lowering device, and it also cuts off further charges and actions by the other party. This entire process is known in Persian as *kutah amædæn*. By practicing

self-lowering along with other-raising in this situation, one relieves
oneself of the responsibility for whatever is making the other person
angry, by "virtue" of inferiority.

An excellent example of this process is pointed out by Browne in
his wonderful travel account, *A Year amongst the Persians*. He recounts
a scene between a learned sheykh and a cobbler, who is attempting
to read a religious text aloud with rather poor results:

> Sheykh Ebrahim bore with this reading or rather chanting as long as
> he could, gulping down his rage and his 'arak together till finally one
> or both of these proved too much for him, and he suddenly turned
> ferociously on the unsuspecting cobbler.
>
> "Beast and idiot!" he cried, "cannot you be silent when there are
> men present and let them talk without interrupting them with your
> abominable gabbling? . . . in every word of Arabic you read you violate
> a rule of grammar. . . .
>
> The poor cobbler was utterly taken aback by this unexpected sally.
> "Forgive me, O Sheykh!" he began. "I am only a poor ignorant
> man. . . ."
>
> "Man!" cried the Sheykh, waxing more and more wroth; "I spit[5] on
> the pates of the father and mother of the dog-mamma! Man, forsooth!
> You are like those maggots which thrust forth their heads from rotten
> fruit and wave them in the air under the impression that they are men.
> I count you not as belonging to the world of humanity!"
>
> "O Sheykh!" exclaimed the poor cobbler. "Whatever you may please
> to say is right. I have eaten dirt.[6] I have committed a fault! I am the
> least of your servants!"
>
> "But I will not accept you are my servant," shouted the Sheykh;
> "you are not in my world at all. I take no cognizance of your ex-
> istence." And so he stormed on, till the wretched cobbler, now re-
> duced to tears, grovelled at his feet, begging for enlightenment and
> instruction, and saying, "You are a great and wise man; your knowl-
> edge is far beyond ours; . . . Tell me what to think, and what to
> believe, and what to do, and I will accept it." Finally the Sheykh was
> appeased, and they embraced and made up their quarrel. (Browne
> 1893: 576–77)

The routine of *kutah amædæn* has many similarities with *xær kærdæn*
in that it involves not only stylistic devices but also content that refers
to the ethics of the status relationship that the person who is under-
taking the routine is attempting to invoke. The sheykh in Browne's
interchange is likewise reinforcing the disparity in status positions in
expressing his anger. Notice that the cobbler in reply does not even
attempt to refute the sheykh's charges, but only speaks of their relative
difference in status and authority.

Yet a third strategy in language involves the use of linguistic style in such a way that a true status inferior becomes situationally raised in status. This sort of routine is rare, because it does not have very much to recommend it in terms of strategic advantage for the higher-status person. It is occasionally practiced in order to engage in collusion with someone who could potentially cause one trouble. In this case, the ethic that is actually invoked is the obligation obtaining between intimate status equals.

Occasionally, raising of a lower-status individual is done by mistake or by a lapse in maintenance of one's own social position. Iranians themselves try and guard against unwarranted departures from what they perceive as proper relative status positions, but many a foreigner teaching in Iran has been chagrined to learn what chaos can be caused by trying to treat students or servants as status equals in linguistic and behavioral routines: the teacher is immediately unable to secure their respect and obedience or assert his or her authority. Whether done on purpose or by mistake, the Persian gloss for this operation is *ru dadæn* (lit. to give face). With *ru dadæn*, as with the other management strategies cited here, the message content of the interaction events refers to the relationship obtaining between status equals in allusion to activities that status equals engage in together: eating, drinking, collusion, sitting in each other's presence without permission, and so forth.

The routines cited here do not represent by any means the total set of verbal strategies that Iranians may use in interactional routines to persuade or convince other people to do something or to adopt a particular position. The process of *partibazi*, based on invoking the language and ethics of *sæmimiæt*, has been described above at some length; it is the basis for endless linguistic interactional routines that fuse elements of style with messages that refer to and reinforce the status relationships being invoked by the verbal style.

Message management routines such as these are the integrated incorporation of elements of stylistic variation in verbal language into ongoing schemes of action. They represent a finished canvas on which the speaker has attempted to create meaning in the course of interaction—meaning that has definite and directed consequences for interaction participants. That which the speaker has produced is a creation—one that he or she hopes will convey an intention, be appropriate, and be effective in the conduct of his or her social life.

VIII

CONCLUSION

THE AESTHETICS OF
IRANIAN VERBAL INTERACTION

Speaker Skills—A Review

It is my hope that the present study has been able to present an account of how speakers of Persian manipulate stylistic dimensions of their language in order to affect interpretations of the ordinary contextual parameters of everyday interaction. In this I have staked out three broad positions:

1. What is eventually perceived as meaning in conversational interaction is the result of a negotiated social process.

2. A good deal of what is perceived to constitute the meaning of utterances in interaction does not result through processes of reference, truth-value testing, or other formal logical process, but rather through manipulation of patterns of stylistic variation within language.

3. Definitive meanings arise for language elements to a large extent as a function of their role in defining the contexts in which they occur.

The descriptive focus of this study has centered on stylistic variation. However, rather than describing variation in terms of contrasts of features within a paradigm, I have chosen to focus on contrasts in conditions for the use of variable elements. The term "conditions for use" has been defined in terms of symbolic structures within Iranian culture rather than in functional or other terms. Thus, the symbolic dimensions of the event as "internal" versus "external," or the definition of individuals in social interaction as "equals" or "nonequals," all defined in Iranian symbolic cultural terms, have taken precedence over definitions external to Iranian cultural sensibility.

This indicates a definite bias in the study toward a phenomenological approach to the formulation of conditions for use in the parameters for variation dealt with above. Such an approach requires a deep understanding of the principles of communication and interaction in Iran which override and encompass the linguistic behavior of specific interaction events.

Functionally, I posited in Chapter 1 that two tendencies were constantly operating in interaction that implied specific speaker skills. One, *appropriateness*, consisted in perceiving expected predictable behavior in interaction and monitoring one's behavior to conform to expectations. The aim of appropriateness skills is to preserve intact the nature of the context of interaction. The second tendency *effectiveness*, consists of skillful maneuvering away from expected, predictable behavior in interaction in ways that serve to redefine the context and hence the effect of interaction.

Throughout the course of this study, examples of both functions have been numerous, from the adjustment of one's pronunciation of consonant clusters and use of proper pronouns as an *appropriate* response to interaction context, to the deliberate use of pronouns and verb forms associated with other than expected status for the *effective* purposes of humor, insult, flattery, or manipulation. One other dimension must be given a final mention, however; this is the dimension of *aesthetics* in the use of speech in interaction and other contexts.

The Bases of Aesthetics in Interaction

In Iran, passing through the territory of interaction successfully is positively valued as a social skill, as I have maintained throughout this study. This being the case, the skillful, efficient use of verbal devices to navigate through that territory constitutes an art that can be appreciated over and above any actual instance of speech usage. In this way, one can easily identify and appreciate the rather weighty *aesthetic* component that adheres in the language of interaction.

Aesthetic sensitivity has rarely been seen as a component of communicational skills, yet this may be one of the central principles in speaker self-orientation. Even judgments of grammaticality in sentences look very much like aesthetic judgments. Indeed, there may be little difference between judging the well-formedness of sentences and the well-formedness of a dancer's moves or of a sculptor's lines. In the case of face-to-face communication, the forms of language can be seen as bearing a relationship to the interaction they are intended to negotiate but remaining independent and free to be well-formed and ill-formed as they may.

The skill needed for the use of language as a navigation device in interaction is subject to aesthetic evaluation in two senses. In an abstract sense, the physical and mental skills needed to use language are appreciated apart from actual use in life. Indeed, tests may be set up that single out and evaluate these skills separately, as in formal debating or oratory contests. The use of language in real life is another art altogether, and it may involve irregular usage in order to achieve success.

The aesthetic principles of speaking constitute the basis for the intersubjective creation of understood meaning on the part of parties in interaction. The interactional terrain is never entirely clearly viewed, because it involves a combination of appropriateness and effectiveness criteria that cannot be assumed to be the same for all parties in interaction. Rough communality of aesthetic judgment about form and configuration of form creates a kind of "overlay" against which the nature of the reality of the interactional terrain can be negotiated by all parties.

The shapes of linguistic variational forms in a given interaction rarely suggest a neat, even, checkerboard distribution of contrasts. As DeCamp states, "The speaker does not monitor his own frequencies and think 'Hm! The atmosphere is getting very formal since the professor entered the room. I'd better increase my frequency of phrase-initial *whom* from five to fifteen percent.' Rather he faces a complex set of discrete decisions (to *ain't* or not to *ain't*), and a set of implicational consequences of those decisions, equally complex . . ." (DeCamp 1970b: 7). When we realize that the final interaction is the result of the dynamic interworking of all speakers making these kinds of decisions, involving different degrees of application of appropriateness and effectiveness skills, we see how each individual interaction manifests itself in a unique configurational shape.

If parties in interaction cannot know what each other's motives, feelings, and goals are, they can at least agree on the relativity of abstract positions of individual items of communicative behavior to each other, and, using these positions as bench marks, account for themselves in terms of them. Thus, it is not surprising that a good deal of interactional behavior consists of continual messages about the state of the interaction itself. One example treated at length in Chapter 7 is that of interaction junctures. Junctures in Iranian verbal interaction are marked by forms that continually serve to inform persons that "the interaction we are now engaged in is being carried on under the same (or different) conditions from when we started." If the interaction conditions have changed, the new juncture form signals the direction in which it has changed, the nature of the direction being determined by general interaction criteria.

One can say that Persian is a language whose variational structures facilitate making oneself understood as an Iranian. This is perhaps the principal basis for the aesthetics of Iranian speech. There is something quintessentially beautiful and satisfying in a polished linguistic routine, even when it disguises a less than noble purpose, such as in the routine of *xær kærdæn*, described at length above.

The routine can be thought of as mere flattery, but it is far more than that. Its aesthetic component is independent of the verbal machinations that tease the person being flattered into taking on the duties of a person of greater status. An instance of *xær kærdæn* must meet standards to the point that the communicative behavior is comprehensible. From there it may be grammatical or ungrammatical, elegant or crude, and this variation may not affect its effectiveness as a verbal routine nor diminish its overall aesthetic quality.

A routine such as *xær kærdæn* achieves its effectiveness through the exploitation of ambiguity in participants' perception of factors entering into interaction events. A person cannot, after all, fall victim to the insincere flattery in such an event without coming to the situation with a penchant for believing that it might be true. The flatterer must play on that belief, matching his language with its shape and strength. This is no small accomplishment.

Notes on the Aesthetics of Iranian Humor

The same words and intonation that are used in a routine of *xær kærdæn* can be used for the production of humor as well, provided that all parties involved are sure—and are sure that others are sure—that appropriateness conventions are being violated for the purpose of humor. This is to say, a paradox is being created through the attempt to impose a proposition contrary to that which is clearly "known" in a given situation. The "victim" pretends to be susceptible to the flattery, though he or she is not, and all know it. This factor creates the effectiveness of the humorous routine.

Aesthetic principles of interaction are the basis for many other forms of humor as well. As mentioned in Chapter 6, the mixing of one variant of linguistic form in one lexical area, such as a pronoun reference, with a variant form from another lexical area, such as verb

usage, can be humorous when the two imply different appropriateness
conventions. This device is used especially effectively in traditional
Iranian comic improvisatory theater (Beeman 1981a, 1981b, 1982).
The principal figure in these theatrical performances, which are carried out primarily at Iranian village wedding ceremonies, is a black-
faced clown. The clown is nearly always in the role of a servant,
although this is not a fixed requirement. Typically, he finds himself
in interaction with some authority figure: the master of the house,
usually an elderly *hæjji*;[1] the mistress of the house; a king, minister,
or member of court.

In these interactions, the clown regularly distorts the pattern of
"appropriate" linguistic and social action, but not in a way that rep-
licates the normal "effective" routines of Persian. In fact, the linguistic
interaction taking place during these humorous performances may
actually take place on three levels. There may be a villain, who uses
all of the tricks and wiles of "effective" speech, a set of reputable
characters, including the *hæjji*, who use "appropriate" speech, and the
clown, who distorts *both* kinds of speech in his interactions. To cite
an example from a typical play:

Vizier: (instructing the clown) *Begid: tæshrif bebærid in tæræf.*
         "Say: Please bring your presence to this side."
Clown: *Akhe, nemitonæm! Sængin-e dige!*
         "Ow, I can't! It's too heavy!"
Vizier: *Che hæst, sangin mibašæd?*
         "What is that, that would be too heavy?"
Clown: *Tæskiš, dige!Ranændegi-æm bælæd nissæm.*
         "His taxi, of course! And I don't drive either!"

In the above interchange, the vizier speaks in language appropriate
for high-status persons in highly "external" (Pole A) situations. The
clown uses language appropriate for intimate equals and the phonology of "internal" (Pole B) situations [*nissæm* for *nistæm* (I'm not, I
don't), etc.]. He further confuses the word *tæšrif* (one's presence) with
tæksi (taxi) and gives the latter a common rural-bumpkin pronunciation, *tæski*, which with the third person singular possessive ending
becomes *tæskiš*. All of this garbling makes the obsequious language of
the vizier look completely ridiculous, even as it is ridiculous itself.

The clown's humor involves a paradox. He is thwarting the system
of social and linguistic hierarchy and yet getting away with the act.
Part of his ability to do this lies in his ability to establish himself as an

individual who is totally outside the normal system of social interaction. He dresses in an outlandish way; his black face marks him as a para- or extra-normal being. His movements on stage are wild and abnormal, and his speech, as mentioned above, is not just the opposite of appropriate speech (which might be labeled rude or impolite) or the opposite of effective speech (which might be labeled crude or clumsy) but is totally outside both systems—a true antistructural statement.

By existing totally apart from normal language use, the clown allows the audience to distance itself from the structure of normal speech interaction and laugh at its conventions and mechanisms. The clown, of course, exposes far more than just the linguistic system—his mockery extends to the entire set of Iranian cultural structures underlying linguistic usage. This is the key to the aesthetics of his humor. In order to create satire, one must know the original system very well indeed. The mockery as antistructure in its mirroring of structure shows an extraordinary elegance in use—a highly developed aesthetic.

The Aesthetics of Revolutionary Rhetoric

The black-faced clown demonstrates how the structures of language can be used to generate antistructural statements of high aesthetic quality. As a final example of aesthetics in language use, I turn to the rhetoric of the Iranian revolution of 1978–1979. The argument that follows is treated at greater length in another essay (Beeman 1983), but I present a brief summary here as a counter to the example of the clown above. If the clown uses the structures of language to mock the system, the revolutionary leaders of Iran can be seen to have used those same structures to generate a reinforcement of the cultural system. Their rhetorical statement was so strong that it was eventually able to topple the regime of the shah, which could not demonstrate to the public that it was able to measure up to the high standards demanded by that cultural system, as powerfully defined by the revolutionary clergy.

The Iranian Revolution of 1978–1979, resulting in the deposition of the Pahlavi regime and its replacement by clerical leaders of the Islamic Republic of Iran, was not so much a struggle for power, governmental control, or even morality as it was a struggle for definition of the context of Iranian culture. The principal battleground in the revolution was the clerical pulpit. The words of the men there inspired the demonstrations in the streets of the cities of the nation that eventually brought down the existing government. Though death also came in dramatic ways to revolutionaries, they were inspired to their martyrdom by men with the powerful ability to alter their most basic notions about themselves and their roles as citizens of Iran.

There is no question that the causes of the revolution were rooted in very real economic and political problems facing the Iranian nation (cf. Beeman 1982: 151–203, 1983; Keddie 1981a, 1981b; Rubin 1980), but these problems were brought home to the public as far more than questions of money and power. They were transformed into symbolic issues of profound depth through the rhetoric of the clergy.

The rhetoric of the revolutionary leaders was powerful because it dealt with the core symbolic issues of Iranian civilization as described throughout this study—the internal versus the external, hierarchy versus equality. The Pahlavi regime and even some of the nationalist intellectuals that replaced the Pahlavis in the first government following their deposition were insensitive to these issues, and they spoke to Iranian citizens in terms of an alien, largely western set of categories—modern versus traditional, world power versus second-class nation, democracy versus dictatorship, to name a few. The rhetoric of the Islamic leaders struck deep in the hearts of Iranian citizens of all social classes—in many ways it was irresistible—because it dwelt on all that was meaningful in Iranian life.

In Chapter 4 I alluded to the fact that part of the power of the rhetoric of Ayatollah Ruhollah Khomeini derived from his ability to identify the cause of the revolution with the martyrdom of Imam Hosein. Imam Hosein represents the epitome of the pure, inner core of the *baten* for individuals. But Khomeini's skill elevated Hosein's struggle to the struggle of a nation to resist the forces of corruption from external sources. In this case, the principal external force was the United States, of which the shah was seen as an agent.

The implicit message for Iranians was that in casting out the shah, one also casts out one's own impurities. One purifies one's own life and eliminates corruption. Iranians are in fact excessively concerned about personal morality and personal purity, even in the midst of widespread corruption (cf. Bateson et al. 1977). The internal *baten* and external *zaher* are both seen as necessary and exerting an equal pull on men. Few can resist the pull of the external, though that is not the road to salvation and enlightenment.

Thus the rhetoric of the revolution served to draw attention to the fact that Iran itself was an internal *baten* cultural space that could only be purified through the clear exclusion of external *zaher* elements, like Western thinking, cultural values, and mores. The shah was re-defined as part of that external intrusion. Once this redefinition had been accomplished, his expulsion was assured.

The rhetoricians of the Revolution were able to redefine the Pahlavi regime in another way as well. The shah, as the nation's leader, was the supreme representative of the high-status individual in Iranian society. No one was higher than he. As was illustrated in several ex-amples in Chapter 3, he and his family not only gave orders, and received tribute and service, but they also were expected to provide favors and rewards and respond to petitions. As the highest-status persons in the land, they were to be obeyed, but they also were charged with the welfare of their citizens.

In Iran, where hierarchical relationships are accepted as a norm, there is no necessary stigma attached to being in an inferior position to another unless the position is undeserved or imposed on one against his will. For this reason, both parties in the relationship respect each other. Indeed, lack of respect for one another is enough to bring about a breach in the relationship. Contempt on the part of the su-perior or subordination on the part of the inferior will cause a rupture.

The question of relative status and the obligations of different social positions is of real importance in Shi'a religious doctrine and is tied to the notion of inner purity as well. Those who achieve positions of superiority among men should do so because of the superiority of their knowledge, understanding, and character. Those who attain their position dishonestly or through the use of brute force are illegitimate. Such persons may be likened to the Sunni caliphs who opposed the legitimate rule of Imam Hosein.

In the end, however, supreme authority comes from only God. This authority is transmitted to his representatives on earth. In Shi'a the-ology, this line of authority becomes invested in the Imamate; in tra-ditional Sunni doctrine, in the Caliphate. Anything that disturbs the legitimate exercise of authority can, by the exercise of religious doc-trine, be declared corrupt.

In Iranian *Ithna'æšæræ* (lit. twelve) Shi'ism, the twelfth Imam, Mahdi, is said to have gone into hiding; he will return at the end of the world to judge the sins of men. In the absence of the Imams, then, Shi'a theologians have argued since the seventeenth century that those in-dividuals who are wisest, purest, and most knowledgeable in the law of God should be the legitimate leaders of society.

The dramatic innovation of Ayatollah Ruhollah Khomeini was to suggest that in the absence of the Imam Mahdi, a so-called *velayæt-e fæqih* (regency of the chief jurisprudent) should be established to rule over men. It is a paradox within the Islamic Republic that most of the religious leaders who would be eligible for the title of *fæqih* reject Khomeini's innovation. Nevertheless, most would agree that it is at least the duty of religious leaders to admonish the people not to follow corrupt leaders or submit to corrupting forces. As superior individuals within the framework of Iranian society, they would be shirking both their religious and social duties to do less, for it would be tantamount to failing to protect and care for their legitimate followers.

My purpose is not to discuss the merits of the legal basis of the Islamic Republic, but rather to point out that the question raised by the leaders of the revolution is a question about the legitimization of hierarchical relationships in Iran. Nowhere is the basic notion of hierarchy challenged. The only serious question that is raised concerns the basis by which one may attain and maintain a superior position.

The rhetoric concerning the deposed shah centered exclusively on the failings of the shah's government to fulfill its role as superior leader in the Iranian social hierarchy. The much-touted economic development of the 1970s was painted as an exploitative relationship that made the wealthy wealthier and left the poor, who supported them, in worse poverty. Moreover, the regime was portrayed as corrupting public morality and working to eliminate Islam itself.

It is easy to see this as a largely materialistic picture of the greedy rich against the moral poor. This assessment of the rhetoric of the revolution is deceptive, however. The protests that toppled the Pahlavi regime touched every stratum of society in the end and spread throughout the nation. It touched something far deeper than a mere desire for a larger piece of Iran's wealth.

The principal result of the portrayal of the shah as an illegitimate leader was righteous indignation resulting from a sense of betrayal. The shah had betrayed his hierarchical role as a leader to his people by failing to protect their economic and spiritual interests, eventually resorting to violent attacks against them when no other mechanism existed. In violating the obligations of a superior, he relinquished all rights to the respect due to a person in that position. Just as in everyday interpersonal relationships, which can rupture in an instant of ill-faith, the shah lost his standing with the public very quickly.

The clerical leaders, who are masters of the art of rhetoric (cf. Beeman 1981a) and practiced at mobilizing the population to high expressions of emotional commitment, thus were able to construct a revolutionary cosmology that placed Khomeini and the clerical leaders both at the spiritual center—the legitimate internal *baten*—of the nation and at the pinnacle of a hierarchy of legitimate authority.

The shah and the United States, by contrast, were relegated to the vilest reaches of the corrupting, external *zaher*. In this position, at the nadir of the spiritual universe, they became deprived of any legitimate authority whatsoever. Indeed, the United States was directly addressed as "The Great Satan"—the great illegitimate corrupter—the antithesis of the legitimate Iranian cultural universe.

This rhetoric is a masterful example of effective communication in Iranian life. To be sure, the basis of a rhetoric that juxtaposed legitimate religious authority with illegitimate secular authority had been a feature of Iranian life for several centuries (cf. Beeman 1983; Fischer 1980: Chapter 6). Nevertheless, during the reign of the Pahlavis, direct open public criticism of the monarch had rarely been heard. Clerical rhetoric produced the changed conditions needed to promote the acceptance of its own truth. As it was promulgated in public speech, leaflets, cassette recordings, and secret radio broadcasts, the shah's government began to attack and suppress it. When the killing of unarmed women and youths began, the truth of the rhetoric was verified, and even those who were slow to accept it became convinced.

Once the rhetoric of the revolutionary symbolic world was accepted, there was no place at all for the shah. He was literally "defined out" of the Iranian cultural universe. This act was a tour de force of rhetoric in Iranian cultural history. As an example of the aesthetics of communication it is breathtaking. Whether one can accept the philosophy of the Shi'a religious revolutionaries or not, Ayatollah Ruhollah Khomeini remains one of the premier masters of communication of our age.

Language and Magic—A Final Note

In the first chapter of this work, I invoked the notion of language and magic as a way of speaking about the power of rhetoric to transform and shape reality. In the course of this discussion, I hope that I have been able to show that there is a great deal of this kind of magic operating in the symbolic use of variation in Iranian interaction. The use of pronouns and verbs transforms status and allows people to make social obligations incumbent on people who would never acquiesce to them without the use of this kind of language.

Likewise, great communicators, such as the black-faced clown in Iranian traditional comic theatre, who can turn the social universe on its head with a few words, or like Ayatollah Ruhollah Khomeini, who can turn the greatest powers in his cultural universe into devils and cast them out with his powerful imagery, are the wonders of our age. Their feats rank with the most astounding, mysterious events in history.

BIBLIOGRAPHY

Aberle, David
  1957 The Influence of Linguistics on Early Culture and Personality Theory. *In* Essays in the Science of Culture. Gertrude E. Dole and Robert Carneiro, eds. New York: Thomas Y. Crowell.
Abrahams, Roger
  1970 Positively Black. Englewood Cliffs, New Jersey: Prentice-Hall.
  1974 Black Talking on the Streets. *In* Explorations in the Ethnography of Speaking. Richard Bauman and Joel Sherzer, eds. Cambridge: Cambridge University Press.
Ajami, Isma'il
  1963 Sima-ye Beh Abad pas az Eslahat-e Arzi. Tehran: Institute for Social Studies and Research, Rural Research Group.
  1966 Khososiat-e Ijtema-i-ye Khanevadeh-ha-ye Do Rusta'i-ye Nemoune-ye Mashhad. Shiraz: Department of National Development, Pahlavi University.
  1969a Sheshdangi. Shiraz: Pahlavi University Press.
  1969b Social Classes, Family Demographic Characteristics and Mobility in Three Iranian Villages. Sociologia Ruralis 9:62−72.
Alberts, R. C.
  1963 Social Structure and Culture Change in an Iranian Village. Ph.D. Dissertation. Department of Anthropology, University of Wisconsin.
Altman, G. and A. Riška
  1966 Toward a Typology of Courtesy in Language. Anthropological Linguistics 8(1):1−10.
Apor, E.
  1970 Some Problems of Word Formation in Modern Persian. *In* Actes du Xᶜ Congrès International Des Linguistics, Volume IV:617−620. Bucharest: Editions de L'academie de La Republique Socialiste de Roumanie.
Arasteh, Reza
  1962 Educational and Social Awakening in Iran. Leiden: Brill.
  1964a Man and Society in Iran. Leiden: Brill.
  1964b The Struggle for Equality in Iran. Middle East Journal 18(2):189−205.
  1966 Comment on Barth's Review of Man and Society in Iran (letter). American Anthropologist 68(2):517−518.
Archer, William Kay and Forugh al-Zaman Minou-Archer
  1972 Some Observations Concerning Stylistics Amongst the Persians. *In* Current Trends in Stylistics. Braj B. Kachru and Herbert Stahlke, eds. Edmonton, Alberta, Canada: Linguistic Research.
Ashraf, Ahmad
  1966 An Evaluation of Land Reform. *In* Seminar on Evaluation of Directed Social Change. Nader Ashraf-Naderi, ed. Tehran: Institute for Social Studies and Research.
Austin, J. L.
  1962 How to Do Things with Words. New York: Oxford University Press.

Avery, Peter
    1965   Modern Iran. New York: Praeger.
Bach, Kent and Robert M. Harnish
    1979   Linguistic Communication and Speech Acts. Cambridge, Massachu-
           setts: MIT Press.
Bahar, Mohammed T.
    1955   Sabk Shenasi (Stylistics). Tehran: Chapkhane-ye Khod-Kar.
Bailey, Charles-James N.
    1973   Variation and Linguistic Theory. Arlington, Virginia: Center for
           Applied Linguistics.
Baldwin, George B.
    1963   The Foreign Educated Iranian: A Profile. Middle East Journal
           17(3):264–278.
    1967   Planning and Development in Iran. Baltimore: Johns Hopkins Press.
Bales, Robert F.
    1950   Interaction Process Analysis: A Method for the Study of Small Groups.
           Reading, Massachusetts: Addison-Wesley.
Banuazizi, Ali
    1977   Iranian National Character Studies: An Evaluation. *In* Psychological
           Dimensions of Near Eastern Studies. L. C. Brown and J. N. Itzkow-
           itz, eds. Princeton, New Jersey: Darwin Press.
Barth, Fredrick
    1961   Nomads of South Persia. Oslo: George Allen and Unwin and Uni-
           versity of Oslo Press.
Barthes, Roland
    1964   Elements de Semiologie. Paris: Editions du Seuil. Also translated as
           Elements of Semiology. New York: Hill and Wang, 1967.
Basso, Keith and Henry Selby, eds.
    1976   Meaning in Anthropology. Albuquerque: University of New Mexico
           Press.
Bateson, Catherine, et al.
    1977   Safa-yi Batin: A Study of the Interrelations of a Set of Iranian Ideal
           Character Types. *In* Psychological Dimensions of Near Eastern Stud-
           ies. L. C. Brown and J. N. Itzkowitz, eds. Princeton, New Jersey:
           Darwin Press.
Bateson, Gregory
    1936   Naven. Stanford, California: Stanford University Press.
    1956a A Theory of Play and Fantasy. Psychiatric Research Reports
           2:39–51.
    1956b The Message "This is Play." *In* Transactions of the Second Confer-
           ence on Group Processes, Josiah Macy Foundation. New York: Josiah
           Macy Foundation.
    1966   Information Codification and Metacommunication. *In* Communi-
           cation and Culture. Alfred G. Smith, ed. New York: Holt, Rinehart
           and Winston.
    1970   Form, Substance and Difference. Nineteenth Annual Alfred Kor-
           zybsky Memorial Lecture, Oceanic Institute: Contribution #65.
           Honolulu: Oceanic Institute.
    1972   Steps to an Ecology of Mind. San Francisco: Chandler.
Bateson, Gregory, Don D. Jackson, Jay Haley and John H. Weakland
    1956   Toward a Theory of Schizophrenia. Behavioral Science 1:251–264.
Bateson, Gregory, R. Birdwhistell, H. Brosin, O. F. Hockett and N. McQuown
    1958   The Life History of an Interview. Ms.

Bauman, Richard and Joel Sherzer, eds.
1974 Explorations in the Ethnography of Speaking. Cambridge: Cambridge University Press.
Bausani, Alessandro
1947 Di una Possibile Origine dell'Accentuazione sull'Ultime Sillaba in Persiano Moderno. Oriente Moderno 27 (4–6):123–130.
Bayne, E. A.
1968 Persian Kingship in Transition. New York: American Universities Field Staff.
Bazell, C. E.
1954 The Sememe. Litera 1:17–31.
Bean, Susan
1970 Two's Company, Three's a Crowd. American Anthropologist 72:562–564.
1978 Symbolic and Pragmatic Semantics: A Kannada System of Address. Chicago: University of Chicago Press.
Becker, Ernest
1968 The Structure of Evil: An Essay on the Unification of the Science of Man. New York: George Braziller.
Beeman, William O.
1968 The Village of Laz: An Anthropological Study of an Island Community in the Persian Gulf. Unpublished B.A. Thesis. Department of Anthropology, Wesleyan University, Middletown, Connecticut.
1971 Interaction Semantics: A Preliminary Approach to the Observational Study of Meaning. M.A. Thesis. Department of Anthropology, University of Chicago.
1976a Status, Style and Strategy in Iranian Interaction. Anthropological Linguistics 18(7):305–322.
1976b What is (Iranian) National Character? A Sociolinguistic Approach. Iranian Studies 9(1):22–48.
1977 The Hows and Whys of Persian Style: A Pragmatic Approach. In Studies in Language Variation. Ralph W. Fasold and Roger W. Shuy, eds. Washington: Georgetown University Press.
1979 Cultural Dimensions of Performance Conventions in Iranian Ta'ziyeh. In Ta'ziyeh: Ritual and Drama in Iran. Peter J. Chelkowski, ed. New York: New York University Press.
1980 Martyrdom vs. Intervention—The Cultural Logic Behind Iranian Resistance to American Military Threats. Leviathan, Fall 1980, 1–6.
1981a A Full Arena: The Development and Meaning of Popular Performance Traditions in Iran. In Modern Iran: The Dialectics of Continuity and Change. Michael Bonine and Nikki Keddie, eds. Albany: State University of New York Press.
1981b Why Do They Laugh? An Interactional Approach to Humor in Traditional Iranian Improvisatory Theater. Journal of American Folklore 94 (4):506–526.
1982 Culture, Performance and Communication in Iran. Tokyo: Institute for the Study of Languages and Cultures of Asia and Africa (ILCAA).
1983 Images of the Great Satan: Symbolic Representations of the United States in the Iranian Revolution. In Religion and Politics in Iran. Nikki R. Keddie, ed. New Haven, Connecticut: Yale University Press.
Beeman, William O. and Amit Bhattacharyya
1978 Toward an Assessment of the Social Role of Rural Midwives and its

Implication for the Family Planning Program: An Iranian Case Study. Human Organization 37(3):295–300.

Bellman, Beryl
1975   Village of Curers and Assassins. The Hague: Mouton.

Ben-Amos, Dan and Kenneth Goldstein
1975   Folklore: Performance and Communication. The Hague: Mouton.

Benes, Eduard and Josef Vachek, eds.
1971   Stilistik and Soziolinguistik. Berlin: List Verlag.

Bennett, Jonathan
1976   Linguistic Behavior. Cambridge: Cambridge University Press.

Berger, Peter L. and Thomas Luckmann
1966   The Social Construction of Reality. New York: Doubleday.

Bernstein, Basil
1960   Language and Social Class. British Journal of Sociology 11:271–276.
1961   Aspects of Language and Learning in the Genesis of Social Process. Journal of Child Psychology and Psychiatry 1:313–324.
1965   A Socio-linguistic Approach to Social Learning. *In* Penguin Survey of the Social Sciences. J. Gould, ed. London: Penguin.
1971a   Social Class, Language and Socialization. *In* Current Trends in Linguistics, Volume XII. A. S. Abramson, et al., associate eds. The Hague: Mouton.
1971b   Class, Codes and Control, Volume I. London: Routledge and Kegan Paul.
1972   Social Class, Language and Socialization. *In* Language and Social Context. Pier Paolo Giglioli, ed. Harmondsworth, England: Penguin.

Bickerton, Derek
1971   Inherent Variability and Variable Rules. Foundations of Language 7:457–492.
1972a   The Structure of Polylectal Grammars. *In* Sociolinguistics: Current Trends and Prospects. Roger Shuy, ed. Washington: Georgetown University Press.
1972b   The Structure of Polylectal Grammars. *In* Georgetown University Monograph Series on Languages and Linguistics, Monograph 25. Roger W. Shuy, ed. Washington: Georgetown University Press.
1973   Quantitative Versus Dynamic Paradigms: The Case of Montreal *que*. *In* New Ways of Analyzing Variation in English. Charles-James N. Bailey and Roger Shuy, eds. Washington: Georgetown University Press.

Bill, James
1969a   The Plasticity of Informal Politics: The Case of Iran. Paper prepared for the Conference on the Structure of Power in Islamic Iran, University of California, Los Angeles, June 26–28.
1969b   Class Analysis and the Dialectics of Modernization in the Middle East. Paper prepared for the Sixty-Fifth Annual Meeting of the American Political Science Association, New York, September 2–6.
1972   The Politics of Iran Groups, Classes and Modernization. Columbus, Ohio: Charles E. Merrill.

Binder, Leonard
1962   Iran: Political Development in a Changing Society. Los Angeles: University of California Press.

Birdwhistell, Ray
1960   Kinesics and Communication. *In* Explorations in Communication:

An Anthology. Edmund Carpenter and Marshall McLuhan, eds. Boston: Beacon.

1970   Kinesics and Context. Philadelphia: University of Pennsylvania Press.

Bloomfield, Leonard
1927   Literate and Illiterate Speech. American Speech 10:432–39.
1933   Language. New York: Holt, Rinehart and Winston.

Blount, Ben G.
1981   Sociolinguistic Theory in Anthropology. International Journal of the Sociology of Language 31:91–108.

Blount, Ben and Mary Sanchez, eds.
1975   Sociocultural Dimensions of Language Use. New York: Academic Press.

Blumer, Herbert
1969   Symbolic Interactionism: Perspective and Method. Englewood Cliffs, New Jersey: Prentice-Hall.

Boas, Franz
1911   Introduction to Handbook of American Indian Languages. Washington: Smithsonian Institution.

Borhanian, Khosro
1959   Die Gemeinde Hamidieh in Khuzistan. Doctoral Dissertation. Cologne, Germany: University of Cologne.

Boyle, John Andrew
1952   Notes on the Colloquial Language of Persia as Recorded in Certain Recent Writings. Bulletin of the School of Oriental and African Studies 14:451–462.
1966   Grammar of Modern Persian. Wiesbaden, West Germany: Otto Harrassowitz.

Braroe, Niels W.
1975   Indians and Whites. Palo Alto, California: Stanford University Press.

Bright, William
1960   Social Dialect and Language History. Current Anthropology I (5–6):424–425.
1966   Sociolinguistics—Proceedings of the UCLA Sociolinguistics Conference, 1964. The Hague: Mouton.

Brittan, Arthur
1973   Meanings and Situations. London: Routledge and Kegan Paul.

Brown, Roger and A. Gilman
1960   The Pronouns of Power and Solidarity. *In* Style in Language. T. A. Sebeok, ed. Cambridge, Massachusetts: MIT Press.

Brown, Roger and Margurete Ford
1961   Address in American English. Journal of Abnormal and Social Psychology 62:375–385.

Browne, Edward G.
1893   A Year amongst the Persians. London: A. and C. Black.
1906–1924   A Literary History of Persia. (4 volumes) Cambridge: Cambridge University Press.

Buchler, Justus, ed.
1955   Philosophical Writings of Peirce. New York: Dover.

Buckler, Ira R. and R. Freeze
1966   The Distinctive Features of Pronominal Systems. Anthropological Linguistics 8(8):17–29.

Carroll, John B., ed.
1956   Language, Thought and Reality: Selected Papers of Benjamin Lee Whorf. New York: Wiley.

Cedergren, Harriet and David Sankoff
  1974   Variable Rules: Performance as a Statistical Reflection of Compe-
         tence. Language 50:333–355.
Cerulli, Enrico
  1956   Origines et developpement de la classe moyenne en Iran. Inter-
         national Institute of Differing Civilizations, Twenty-Ninth Session,
         London.
Chelkowski, Peter
  1971   Dramatic and Literary Aspects of Ta'ziyeh-Khani—Iranian Passion
         Play. Review of National Literatures 2:121–138.
  1975   Ta'ziyeh: Indigenous Avant-Garde Theatre of Iran. Tehran: Festival
         of Arts Series.
  1980   Iran: Mourning Becomes Revolution. Asia May/June: 3(1):30–37.
Chelkowski, Peter, ed.
  1979   Ta'ziyeh: Ritual and Drama in Iran. New York: New York University
         Press.
Cherry, Colin
  1957   Human Communication. Cambridge, Massachusetts: MIT Press.
Chomsky, Noam
  1957   Syntactic Structures. The Hague: Mouton.
  1965   Aspects of the Theory of Syntax. Cambridge, Massachusetts: MIT Press.
Cicourel, Aaron
  1973   Cognitive Sociology. New York: Free Press.
Clemmer, Richard O.
  1968   German Pronominal Address. *In* Proceedings of the 1967 Annual
         Spring Meeting of the American Ethnological Society. Seattle: Uni-
         versity of Washington Press.
Crick, Malcolm
  1976   Explorations in Language and Meaning. New York: John Wiley and
         Sons.
Curzon, G. N.
  1892   Persia and the Persian Question. (2 volumes.) London: George Allen
         and Unwin.
Das, Sisir Kumar
  1968   Forms of Address and Terms of Reference in Bengali. Anthropo-
         logical Linguistics 10(4):19–31.
DeCamp, David
  1968   Toward a Generative Analysis of a Post-Creole Speech Continuum.
         Paper prepared for the Conference on Pidginization and Creoliza-
         tion of Languages, Mona, Jamaica, April.
  1969   Is a Sociolinguistic Theory Possible? Paper prepared for the Twen-
         tieth Annual Round-Table Meeting on Linguistics and Language
         Studies, Georgetown University, Washington.
  1970a Implicational Scales and Sociolinguistic Linearity. Latin American
         Research Review 3:25–46.
  1970b Is a Sociolinguistic Theory Possible? Monograph Series on Lan-
         guages and Linguistics 20:157–174.
  1971   Toward a Generative Analysis of a Post-Creole Speech Continuum.
         In Pidginization and Creolization of Languages. Dell Hymes, ed.
         Cambridge: Cambridge University Press.
  1973   What Do Implicational Scales Imply? *In* New Ways of Analyzing
         Variation in English. Charles-James N. Bailey and Roger Shuy, eds.
         Washington: Georgetown University Press.

Dewey, John
  1946 Peirce's Theory of Linguistic Signs, Thought and Meaning. The Journal of Philosophy 43:56–75.
Djamalzadeh, M. A.
  1951 An Outline of the Social and Economic Structure of Iran. International Labor Review 63:26–40.
Douglas, Mary
  1966 Purity and Danger: An Analysis of Concepts of Pollution and Taboo. London: Routledge.
  1968 The Social Control of Cognition: Some Factors in Joke Perception. Man 3(3):361–376.
  1970 Natural Symbols. London: Barrie and Rockliff, The Crescent Press.
  1975 Deciphering a Meal. *In* Implicit Meanings. London: Routledge.
Dumont, Louis
  1970 Homo Hierarchicus. Chicago: University of Chicago Press.
Duncan, Starkey
  1972 Some Signals and Rules for Taking Speaking Turns in Conversations. Journal of Personality and Social Psychology 23:283–292.
  1973a Interaction Units During Speaking Turns in Dyadic, Face-to-Face Conversations. Paper presented at the Ninth International Congress of Anthropological and Ethnological Sciences, Chicago, June.
  1973b Language, Paralanguage and Body Motion in the Structure of Conversations. Paper presented at the Ninth International Congress of Anthropological and Ethnological Sciences, Chicago, June.
Ervin-Tripp, Susan
  1969 Sociolinguistics. Advances in Experimental Social Psychology 4:91–165.
  1972 On Sociolinguistic Rules: Alternation and Co-Occurrence. *In* Directions in Sociolinguistics. John J. Gumperz and Dell Hymes, eds. New York: Holt, Rinehart and Winston.
Evans-Pritchard, E. E.
  1948 Nuer Modes of Address. The Uganda Journal 12:166–171.
Ferguson, Charles A.
  1957 Word Stress in Persian. Language 33(2):123–135.
  1959 Diglossia. Word 15:325–340.
Fillimore, Charles
  1966 Deictic Categories in the Semantics of Come. Foundations of Language 2:219–27.
  1968 The Case for Case. *In* Universals in Linguistic Theory. E. Bach and R. Harms, eds. New York: Holt, Rinehart and Winston.
  1970 Subjects, Speakers and Roles. Working Papers in Linguistics, Ohio State University Computer Information Science Research Center 4:31–63.
  1971a Santa Cruz Lectures on Deixis. Bloomington: Indiana University Linguistics Club.
  1971b Verbs of Judging: An Exercise in Semantic Description. *In* Studies in Linguistic Semantics. C. J. Fillmore and D. T. Langendoen, eds. New York: Holt, Rinehart and Winston.
  1972 A Grammarian Looks to Sociolinguistics. *In* Sociolinguistics: Current Trends and Prospects. Roger Shuy, ed. Washington: Georgetown University Press.
Firth, J. R.
  1968 Selected Papers of J. R. Firth 1952–59. London: Longmans.

Fischer, John L.
  1968   Social Influence in the Choice of a Linguistic Variant. Word
          14:47–56.
Fischer, Michael
  1973   Zoroastrian Iran between Myth and Praxis. Ph.D. Dissertation. De-
          partment of Anthropology, University of Chicago.
  1977   Persian Society: Transition and Strain. *In* Twentieth-Century Iran.
          H. Amirsadeghi and R. W. Ferrier, eds. London: Heinemann.
  1980   Iran: From Religious Dispute to Revolution. Cambridge, Massachu-
          setts: Harvard University Press.
Fisher, W. E., ed.
  1968   The Cambridge History of Iran, Volume I, The Land of Iran. Cam-
          bridge: Cambridge University Press.
Fishman, Joshua
  1968   Readings in the Sociology of Language. The Hague: Mouton.
  1972   The Sociology of Language. Rowley, Massachusetts: Newbury House.
Fought, John G.
  1972   Categories of Deictic Fields. Paper presented at the Seventieth An-
          nual Meeting of the American Anthropological Association, To-
          ronto, November.
Friedrich, Paul
  1963   An Evolutionary Sketch of Russian Kinship. *In* Symposium on Lan-
          guage and Culture. Proceedings of the 1962 Annual Meeting of the
          American Ethnological Society. Seattle: University of Washington
          Press.
  1966   Structural Implications of Russian Pronominal Usage. *In* Sociolin-
          guistics—Proceedings of the UCLA Sociolinguistics Conference 1964.
          William Bright, ed. The Hague: Mouton.
  1969   On the Meaning of the Tarascan Suffixes of Space. Memoir 23,
          International Journal of American Linguistics. Baltimore: Waverly
          Press.
  1971   Dialectical Variation in Tarascan Phonology. International Journal
          of American Linguistics 37(3):164–187.
  1972   Social Context and Semantic Feature: The Russian Pronominal Usage.
          In Directions in Sociolinguistics: The Ethnography of Communi-
          cation. John Gumperz and Dell Hymes, eds. New York: Holt,
          Rinehart and Winston.
  1979   The Lexical Symbol and Its Non-arbitrariness. *In* Language, Con-
          text and the Imagination: Essays by Paul Friedrich. Stanford, Cal-
          ifornia: Stanford University Press.
Gallie, W. B.
  1952   Peirce and Pragmatism. Harmondsworth, England: Pelican Books.
Garfinkel, Harold
  1967   Studies in Ethnomethodology. Englewood Cliffs, New Jersey:
          Prentice-Hall.
Gastil, Raymond D.
  1958a Iranian General Belief Modes as Found in Middle Class Shiraz. Ph.D.
          Thesis. Department of Sociology, Harvard University.
  1958b Middle Class Impediments to Iranian Modernization. Public Opin-
          ion Quarterly 22:325–329.
  1959   Language and Modernization: A Comparative Analysis of Persian
          and English Texts. Cambridge, Massachusetts: Center for Interna-
          tional Affairs, Harvard University (mimeo).

Geertz, Clifford
  1960   The Religion of Java. Glencoe, Illinois: The Free Press.
  1966   Religion as a Cultural System. *In* Anthropological Approaches to the Study of Religion. M. Banton, ed. London: Tavistock.
  1973   The Interpretation of Cultures. New York: Basic Books.
Goffman, Erving
  1953   Communication and Conduct in an Island Community. Unpublished Ph.D. Dissertation. Department of Sociology, University of Chicago.
  1959   The Presentation of Self in Everyday Life. New York: Doubleday Anchor Books.
  1961   Encounters: Two Studies in the Sociology of Interaction. Indianapolis: Bobbs-Merrill.
  1963a Behavior in Public Places. New York: The Free Press.
  1963b Stigma. Englewood Cliffs, New Jersey: Prentice-Hall.
  1964   The Neglected Situation. American Anthropologist 66 (6,2):133–136.
  1967   Interaction Ritual: Essays on Face-to-Face Behavior. Garden City, New York: Doubleday Anchor Books.
  1969   Strategic Interaction. Philadelphia: University of Pennsylvania Press.
  1974   Frame Analysis. Cambridge, Massachusetts: Harvard University Press.
Greenberg, Joseph A.
  1948   Linguistics and Ethnology. Southwestern Journal of Anthropology 40:140–148.
  1954   Concerning Inferences from Linguistic to Non-linguistic Data. *In* Language in Culture. Harry Hoijer, ed. Chicago: University of Chicago Press.
  1966   Language Universals. (Janua Linguarum, Series Minor, 59.) The Hague: Mouton.
Greenberg, Joseph, ed.
  1963   Universals in Language. Cambridge, Massachusetts: MIT Press.
Greimas, A. J.
  1966   Semantique Structurale. Paris: Larousse.
Gumperz, John J.
  1958   Dialect Differences and Social Stratification in a North Indian Village. American Anthropologist 60:668–682.
  1961   Speech Variation and the Study of Indian Civilization. American Anthropologist 63:976–988.
  1962   Types of Linguistic Communities. Anthropological Linguistics 4(1):28–40.
  1968   The Speech Community. *In* International Encyclopedia of the Social Sciences 9:381–386. New York: Macmillan and The Free Press.
  1970   Verbal Strategies in Multilingual Communication. *In* Report of the Twenty-First Annual Round Table Meeting on Linguistic and Language Studies. James E. Alatis, ed. Washington: Georgetown University Press.
  1982   Discourse Strategies. Cambridge: Cambridge University Press.
Gumperz, John J., ed.
  1982   Language and Social Identity. Cambridge: Cambridge University Press.
Gumperz, John J. and Dell Hymes, eds.
  1964   The Ethnography of Communication. American Anthropologist 66 (6,2).

1972   Directions in Sociolinguistics: The Ethnography of Communication.
       New York: Holt, Rinehart and Winston.
Gumperz, John J. and C. M. Naim
1960   Formal and Informal Standards in Hindi Regional Language Area.
       In Linguistic Diversity in South Asia. Charles A. Ferguson and John
       J. Gumperz, eds. Bloomington: Indiana University Research Center
       in Anthropology, Folklore and Linguistics Publication 13.
Haas, William S.
1946   Iran. New York: Columbia University Press.
Haim, Sulaiman
1954   Shorter Persian-English Dictionary. Tehran: Beroukhim.
Hall, Edward T.
1959   The Silent Language. New York: Doubleday.
1966   The Hidden Dimension. New York: Doubleday.
Halliday, Michael
1970   Functional Diversity in Language as Seen from a Consideration of
       Mood or Modality in English. Foundations of Language 6:322–61.
1973   Explorations in the Functions of Language. London: Arnold.
1978   Language as Social Semiotic: The Social Interpretation of Language
       and Meaning. London: Arnold.
Hambley, Gavin
1964   Attitudes and Aspirations of the Contemporary Iranian Intellectual.
       Journal of the Royal Central Asian Society 51(2):127–140.
Hamp, Eric. P.
1958   Stress Continuity in Iranian. Journal of the American Oriental So-
       ciety 78:115–118.
Hanessian, John
1963   Yosouf-Abad, An Iranian Village, Parts I–VI. American Universities
       Field Staff Report Service, Southwest Asia Series, Volume VII, Num-
       bers 1–6, Iran. New York: American Universities Field Staff.
Harrison, Bernard
1972   Meaning and Structure: An Essay in the Philosophy of Language.
       New York: Harper and Row.
Hayden, L. J.
1949   Living Standards in Rural Iran: A Case Study. Middle East Journal
       3:140–150.
Helmreich, Robert, Roger Bakeman and Larry Scherwitz
1973   The Study of Small Groups. *In* Annual Review of Psychology 24.
       Palo Alto, California: Annual Reviews.
Herman, Simon R.
1968   Explorations in the Social Psychology of Language Choice. *In* Readings
       in the Sociology of Language. Joshua Fishman, ed. The Hague: Mouton.
Hillman, Michael
1981   Language and Social Distinctions in Iran. *In* Modern Iran: The
       Dialectics of Continuity and Change. Michael Bonine and Nikki
       Keddie, eds. Albany: State University of New York Press.
Hillman, Michael et al.
1972   Elementary Modern Persian. Tehran: U.S. Peace Corps.
Hjelmslev, Louis
1961   Prolegomena to a Theory of Language. Madison: University of Wis-
       consin Press.
Hockett, Charles. F.
1954   Chinese versus English: An Exploration of the Whorfian Thesis. *In*

Language in Culture. Harry Hoijer, ed. Chicago: University of Chicago Press.
    1958   A Course in Modern Linguistics. New York: Macmillan.
Hodge, Carleton
    1957   Some Aspects of Persian Style. Language 33(3):355–359.
    1960   Spoken Persian, Part I. Washington: Center for Applied Linguistics.
Hoijer, Harry
    1954   The Sapir-Whorf Hypothesis. *In* Language in Culture. Harry Hoijer, ed. Chicago: University of Chicago Press.
Hoijer, Harry, ed.
    1954   Language in Culture. Chicago: University of Chicago Press.
Hymes, Dell
    1959   On Typology of Cognitive Styles in Language (with Examples from Chinookan). Anthropological Linguistics 3:22–54.
    1962   The Ethnography of Speaking. *In* Anthropology and Human Behavior. Thomas Gladwin and William C. Sturtevant, eds. Washington: Anthropological Society of Washington.
    1964   Toward Ethnographies of Communication: The Analysis of Communicative Events. American Anthropologist 66 (6,2):12–25.
    1966   On Communicative Competence. Paper presented at Research Planning Conference on Language Development Among Disadvantaged Children, Yeshiva University, June 7–8.
    1972   Models of Interaction of Language and Social Life. *In* Directions in Sociolinguistics. John J. Gumperz and Dell Hymes, eds. New York: Holt, Rinehart and Winston.
    1974   Foundations in Sociolinguistics. Philadelphia: University of Pennsylvania Press.
Hymes, Dell, ed.
    1964   Language in Culture and Society. New York: Harper and Row.
    1972   Reinventing Anthropology. New York: Pantheon Books.
Irvine, Judith
    1974   Strategies of Status Manipulation in the Wolof Greeting. *In* Explorations in the Ethnography of Speaking. Richard Bauman and Joel Sherzer, eds. London: Cambridge University Press.
    1979   Formality and Informality in Communicative Events. American Anthropologist 81(4):773–790.
Ivanow, W.
    1931   Notes on the Phonology of Colloquial Persian. Islamica 4:576–595.
Jacobs, Norman
    1966   The Sociology of Development: Iran as an Asian Case Study. New York: Frederick A. Praeger.
Jakobson, Roman
    1932   Zur Struktur des Russischen Verbums. *In* Charisteria V. Mathesio oblata. Paris: Mouton.
    1939   Signe zero. *In* Melanges de linguistique, offerts à Charles Bally. Paris: Mouton.
    1957   Shifters, Verbal Categories and the Russian Verb. Cambridge, Massachusetts: Harvard University Russian Language Project.
    1960   Concluding Statement: Linguistics and Poetics. *In* Style in Language. Thomas Sebeok, ed. Cambridge, Massachusetts: MIT Press.
    1962   Selected Writings. The Hague: Mouton.
Jakobson, Roman and Morris Halle
    1956   Fundamentals of Language. The Hague: Mouton.

Jay, Robert
   1972   Personal and Extrapersonal Vision in Anthropology. *In* Reinventing Anthropology. Dell Hymes, ed. New York: Pantheon Books.
Jazayery, Mohammad Ali
   1966   Western Influence on Contemporary Persian: A General View. Bulletin of the School of Oriental Studies, Harvard University 29(1):79–96.
   1969   Persian Verbs Derivable from Other Parts of Speech. *In* American Oriental Society Middle West Branch, Semi-Centennial Volume, Asian Research Institute, Oriental Series #3. Denis Sinor, ed. Bloomington: Indiana University Press.
   1970   Observations on Stylistic Variation in Persian. *In* Actes du Xᵉ Congrès International des Linguistes, Volume IV: 447–547. Bucharest: Editions de L'Academie de la Republique Socialiste de Roumanie.
Jesperson, Otto
   1922   Language: Its Nature, Development and Origin. New York: W. W. Norton.
   1924   The Philosophy of Grammar. London: George Allen and Unwin.
Joos, Martin
   1959   The Isolation of Styles. Monograph Series on Languages and Linguistics (Georgetown University) 12:107–113.
   1962   The Five Clocks. Bloomington: Indiana University Research Center in Anthropology, Folklore and Linguistics Publication 22/International Journal of American Linguistics 28:2(V).
Jørgensen, Eli Fischer
   1952   On the Definition of Phoneme Categories on a Distributional Basis. Acta Linguistica 7:8–39.
Junker, Heinrich and Buzurg Alavi
   1957   Persisches Worterbuch. Leipzig: VEB Verlag Enzyklopadie.
Kantor, Jacob Robert
   1936   An Objective Psychology of Grammar. Bloomington: Indiana University Press.
Keddie, Nikki R.
   1963   Symbol and Sincerity in Islam. Studia Islamica 19:27–63.
   1972a   Sayyid Jamal ad-Din 'Al-Afghani: A Political Biography. Berkeley: University of California Press.
   1972b   Stratification, Social Control and Capitalism in Iranian Villages: Before and After Land Reform. *In* Rural Politics and Social Change in the Middle East. Richard Antoun and Iliya Harik, eds. Bloomington: Indiana University Press.
   1980   Iran: Religion, Politics and Society. London: Frank Cass.
   1981a   Religion, Society and Revolution in Modern Iran. *In* Modern Iran: The Dialectics of Continuity and Change. Michael Bonine and Nikki Keddie, eds. Albany: State University of New York Press.
   1981b   Roots of Revolution: An Interpretative History of Modern Iran. New Haven, Connecticut: Yale University Press.
Keddie, Nikki R., ed.
   1972   Scholars, Saints and Sufis. Berkeley: University of California Press.
   1983   Religion and Politics in Iran. New Haven, Connecticut: Yale University Press.
Kempson, Ruth
   1977   Semantic Theory. Cambridge: Cambridge University Press.

Khosrovi, Khosro
    1969   La reforme agraire et l'apparition d'une nouvelle classe en Iran.
           Etudes Rurales 34:122–126.
Khuri, Fuad
    1968   The Etiquette of Bargaining in the Middle East. American Anthro-
           pologist 70:698–706.
Kielstra, Nico
    n.d.   A Dialectical Model of Attitudes Toward Authority in a Persian Vil-
           lage. Ms.
Krámský, Jiři
    1939   A Study in the Phonology of Modern Persian. Archiv Orientalni
           11:66–83.
    1948   A Phonological Analysis of Persian Monosyllables. Archiv Orientalni
           16:103–134.
    1966   Some Remarks on the Problem of Quantity of Vowel Phonemes in
           Modern Persian. Archiv Orientalni 34:215–220.
Kucera, Henry
    1973   Language Variability, Rule Interdependency and the Grammar of
           Czech. Linguistic Inquiry 4:499–521.
Kuhn, Thomas
    1962   The Structure of Scientific Revolutions, International Encyclopedia
           of Unified Science, Volume VI, Number 2. Chicago: University of
           Chicago Press.
Labov, William
    1963   The Social Motivation of Sound Change. Word 19:273–309.
    1964   Phonological Correlates of Social Stratification. In The Ethnography
           of Communication. John J. Gumperz and Dell Hymes, eds. Amer-
           ican Anthropologist 66 (6,2):164–176.
    1965   On the Mechanism of Linguistic Change. Georgetown University
           Monographs on Languages and Linguistics 18:91–114. Washing-
           ton: Georgetown University Press.
    1966   The Social Stratification of English in New York City. Washington:
           Center for Applied Linguistics.
    1968   On the Mechanism of Linguistic Change. Georgetown University
           Monographs on Languages and Linguistics Number 18. Washing-
           ton: Georgetown University Press.
    1969   The Logic of Non-Standard English. In Report on the Twentieth
           Annual Round Table Meeting on Linguistics and Language Studies.
           James Alatis, ed. Washington: Georgetown University Press.
    1970   The Study of Language in its Social Context. Studium Generale
           23:66–84.
    1971   On the Adequacy of Natural Languages. Ms.
    1972   Sociolinguistic Patterns. Philadelphia: University of Pennsylvania
           Press.
    1973   Language in the Inner City. Philadelphia: University of Pennsylvania
           Press.
Ladefoged, Peter
    1974   Current Issues and Trends in Phonetics. Lecture delivered at Brown
           University, Providence, Rhode Island, February 11.
Lakoff, Robin
    1972   Language in Context. Language 48:907–927.
    1973   Language and Woman's Place. Language in Society 2:45–80.

Lambton, A. K. S.
  1953a Landlord and Peasant in Persia. Oxford: Oxford University Press.
  1953b Persian Grammar. Cambridge: Cambridge University Press.
  1963 Some Reflections on the Question of Rural Development and Land
         Reform in Iran. CENTO Symposium on Rural Development. Teh-
         ran: CENTO.
  1969 The Persian Land Reform, 1962–1966. Oxford: Clarendon Press/
         Oxford University Press.
Lazard, Gilbert
  1957 Grammaire du Persan Contemporain. Paris: Klincksieck.
  1970 Persian and Tajik. *In* Linguistics in South West Asia and North Africa
         (Volume VI of Thomas A. Sebeok, ed., Current Trends in Linguis-
         tics). Charles A. Ferguson, Carleton T. Hodge and Herbert R. Paper,
         eds. The Hague: Mouton.
Leach, Edmund R.
  1961 Rethinking Anthropology. London: The Athlone Press.
Lebra, Takie Sugiyama
  1976 Japanese Patterns of Behavior. Honolulu: University Press of Hawaii.
Lee, Dorothy
  1959 Freedom and Culture. Englewood Cliffs, New Jersey: Prentice-Hall.
Lee, Hong Bae
  1970 A Study of Korean Syntax: Performatives, Complementation, Ne-
         gation, Causation. Ph.D. Dissertation. Department of Linguistics,
         Brown University, Providence, Rhode Island.
Lefebvre, Henri
  1966 Le Langage et la Société. Paris: Gallimard.
Lentz, Wolfgang
  1958 Das Neupersische. *In* Handbuch der Orientalistik I, 4, Part 1. B.
         Spuler, ed. Leiden: Brill.
Levi-Strauss, Claude
  1963 Structural Anthropology. Tr. Claire Jacobson and Brooke Grundfest
         Schoepf. Garden City, New Jersey: Doubleday.
  1966 The Savage Mind. Chicago: University of Chicago Press.
Loeb, Laurence D.
  1969 Mechanisms of Rank Maintenance and Social Mobility Among Shi-
         razi Jews. Paper presented at the Sixty-Eighth Annual Meeting of
         the American Anthropological Association, New Orleans, November.
  1977 Outcaste: Jewish Life in Southern Iran. New York: Gordon and
         Breach.
Lucidi, M.
  1951 L'Accento nel Persiano Moderno. Ricerche Linguistiche 2:108–140.
McCawley, James
  1969 Semantic Representation. Paper prepared for Presentation of
         Wenner-Gren Symposium Cognitive Studies and Artificial Intelli-
         gence Research, Chicago, March 2–8.
McQuown, Norman A., ed.
  1971 The Natural History of an Interview. Microfilm Collection of Manu-
         scripts on Cultural Anthropology. Fifteenth Series. Chicago: Uni-
         versity of Chicago/Joseph Regenstein Library, Department of
         Photoduplication.
Malek, Hossein and Javad Safi-Nezhad
  1970 Vahed-ha-ye Andazeh Giri dar Roosta-ha-ye Iran. Tehran: Institute
         for Social Studies and Research.

Malinowski, Bronislaw
  1923   Appendix to C. K. Ogden and I. A. Richards, The Meaning of
         Meaning. New York: Harcourt, Brace.
  1935   Coral Gardens and Their Magic, Volume II, The Language of Magic
         and Gardening. New York: American Book Company.
Mandelbaum, David G., ed.
  1949   Selected Writings of Edward Sapir in Language, Culture and Per-
         sonality. Berkeley: University of California Press.
Manis, Jerome G. and Bernard N. Meltzer
  1967   Symbolic Interaction: A Reader in Social Psychology. Boston: Allyn
         and Bacon.
Manners, Robert and David Kaplan
  1968   Theory in Anthropology. Chicago: Aldine.
Marsden, David
  n.d.   A Moral Statement as Given by a Troupe of Players at a Village
         Wedding, Tarbour, Kushk-e-Mullah, Fars. Ms.
Martin, Samuel
  1958   Speech Levels and Social Structure in Japan and Korea. Paper read
         at Annual Meeting of the Asian Studies Association, New York City,
         April 1, 1958. Reprinted *In* Dell Hymes, ed., Language in Culture
         and Society. New York: Harper and Row, 1964.
Massé, Henri
  1954   Persian Beliefs and Customs. New Haven, Connecticut: Human Re-
         lations Area Files.
Mathiot, Madeline
  1962   Noun Classes and Folk Taxonomy in Papago. American Anthro-
         pologist 54(2):154–163.
  1968   An Approach to the Cognitive Study of Language. Bloomington:
         Indiana University Research Center in Anthropology, Folklore, and
         Linguistics Publication 45/International Journal of American Lin-
         guistics 34:1(II).
Matthews, W. K.
  1956   The Systematization of Persian Phonemes. Le Maître Phonetique
         3(5):2–6.
Maturana, Humberto
  1969   Neurophysiology of Cognition. Paper prepared for Wenner-Gren
         Symposium on Cognitive Studies and Artificial Intelligence Re-
         search, Chicago, March 2–8.
Mead, George Herbert
  1934   Mind, Self, and Society. Chicago: University of Chicago Press.
Mead, Margaret
  1962   National Character. *In* Anthropology Today. Sol Tax, ed. Chicago:
         University of Chicago Press.
Miller, William Green
  1964   Hosseinabad: A Persian Village. Middle East Journal 18(4):493–
         498.
  1969   Political Organization in Iran: From Dowreh to Political Party. Mid-
         dle East Journal 23 (Spring/Summer):159–167, 343–350.
Mills, C. Wright
  1964   Sociology and Pragmatism. New York: Paine-Whitman.
Millspaugh, Arthur C.
  1925   The American Task in Persia. New York: Century.
  1946   Americans in Persia. Washington: Brookings Institution.

Milner, G. B.
  1961 The Samoan Vocabulary of Respect. Journal of the Royal Asian
         Society 91:296–317.
Mitchell, T. F.
  1957 The Language of Buying and Selling in Cyrenaica: A Situational
         Statement. Hesperis 44:31–71.
Modaressi-Tehrani, Yahya
  1978 A Sociolinguistic Analysis of Modern Persian. Ph.D. Dissertation.
         Department of Linguistics, University of Kansas.
Moerman, Michael
  1968 Being Lue: Uses and Abuses of Ethnic Identification. *In* June Helm,
         ed., Essays on the Problem of Tribe. Seattle: University of Wash-
         ington Press.
Morganstierne, Georg
  1923 Iranian Notes. Acta Orientalia 1:245–285.
Morier, J.
  1937 The Adventures of Hajji Baba of Isphahan. (London 1824.) New
         York: Random House.
Moyne, John and Guy Carden
  1974 Subject Reduplication of Persian. Linguistic Inquiry 5:205–249.
Naraghi, Ehsan
  1951 Elite ancienne et elite nouvelle dans l'Iran actual. Revue des Etudes
         Islamiques 25:69–80.
  1957 Les Classes Moyennes en Iran. Cahiers International de Sociologie
         22:215–232.
Natanson, Maurice
  1967 Introduction to the Collected Papers of Alfred Schutz. The Hague:
         Nijhoff.
Newton, John, et al.
  n.d. Ta'arof Expressions in Persian. Tehran: American Peace Corps.
Nezami-Nav, M. Assad
  1969 The Persian Political Elite. Ph.D. Dissertation. Department of So-
         ciology, University of Chicago.
Nida, Eugene A.
  1964 Toward a Science of Translation. Leiden: Brill.
Noorduyn, J.
  1963 Categories of Courtesy in Sundanese. Bible Translator 14(4):1–2.
Nyberg, H. S.
  1939 Einige Bemerkungen zum Neupersischen Akzent. *In* Reichsturk-
         jische Lautstudien. Bjorn Collinder, ed. Wiesbaden, West Germany:
         Otto Harrassowitz.
Nye, Gertrude E.
  1955 The Phonemes and Morphemes of Modern Persian: A Descriptive
         Study. Ph.D. Dissertation. Department of Linguistics, University of
         Michigan.
Oblensky, Serge
  1963 Persian Basic Course. Washington: Foreign Service Institute.
Ogden, C. K. and I. A. Richards
  1923 The Meaning of Meaning. New York: Harcourt, Brace.
Ono, Morio
  n.d. On the Socio-Economic Structure of Iranian Villages. Ms.
Palmer, E. H.
  1924 A Concise Dictionary of the Persian Language. London: Blackwells.

Paper, Herbert and M. A. Jazayery
1955 The Writing System of Modern Persian. American Council of Learned Societies Publication Series B, Aids, Number 4. Ann Arbor: University of Michigan.

Peirce, Charles Sanders
1878 How to Make Our Ideas Clear. Popular Science Monthly (January): 286–302.
1955 The Philosophy of Peirce, Selected Writings. Justus Buchler, ed. London: Routledge and Kegan Paul.
1958 Values in a Universe of Chance: Selected Writings. Philip P. Wiener, ed. New York: Doubleday.

Peristiany, J., ed.
1966 Honor and Shame. Chicago: University of Chicago Press.
1968 Contributions to Mediterranean Sociology. Paris: Mouton.

Pike, Kenneth L.
1967 Language in Relation to a Unified Theory of Human Behavior. (Janua Linguarum, Series Maior, 24.) The Hague: Mouton.

Pittenger, Robert E., C. F. Hockett and J. J. Danehy
1960 The First Five Minutes: A Sample of Microscopic Interview Analysis. Ithaca, New York: Martineau.

Pourkarim, Hushang and Mohammed Hassen Sani'ad-Dowleh
1962 Fashandak be Zamineh-ye Joghrafiai-ye Taleghan. Tehran: Institute of Social Studies and Research, Publication #6.

Price, Henry H.
1953 Thinking and Experience. London: Hutchinson's University Library.

Prideaux, Gary D.
1970 The Syntax of Japanese Honorifics. The Hague: Mouton.

Quine, W. V.
1953 From a Logical Point of View. Cambridge, Massachusetts: Harvard University Press.
1960 Word and Object. Cambridge, Massachusetts: MIT Press.
1971 The Inscrutability of Reference. *In* Semantics: An Interdisciplinary Reader in Philosophy, Linguistics, and Psychology. Danny D. Steinberg and Leon A. Jakobovits, eds. Cambridge: Cambridge University Press.

Rahman, Fazlur
1968 Islam. New York: Doubleday Anchor.

Rastorgueva, V. S.
1964 A Short Sketch of the Grammar of Persian. International Journal of American Linguistics 30 (1,2).

Redard, Georges, ed.
1964 Indo-Iranica, Melanges presentes a Georg Morgenstierne a l'occasion de son sointe-dixieme anniversaire. Wiesbaden, West Germany: Otto Harrassowitz.

Redfield, Robert
1941 The Folk Culture of Yucatan. Chicago: University of Chicago Press.

Ritter, Helmut
1933 Philologika, VII: Arabische und Persische Schriften über die profane und die mystische Liebe. Der Islam 21:84–109.

Roberts, John M., et al.
1956 Zuni Daily Life. Lincoln: University of Nebraska Press.

Robinson, Ian
1975 The New Grammarians' Funeral. Cambridge: Cambridge University Press.

Robinson, W. P.
   1974   Language and Social Behavior. Harmondsworth, England: Penguin
          Books.
Rosenthal, F.
   1964   Gifts and Bribes: The Muslim View. Proceedings of The American
          Philosophical Society 108(2):135–144.
Ross, John R.
   1972   The Category Squish: Endstation Hauptwort. *In* Papers from the
          Eighth Regional Meeting of the Chicago Linguistic Society. Chicago:
          Chicago Linguistic Society.
   1973   Primacy. Ms.
   1974   World Order. Paper presented at Third Annual NWAVE Confer-
          ence, Georgetown University, Washington, October.
Roudolph-Touba, Jacqueline and William O. Beeman
   1971   Problems of Children and Youth in the Iranian Family: A Pilot Study
          in the Villages of the Kashan Desert Region. Tehran: Plan Orga-
          nization and the Institute of Social Studies and Research.
Rubin, Barry R.
   1980   Paved with Good Intentions: The American Experience and Iran.
          New York: Oxford University Press.
Ruesch, Jurgen and Gregory Bateson
   1951   Communication: The Social Matrix of Psychiatry. New York: W. W.
          Norton and Company.
Rypka, Jan
   1968   History of Iranian Literature. Dorerecht, Holland: D. Reidel.
Sacks, Harvey
   1970   Mimeographed lectures, §285.
   1974   An Analysis of the Course of a Joke's Telling in Conversation. *In*
          Explorations in the Ethnography of Speaking. Richard Bauman and
          Joel Sherzer, eds. Cambridge: Cambridge University Press.
Sa'edi, Gholamhossein
   1956   Dandil. Tehran.
   1963   Ilkhchi. Tehran: Institute for Social Studies and Research, Publi-
          cation #15.
   1965   Khiav ya Meshkin-Shahr. Tehran: Institute for Social Studies and
          Research, Publication #30.
   1966   Ahl-e Hava. Tehran: Institute for Social Studies and Research, Pub-
          lication #36.
Safi-Nezhad, Javad
   1966   Taleb-Abad. Tehran: Institute for Social Studies and Research, Pub-
          lication #38.
Sampson, Geoffrey
   1980   Making Sense. Oxford: Oxford University Press.
Sankoff, David, ed.
   1978   Linguistic Variation: Models and Methods. New York: Academic Press.
Sankoff, Gillian
   1973   Above and Beyond Phonology in Variable Rules. *In* New Ways of
          Analyzing Variation in English. Charles-James N. Bailey and Roger
          Shuy, eds. Washington: Georgetown University Press.
Sapir, Edward
   1921   Language. New York: Harcourt, Brace.
   1929   The Status of Linguistics as a Science. Language 5:207–214.

1931   The Function of an International Auxiliary Language. Psyche II
        (4):4–15.
1933   Language. *In* Encyclopedia of the Social Sciences, Volume II. New
        York: Macmillan.
1949   Selected Writings in Language, Culture, and Personality. D. G. Man-
        delbaum, ed. Berkeley: University of California Press.
Sapir, J. and Christopher Crocker, eds.
1977   The Social Use of Metaphor: Essays on the Anthropology of Rhet-
        oric. Philadelphia: University of Pennsylvania Press.
Sarles, Harvey
1966   The Dynamic Study of Interaction as Ethnoscientific Strategy. An-
        thropological Linguistics 8(8):66–70.
1970a   Facial Expression and Body Movement. *In* Current Trends in Lin-
        guistics, Volume XII. Thomas Sebeok, ed. The Hague: Mouton.
1970b   Communication and Ethology. *In* Anthropology and the Behavioral
        and Health Sciences. Otto von Mering and Leonard Kasdan, eds.
        Pittsburgh: University of Pittsburgh Press.
Saussure, Ferdinand de
1959   Course in General Linguistics. New York: Philosophical Library.
Schegloff, Emanuel
1968   Sequencing in Conversation Openings. American Anthropologist
        70(6):1075–1098.
1972   Notes on a Conversational Practice: On Formulating Place. *In* Stud-
        ies in Social Interaction. David N. Sudnow, ed. New York: Free Press.
Schmidt, Richard
1974   Sociostylistic Variation in Spoken Egyptian Arabic: A Re-examina-
        tion of the Concept of Diglossia. Ph.D. Dissertation. Department of
        Linguistics, Brown University, Providence, Rhode Island.
Schneider, David
1965   American Kin Terms and Terms for Kinsmen: A Critique of Good-
        enough's Componential Analysis of Yankee Kinship Terminology.
        American Anthropologist 67 (5,2):288–308.
1968a   American Kinship: A Cultural Account. Englewood Cliffs, New Jer-
        sey: Prentice-Hall.
1968b   What Should Be Included in a Vocabulary of Kinship Terms. Ms.
1969   Componential Analysis: A State of the Art Review. Paper prepared
        for Wenner-Gren Symposium on Cognitive Studies and Artificial
        Intelligence Research, Chicago, March 2–8.
1970   Kinship, Nationality and Religion in American Culture: Toward a
        Definition of Kinship. *In* Forms of Symbolic Action, Proceedings of
        the 1969 Annual Spring Meeting of the American Ethnological So-
        ciety. Seattle: University of Washington Press.
1976   Notes Toward a Theory of Culture. *In* Meaning in Anthropology.
        Keith H. Basso and Henry A. Selby, eds. Albuquerque: University
        of New Mexico Press.
Scholte, Bob
1970   Toward A Self-Reflective Anthropology: An Introduction with Some
        Examples. Paper presented to the ISA Research Committee on the
        Sociology of Knowledge, Seventh World Congress of Sociology, Varna,
        Bulgaria, September.
1972   Toward a Reflexive and Critical Anthropology. *In* Reinventing An-
        thropology. Dell Hymes, ed. New York: Pantheon Books.

Schutz, Alfred
 1967   Collected Papers I: The Problem of Social Reality. The Hague: Mar-
        tinus Nijhoff.
Scott, Charles T.
 1964   Syllable Structure in Tehran Persian. Anthropological Linguistics
        6(1):28–30.
Searle, John R.
 1969   Speech Acts. Cambridge: Cambridge University Press.
 1979   Expression and Meaning. Cambridge: Cambridge University Press.
Sebeok, Thomas A., ed.
 1960   Style in Language. Cambridge, Massachusetts: MIT Press.
 1964   Approaches to Semiotics. (Janua Linguarum, Series Maior, 15.) The
        Hague: Mouton.
 1966   Current Trends in Linguistics, Volume III, Theoretical Founda-
        tions. The Hague: Mouton.
Shaki, Mansour
 1957   The Problem of the Vowel Phonemes in the Persian Language. Ar-
        chiv Orientalni 25:45–55.
 1963   A Modern Persian Phrase Book. Prague: Statni pedagogicke
        nakladatelstvi.
Shands, Harley
 1968   Outline of a General Theory of Human Communication. Social
        Science Information 7(4):55–94.
Shuy, Roger, ed.
 1972   Sociolinguistics: Current Trends and Prospects. Washington:
        Georgetown University Press.
Silverstein, Michael
 1973   Linguistics and Anthropology. *In* Linguistics and Neighboring Dis-
        ciplines. R. Bartsch and T. Vennemann, eds. Leiden: North Holland
        (Linguistic Series Number 4).
 1976   Shifters, Linguistic Categories and Cultural Description. *In* Meaning
        in Anthropology. Keith H. Basso and Henry A. Selby, eds. Albu-
        querque: University of New Mexico Press.
Simmel, Georg
 1907   Philosophie des Geldes. Leipzig: Duncker and Humbolt.
 1950   The Sociology of Georg Simmel. Kurt Wolf, trans. and ed. Glencoe,
        Illinois: The Free Press.
Slobin, B. F.
 1963   Some Aspects of the Use of Pronouns of Address in Yiddish. Word
        19:193–202.
Smith, David M.
 1973   Speech Communities—A Framework for Viewing Human Inter-
        action. Ms.
Smith, Harvey H. et al.
 1971   Area Handbook for Iran. Washington: U.S. Government Printing
        Office.
Spooner, Brian
 1965a Arghiyan, the Area of Jayarm in Western Khorassan. Iran 3:97–
        108.
 1965b Kinship and Marriage in Eastern Persia. Sociologus Neue Folge
        15(1):22–31.
 1965c Religion in Iran. Iran 3:49–63.

1969a Notes on the Toponymy of the Persian Makran. *In* Iran and Islam
        (Memorial Volume to Vladimir Minorsky). C. E. Bosworth and
        J. Aubin, eds. Edinburgh: Edinburgh University Press.
1969b Politics, Kinship and Ecology in Southeast Persia. Ethnology
        8(2):139–152.
Spuler, B., ed.
1958 Handbuch der Orientalistik, I Abteilung, 4 Band, 1 Abschnitt,
        Iranistik-Linguistik. Leiden: Brill.
Steinberg, Danny and Leon A. Jakobvits, eds.
1971 Semantics: An Interdisciplinary Reader in Philosophy, Linguistics
        and Psychology. Cambridge: Cambridge University Press.
Steingor, B.
1949 The Development of a Measure of Social Interaction. Human Re-
        lations 2:103–122, 319–347.
Sturtevant, William C.
1964 Studies in Ethnoscience. *In* Transcultural Studies in Cognition. A. K.
        Romney and Roy G. D'Andrade, eds. American Anthropologist 66
        (3,2):99–131.
Sudnow, David N.
1972 Studies in Social Interaction. New York: Free Press.
Tahebaz, Sirous
1963 Yoush. Tehran: Institute for Social Studies and Research, Publica-
        tion #9.
Thaiss, Gustav
1971a Ideology and Social Changes in Iran. Paper presented at the Con-
        ference on Iranian Civilization and Culture, New York, December
        10–11.
1971b Networks from a Persian Market. Paper presented at the Seventieth
        Annual Meeting of the American Anthropological Association, New
        York, November 18–21.
Titiev, Mischa
1967 The Hopi Use of Kinship Terms for Expressing Socio-Cultural Val-
        ues. Anthropological Linguistics 9(5):44–49.
Trager, G. L.
1958 Paralanguage: A First Approximation. Studies in Linguistics
        13:1–12.
Traugott, Elizabeth
1973 Some Thoughts on Natural Syntactic Processes. *In* New Ways of
        Analyzing Variation in English. Charles-James N. Bailey and Roger W.
        Shuy, eds. Washington: Georgetown University Press.
Trudgill, Peter
1973 Phonological Rules and Sociolinguistic Variation in Norwich English.
        In New Ways of Analyzing Variation in English. Charles-James N.
        Bailey and Roger W. Shuy, eds. Washington: Georgetown University
        Press.
1974 Sociolinguistics. Harmondsworth, England: Penguin Books.
Turner, Victor
1967 The Forest of Symbols: Aspects of Ndembu Ritual. Ithaca, New
        York: Cornell University Press.
1969 The Ritual Process. Chicago: Aldine.
1974 Dramas, Fields and Metaphors. Ithaca, New York: Cornell Univer-
        sity Press.

Tyler, Stephen A.
    1969   Cognitive Anthropology. New York: Holt, Rinehart and Winston.
    1978   The Said and the Unsaid: Mind, Meaning and Culture. New York:
            Academic Press.
Ullman, Stephen
    1951   The Principles of Semantics. Glasgow: Jackson.
    1966   Language and Style: Collected Papers. New York: Barnes and Noble.
    1967   Semantics. Oxford: Basil Blackwell.
    1973   Meaning and Style: Collected Papers. Oxford: Blackwell.
Untereiner, W. C.
    1958   The Administrative Environment of Iran. Unpublished report. Los
            Angeles: University of Southern California School of Public Admin-
            istration (mimeo).
Upton, Joseph M.
    1961   The History of Modern Iran, an Interpretation. Harvard Middle
            East Monograph Series. Cambridge, Massachusetts: Harvard Center
            for Middle Eastern Studies.
Vahidian, Taqi
    1963   Dastur-e Zaban-e 'Amianeh-ye Farsi (Grammar of Colloquial Per-
            sian). Mashhad: Ketab Forushi-ye Bastan.
Veille, P.
    1966   Naissance, Mort, Sexe dans la Societe et la Culture Populaire en
            Iran. Tehran: Institute for Social Studies and Research (mimeo).
Vogelin, C. F. and F. M. Vogelin
    1965   Languages of the World: Indo-European, Fascile One, #10, Iranian.
            Anthropological Linguistics 7(8):190–218.
Vreeland, Herbert H. et al., eds.
    1957   Iran. New Haven, Connecticut: Human Relations Area Files.
Watson, J. and R. Potter
    1962   An Analytical Unit for the Study of Interaction. Human Relations
            15:245–263.
Watzlawick, Paul, Janet H. Beavin and Don D. Jackson
    1967   Pragmatics of Human Communication. New York: W. W. Norton.
Weinrich, Uriel, William Labov and Marvin I. Herzog
    1968   Empirical Foundations for a Theory of Language Change. *In* Di-
            rections for Historical Linguistics. W. P. Lehman and Yakov Malkiel,
            eds. Austin: University of Texas Press.
Westwood, Andrew F.
    1965   Politics of Distrust in Iran. Annals of the American Academy of
            Political and Social Sciences 358:123–135.
White, Leslie
    1940   The Symbol: Origin and Basis of Human Behavior. Philosophy of
            Science 7:451–463.
    1949   The Science of Culture. New York: Farrar, Straus and Cudahy.
    1973   The Concept of Culture. Minneapolis: Burgess.
Whorf, B. L.
    1956   Language, Thought and Reality: Selected Papers. New York: Wiley.
Wiener, P. P. and F. H. Young, eds.
    1952   Studies in the Philosophy of Charles S. Peirce. Cambridge, Massa-
            chusetts: Harvard University Press.
Wilber, Donald N.
    1955   Iran Past and Present. Princeton, New Jersey: Princeton University
            Press.

1963   Contemporary Iran. New York: Praeger.
1967   Language and Society: The Case of Iran. Behavior Science Notes 2:22–30.
Wilden, Anthony
1970   Epistemology and the Biosocial Crisis: The Difference That Makes a Difference. Ms.
Wilson, J. Christy, Jr.
1956   An Introduction to Colloquial Kaboli Persian. Monterey, California: Foreign Language Institute.
Windfuhr, Gernot L.
1979   Persian Grammar: History and State of its Study. The Hague: Mouton.
1981   Persian Grammar: History and State of its Study, Part I—Trends in Linguistics. State of the Arts Report #12. The Hague: Mouton.
Windfuhr, Gernot L., William Beeman, et al.
1979   Intermediate Persian, Volumes I and II. Ann Arbor: Department of Near Eastern Studies, University of Michigan.
Wolfram, Walter
1969   A Sociolinguistic Description of Detroit Negro Speech. Washington: Center for Applied Linguistics.
1973   On What Basis Variable Rules. *In* New Ways of Analyzing Variation in English. Charles-James N. Bailey and Roger Shuy, eds. Washington: Georgetown University Press.
Yarmohammadi, Lotfollah
1962   A Structural Analysis of Modern Persian. M.A. Thesis. Department of Linguistics, Indiana University.
Yar-Shater, Ehsan, ed.
1971   Iran Faces the Seventies. New York: Praeger.
Yngve, Victor
1969   On Achieving Agreement in Linguistics. *In* Papers from the Fifth Regional Meeting of the Chicago Linguistic Society. R. I. Binnick, et al., eds. Chicago: Department of Linguistics, University of Chicago.
1970   On Getting a Word in Edgewise. *In* Papers from the Sixth Regional Meeting of the Chicago Linguistic Society. Chicago: Chicago Linguistic Society.
1973   I Forget What I Was Going to Say. *In* Papers from the Ninth Regional Meeting of the Chicago Linguistic Society. C. Corum, et al., eds. Chicago: Chicago Linguistic Society.
1975   Human Linguistics and Face-to-Face Interaction. *In* Organization of Behavior in Face-to-Face Interaction. Adam Lendon, Richard M. Harris and Mary Ritchie Key, eds. The Hague: Mouton.
Zonis, Marvin
1971   The Political Elite of Iran. Princeton, New Jersey: Princeton University Press.

NOTES

Preface

1. This is not to deny the large body of data in other social science fields that treat this type of material. Among researchers with interests in this type of data are social psychologists working on problems of small-group interaction (see Helmreich et al. 1973); the symbolic interactionalist school in sociology and psychology (see Brittan 1973 for a concise and useful survey of the field); "ethnomethodologists," such as Douglas (1970), Garfinkel (1967), Erving Goffman (1953, 1959, 1961, 1963a, 1963b, 1967, 1971, 1972, 1974), Sacks (1970, 1974), and Sudnow (1972); and a few current researchers, such as Duncan (1972, 1973a, 1973b) and Yngve (1969, 1970, 1973, 1975), carrying out studies of videotaped interaction sequences. Strangely, early anthropological attempts at this kind of analysis (McQuown 1971) have been all but abandoned. None of this work at present assumes any cross-cultural perspective whatsoever, with the possible exception of Braroe (1975) and Goffman (1953). T. F. Mitchell's study of bazaar language in Cyrenaica is perhaps the most successful study thus far of the language of interaction in its cultural contextual framework (Mitchell 1957).

1. Introduction: The Architecture of Iranian Verbal Interaction

1. Such as "here," "in Toronto," "in back of you," "outside of the bank," "waiting for a bus," "in South America," and many more.

2. See for example, Moerman (1968), which demonstrates that ethnicity for the Lue of Thailand is a factor to be invoked in interaction whenever it serves a social purpose.

3. The importance of this interactional approach to the study of language has been given increased attention in recent years. Beeman (1971) attempted to establish some philosophical foundations for this study in an essay entitled *Interaction Semantics: A Preliminary Approach to the Observational Study of Meaning*, further elaborated in Beeman 1976a and 1976b, portions of which have been incorporated into the present study. A series of studies edited by Bauman and Sherzer (1974) and Blount and Sanchez (1975) show how interaction analysis and a consideration of language usage as performance are effectively used in field studies of sociolinguistic phenomena. Blount (1981), cited above in the main text, provides a particularly strong set of arguments in favor of interaction and performance analysis in the study of language. Malcolm Crick (1976) and Stephen Tyler (1978) have undertaken large-scale surveys of the ways meaning is used as a concept in anthropology, and Crick in particular is critical of the stasis of formal analysis. Philosophers Jonathan Bennett (1976) and Geoffrey Sampson (1980) emphasize the need to understand language in terms of its full function as expressive behavior, and Sampson particularly emphasizes the role of creativity. Ian Robinson (1975) turns many of these positions into a full-fledged attack against the linguistics of Noam Chomsky and the whole dominant school of language that has followed from his writings. Other collections of papers by Basso and Selby (1976), Ben-Amos and

Goldstein (1975) and Sapir and Crocker (1977) emphasize performative aspects of linguistics and the use of metaphor. Specific studies by Abrahams (1970, 1974), Bean (1978), Bellman (1975), and Irvine (1974, 1979) have perhaps come closest to describing how speakers of a language use that language to affect the parameters by which the meanings of their communication are interpreted.

4. Cf. Blount 1981: 104, whose thoughts I paraphrase here.

5. Silverstein makes this point in a slightly more limited way: "Adherence to the norms specified by rules of use reinforces the perceived social relations of speaker and hearer, violations constitute a powerful rebuff or insult, or go to the creation of irony and humor" (Silverstein 1976: 34–35).

6. Cf. Bach and Harnish (1979), who posit a set of illocutionary acts, in Austin and Searle's sense, which they term *effectives. Effectives* are illocutionary acts that effect changes in institutional states of affairs. *Verdictives* are judgments that bind the state of a given institution. My use of the term "effective" is much broader than this. In the sense that interaction contexts can be thought of as "institutions," the two usages overlap, but I mean to speak of effectiveness in communication as the ability to move between expected and unexpected communicational behaviors in order to bring about eventual fulfillment of a communicator's goals. In this sense, my use encompasses specific speech acts but is not limited to one type or usage.

7. This has led to interesting difficulties in communication between Japanese and Iranians. Japanese informants report that early encounters with Iranians are very successful, but Iranians prove to be "shifty" and "untrustworthy" in Japanese eyes over the long run. The difference between the qualitative stress laid on effectiveness as part of a successful repertoire of communication skills in Iran and the stress on appropriateness in Japan may lie at the base of this feeling.

8. The distinction between inside and outside is of course not unique to Iranian culture. It seems to have at least Pan-Asian distribution. Still, even though as a dimension of orientation it is widespread, its particular realization differs widely from culture to culture. The Iranian *zaher* and *baten* do not have the same cultural meaning they have in Indonesia (cf. Geertz 1960, 1966), and they differ considerably from the Japanese *hon-ne* and *tatemae*.

9. See Catherine Bateson et al. (1977) for an extended discussion of this concept in Iranian popular culture. Keddie (1963) offers a discussion of esoteric vs. exoteric aspects of Shi'a religious thought. Additional discussion on linguistic aspects is provided in Beeman (1977, 1982).

10. Friedrich's work, among many studies of pronoun usage, starting with the classic research of Brown and Gillman (1960), remains the richest in its texture and coverage of the field. Friedrich allows for the expression of individual emotion and affectivity, whereas many later formulations (cf. Ervin-Tripp 1969) try to reduce pronoun choice to a simple set of binary decisions or rule applications.

11. See Irvine (1979) for an extremely useful discussion of the use of the concept of "formality" in current anthropological linguistic theory.

2. The Management of Messages

1. This multiple *kædkhoda* situation was by no means uncommon in Fars province. In some villages, multiple ethnic factions (Turkish-speaking tribesmen recently settled, Turkish-speaking tribesmen long settled, indigenous Iranian-speaking villagers) would often all claim their own *kædkhoda*, each of

whom was recognized in some contexts and not in others. One case pointed out to me by a student at Pahlavi University involved five *kædkhodas* claimed by groups from the same village allied in cooperative pump ownership.

2. The distinction between inside (*baten*) and outside (*zaher*) as cognitive dimensions in Iranian social life is fundamental. Excellent analyses of this have been undertaken by Bateson et al. (1977) and Banuazizi (1977). I also treat this at length below.

3. As Lord Curzon noted about the Persians, "Accomplished manners and a more than Parisian polish cover a truly superb faculty for lying and almost scientific imposture" (Curzon 1892: 15).

4. Many Iranians do not realize that Hajji Baba is the creation of a foreigner.

5. The transliteration of the term represents contemporary Persian pronunciation.

6. The traditional woman's outer covering in Iran—a half circular piece of cloth that covers the woman's body from head to foot. Women who wear a *chador* are generally considered more respectable than those in modern dress in traditionally oriented sectors of society, a point made continually throughout the course of the Iranian revolution.

7. Translators have the same problem with a raft of similar words, such as "insecurity," "unreliability," "inconsiderateness," even "dishonesty," all of which one might expect to find represented in the vocabulary of a society beset and troubled by these manifest and pervasive attitudes.

8. See Archer and Archer (1972) for further views on the value of obscurity and multiple meaning in literature.

9. The Iran Center for Management Studies (ICMS).

3. The Management of Interactional Parameters: People

1. Indeed, the entire Iranian revolution of 1978–1979 was played out with a central theme of the glorification of martyrdom. See Beeman (1980) and Chelkowski (1980) for more on this topic.

2. Translated sometimes as *Parliament of the Birds*.

3. The mirror is not without significance in Iranian religious ceremony at weddings, in the New Year's celebration, and elsewhere (cf. Massé 1954).

4. Persons whose relationship to each other is one of inequality would seldom, if ever, engage in this kind of activity together.

5. This makes the function of the news media in Iran considerably different from that of news media in the United States or Western Europe. Newspapers in particular often serve more to convey public announcements than as active forces in the political process. The idea of a "scoop" in American terms is totally out of place in Iran, where to have a piece of information of consequence is to have a degree of power—one not to be diluted through publication for the world at large. There seems to be an idea on the part of the Western world that the press must serve the same functions in every society, and that if the leading daily in Tehran is not like the *Washington Post* or *Le Monde*, something is dreadfully wrong with Iranian society. This attitude smacks of a particularly ugly sort of ethnocentric arrogance—perpetuated, ironically, by the Western press corps itself.

6. I should note here that some *dowrehs* are more formally constituted than others. Zonis notes one group of powerful politicians who have been meeting for lunch for over twenty-five years (Zonis 1971: 233–239). Other groups that function as *dowrehs* are less permanent.

7. A merchant would, of course, pass on his increased wholesale cost, but he could not charge more for a scarce commodity solely because he knew he could get the higher price. He would then incur the indignant wrath of his customers.

8. As one news correspondent said about the former Shah and his cabinet, "He treats them like office boys, and they love it!" (*Time*, June 2, 1974).

9. See also Loeb's full-length monograph on the Jewish community in Shiraz (Loeb 1977).

10. Judith Irvine describes a remarkably similar set of strategic operations in an excellent paper on Wolof greetings (Irvine 1974).

11. Cf. Michael J. Fischer's superb study, *Iran: From Religious Dispute to Revolution* (Fischer, Michael, 1980), which contains an excellent treatment on the role of Shi'ism and Sufistic philosophy in everyday life.

4. The Marking of Parameters: Events

1. It is noteworthy that the meanings of the most mystical poetry are often couched in metaphors that play most heavily on the things of the external world: carnal love, wine, and sensual pleasures.

2. I use the term "myth" not because the event did not happen, but because the actual event has come to be embellished, expanded, and transformed into an all-pervasive symbolic expression of the central doctrines of the faith.

3. It is interesting here that music, which is forbidden in orthodox Islam, both Shi'a and Sunni, is a central feature in the various kinds of public activity occurring at Moharram. In the strictest religious sense, what is being performed is not "music," which in Persian is a term that excludes religious connotation, but "chanting."

4. It is common to invoke the story of the martyrdom of Hosein in sermons. In point of fact, there are professionals in almost every village who are not clergymen, but who come to a home on request specifically to recite the story; the occasion is a *rowzeh*, and the specialists are given the title *rowzeh-xvan*. Often these are persons who are unable to do other work by dint of infirmity. Thus to hire them constitutes religious charity on two counts.

5. The parallels between the Iranian schema for personal conduct and the regulation of emotion and that of the Javanese system as described by Geertz (1960) are difficult to ignore. As he writes:

> If one can calm one's most inward feelings (by being *trima*, *sabar*, and *iklas*) . . . one can build a wall around them; one will be able both to conceal them from others and to protect them from outside disturbance. The refinement of inner feelings has thus two aspects: the attempt to control one's emotions represented by *trima* (acceptance), *sabar* (patience), and *iklas* (detachment); and secondly, an external attempt to build a wall around them that will protect them. On the one hand, one engages in an inward discipline, and on the other in an outward defense. Mysticism is mainly training in the first. . . . Etiquette is training in the second. At the bottom, the refinement of the inner world—the *baten*—makes possible the refinement of the outer, which in turn protects one from being easily upset. (Geertz 1960: 241)

Though both systems have an Indo-European-cum-Islamic base, the parallels throughout both systems are startling, especially in the incidence of both strong mystic traditions and elaborate codes of etiquette. This leads me, at least, to speculate that common modes of orientation of the individual to society may be reflected in common institutionalized behavioral patterns.

6. Persian abounds in expressions that use *rou* (face) as a way of talking about matters of reputation, honor, or decorum. In a real sense, the "face" is external and visible, thus the perfect vehicle for speaking about such externally perceived matters as reputation (which is itself *aberou*, literally "water of the face").

7. *Por-rou'i*, when applied too freely in high-grid situations without the flanking of the courtesies and *tæ'arof* necessary in that context, is simply *bi-ædæb* (impolite). (See the last section of Chapter 4.) To be effective, it must be applied encapsulated in all of the social graces that are required for *zaher* situations.

8. This is true in the sense that no actual information is intended to be conveyed in speech, nor is novel, unexpected behavior being enacted. Both speech and behavior approach total predictability for the participants.

9. Goffman treats considerations of this sort in much greater detail, and with far more thoroughness, than can be accomplished in this brief account. He subdivides this sort of phenomena: "astounding phenomena," stunts, muffings, fortuitousness, and "tensions and joking" (Goffman 1974: 28–39). I am, as should be obvious, indebted to Goffman for this whole line of thinking.

10. This portion of the study was first presented in another form in 1977 (Beeman 1977). Subsequently, in an excellent dissertation, Yahya Modaressi-Tehrani (Modaressi-Tehrani 1978) has analyzed certain stylistic features of Persian according to contexts ranging from informal conversation to formal elicitation through reading of word lists and pronunciation of minimal pairs after Labov (1964, 1970, 1972). Modaressi-Tehrani basically supports the findings given in this chapter and in Chapters 5 and 6. The present study attempts to describe linguistic reality in Iranian cultural symbolic terms to the greatest extent possible; therefore I have tried to avoid using a non-Iranian definition of contextual variation—even to the point of eschewing words like "formal" and "informal," which I believe distort understanding of the real nature of the two poles. Nevertheless, Modaressi-Tehrani's findings show that when reading word lists and minimal pairs, informants produce a speech pattern close to the one that I have identified as occurring at Pole A. Informal conversation corresponds to language produced in Pole B situations. Modaressi-Tehrani further notes that the linguistic changes noted in "informal" style are more pronounced when informants are young, relatively uneducated, and male (Modaressi-Tehrani 1978: 132).

5. Persian Socio-Phonology

1. Hodge takes the position that stress is primary or weak and that primary stress has three allophones: secondary, tertiary, and loud. Ferguson, in his article on Persian stress, admits that two degrees of stress, primary and secondary, may be structurally significant, but says that for the purposes of his argument, only a distinction between stressed and unstressed syllables in Persian words need be made.

2. Yarmohammadi (1962) lists [w] and [y] as nonvocalic allophones of /u/ and /i/ on fairly supportable morphological grounds.

3. The existence of this variable is admittedly disputable. In such words as *vaqt* (time) there is probably *never* a realization *[vaqt]—the word is invariably pronounced [vaxt]. Other /qt/ combinations are rare.

4. (ṗ) indicates a weakly pronounced lablo-dental stop.

5. The case of certain verbs, such as *xᵛastan*, will be taken up in the following chapter. *Xᵛastan* in particular deletes /h/ in present tense forms with such regularity today that their inclusion is stylistically more remarkable than their exclusion. Thus, *mixam* (I want) is heard normally in interaction, whereas *mixaham* is encountered only in styles that Joos (1959) would term "frozen."

6. One would expect the full retention of /ˀ/ in *mæˀzeræt* in the more formal expression. In Gavaki, /ˀ/ was rarely used except for exaggerated effect. Its retention in urban speech was more regular.

7. The plural "suffix" /ha/ and the direct object particle /ra/ may be written attached to the word they modify or separately, but immediately following. In formal Persian, in fact, phrase internal juncture precedes them, and the division is neither as sharp as a word boundary nor as weak as syllable division. The status of these particles in informal Persian has been treated above.

8. In Persian these are called *zebar*, *zir*, and *pish*, respectively.

9. This may be true only for that set of Arabic forms used in Persian.

10. In fact, certain vocabulary items are stylistically and cognitively "marked" as being more Arabic, and it is these words that are used more in Style A. Many thousands of words have passed into Persian from Arabic, have become totally absorbed, and are no longer stylistically marked for this Arabic quality. This phenomenon lends support to the thesis, presented throughout this study, that conscious cognitive factors actively govern stylistic shifts.

11. Modaressi-Tehrani correctly points out that there are a number of cases in Persian where the Persian-based word is actually perceived as more "formal" (corresponding to Pole A situations) than the Arabic-based equivalent. He notes, "the words /amixtæn/ 'to mix', /gerami/ 'dear', /bastani/ 'ancient', and /hengam/ 'time' were judged (by 100 percent of the informants) to be more formal than their foreign synonyms (Arabic or Turkish), which were /qati-kærdæn/, /æziz/, /qædimi/, /moqˀ/[sic] (or /væqt/) respectively" (Modaressi-Tehrani 1978: 62). He also notes other cases where Persian and Arabic forms may have more than one "formal" stylistic equivalent, drawn from both Persian- and Arabic-based roots. This does not change the fact that there is a general *tendency* toward Arabicization in more Pole A situations, as I have claimed, but, along the lines suggested by Modaressi-Tehrani, this tendency should not be considered to be an absolute rule.

In light of this, it should be noted that further changes are underway as a result of the revolutionary events of 1978 and 1979, which produced a curious effect on this variable. Suddenly, to use more "Arabic" words and "Arabic" pronunciation was a sign of support for the revolution. Many persons unused to exercising this stylistic variable, but wanting to be properly revolutionary, came out with some very bizarre verbal production in the early days of Aya-tollah Khomeini's reign.

6. Persian Socio-Morphology

1. Contrasted with, for example, the complex Javanese stylistic system as outlined by Geertz (1960).

2. Persian does not make a gender distinction in third person pronominal reference. Note too, that the enclitic pronoun is unacceptable in the most formal contexts as the object of a verb. Normally, the sentence would read *ura zædæm* (I hit him, her, it).

3. A full discussion of tense and aspect in the Persian verb is beyond the scope of this discussion, although it is my belief that current interpretations are far from correct.

4. For instance, it has no negative.

5. A colloquialism in this case is a regular feature of speech that can be seen as an identifying mark of the language habits of a social group or subgroup. Unlike the sound shifts dealt with in this chapter, these features alternate with others only as the gross code of which they are a feature alternates with other gross codes, such as village speech alternating with urban speech. They are not normally available as linguistic strategies except as part of a total gross code switch, although they may have a tendency to be introduced particularly as context is perceived as less restricted, more group oriented, and more *ændærun*, i.e., Pole B situations outlined in the previous chapters and specifically excluded in Pole A situations. Thus, villagers from around Shiraz tend to eliminate regional colloquialisms from their speech in dealing with urban officials. Modaressi-Tehrani treats the final particle /-eš/ as an informal variant of the "formal" suffix /-æš/, noting that in formal styles the latter is used, whereas in informal styles the former is used. He too notes that /-eš/ is a redundant particle in the third person past singular (/rafteš/) "Since this is true only in spoken informal Persian, the informal variant [eš] is the only variant which is normally realized" (Modaressi-Tehrani 1978: 133). Indeed, of three variables that Modaressi-Tehrani deals with, mean realization of [-eš] as opposed to [-æš] was extremely high in informal conversation (90.7 percent mean), and among the entire population with only a high-school education or less (100 percent of informants with ten to twelve years of school—ibid.: 146). Since the present study is based primarily on conversational styles, the extreme formal variant [-æš] that was detected in Modaressi-Tehrani's word lists and minimal pairs is not dealt with in my paradigm.

The substitution of [u] for [a] before the nasals [m] and [n] is another feature treated as a variable by Modaressi-Tehrani, and indeed he suggests that the raising of [u] to [a] and [æ] to [e] in the suffix [æš]/[es] may be related phenomena in that (1) they both represent raising of a low vowel, (2) they are realized more by males than by females, and (3) they are predominant features of Tehrani Persian, found less in regional dialects (Modaressi-Tehrani treated the dialect of Qazvin in his study). He thus suggests that prenasal vowels and the possessive suffix may be prestige variants (Modaressi-Tehrani 1978: 155).

6. The distinction between the pluralizing particle /-an/ for animate objects and /-ha/ for inanimate objects is rapidly disappearing. Accordingly, the two demonstrative adjectives /inan/ and /anan/ are rarely encountered.

7. This is not to imply that status distinctions are not made in the English socio-linguistic usage. Such distinctions definitely exist, but they are not reflected strongly by means of lexical substitution within the verbal system.

8. John Perry also reports *šoma ræfti* as another intermediate form (personal communication).

9. In fact, the use of *u* in speech is quite infrequent.

10. A kind of appropriateness criterion different from the Iran situation is indicated in the nineteenth-century maxim "Women glow, men perspire, horses sweat."

11. A distinctly northern dialect feature that has spread as a result of Tehran's overwhelming importance in this century.

7. The Socio-Syntax of Iranian Interaction

1. These and other devices may be particular to specific cultural traditions. Certainly irony, puns, and topical humor require deep cultural knowledge to be appreciated.

2. Note that all second person singular endings are used in this passage, as well as Pole B sound deletions. The latter phenomenon is not totally explicable in this case without fuller knowledge of the persons in the room and the business being transacted. However, my impression was that the villager was never really "in" the communication event that included the others in the room. Thus communications between him and the official could be considered separately.

3. As in the examples given in the last chapter, *jenab-e to*, and *arz mikonam xedmatæt*, where other-raising forms are combined with second person singular pronoun reference.

4. Jim Prior (personal communication).

5. This is most probably the verb *ridæn*—properly "to shit." Browne calls this "a slightly refined translation."

6. Also probably *goh* (excrement).

8. Conclusion: The Aesthetics of Iranian Verbal Interaction

1. *Hajji* is a title applied formally to an individual who has made the obligatory (for Muslims) pilgrimage to Mecca. It is also generally applied to elderly, wealthy men and is a term of address for merchants, heard frequently in the bazaar.

INDEX OF SUBJECTS

INDEX OF NAMES

INDEX OF PERSIAN TERMS
AND EXPRESSIONS